CONSUMERS AND LUXURY

MANCHESTER
UNIVERSITY PRESS

Consumers and luxury

CONSUMER CULTURE IN EUROPE 1650–1850

EDITED BY
MAXINE BERG AND HELEN CLIFFORD

Manchester University Press

MANCHESTER AND NEW YORK

distributed exclusively in the USA by St. Martin's Press

Published by Manchester University Press
Oxford Road, Manchester M13 9NR, UK
and Room 400, 175 Fifth Avenue, New York, NY 10010, USA
http://www.man.ac.uk/mup

Distributed exclusively in the USA by
St. Martin's Press, Inc., 175 Fifth Avenue, New York,
NY 10010, USA

Distributed exclusively in Canada by
UBC Press, University of British Columbia, 6344 Memorial Road,
Vancouver, BC, Canada V6T 1Z2

British Library Cataloguing-in-Publication Data
A catalogue record for this book is available from the British Library

Library of Congress Cataloging-in-Publication Data applied for

ISBN 0 7190 5273 4 *hardback*
       0 7190 5274 2 *paperback*

First published 1999

05 04 03 02 01 00 99   10 9 8 7 6 5 4 3 2 1

Typeset in 11/13pt Goudy
by Graphicraft Limited, Hong Kong
Printed in Great Britain
by Biddles Ltd, Guildford and King's Lynn

CONTENTS ◎◎

LIST OF ILLUSTRATIONS ◎◎

LIST OF CONTRIBUTORS ⊚⊚

Maxine Berg is Professor of History at the University of Warwick. She has written widely on the economic and social history of eighteenth- and early nineteenth-century Britain and Europe. She is now writing a book on semi-luxury commodities and their markets in eighteenth-century Britain. Recent publications include *The Age of Manufactures, Industry, Innovation and Work in Britain 1770–1820* (1994) and *Technological Revolutions in Europe: Historical Perspectives*, edited with K. Bruland (1998).

Marina Bianchi is Associate Professor of Economics at the University of Cassino, Italy, where she teaches microeconomics and industrial organisation. She has recently edited a book published by Routledge, entitled *The Active Consumer: Novelty and Surprise in Consumer Choice* (1998). Other publications include 'How to Learn Sociality: True and False Solutions to Mandeville's Problem', *History of Political Economy* (1993) and 'Collecting as a Paradigm of Consumption', *Journal of Cultural Economics* (1997).

Helen Clifford is a tutor and a member of the Research Department at the Victoria and Albert Museum, currently teaching on the joint V & A/RCA MA in the History of Design. Her PhD thesis was on manufacture and consumption in the London precious metals trades and she has curated major exhibitions on historic and contemporary silver. Her current area of research interest concerns the seventeenth- and eighteenth-century Luxury trades, the communication of design information and business history. She has published on aspects of design history in the *Burlington Magazine*, *Studies in the Decorative Arts*, *Business Archives* and *Apollo*.

Neil De Marchi is Professor of Economics at Duke University. He is currently working on the development of early modern art markets. Recent publications include 'The Role of Dutch Auctions and Lotteries in Shaping the Art Markets of 17th Century Holland' and 'Novelty and Fashion Circuits in the Mid-Seventeenth Century Antwerp–Paris Art Trade' (with Hans J. Van Miegroet).

Fiona Ffoulkes originally studied fashion design and worked as a television costume designer, and did an MA in History of Textiles and Dress at Winchester School of Art in 1995. She has been a visiting lecturer in the history of art and design since 1993 and is currently carrying out research for a PhD entitled 'Dressing Royalty: The Luxury Clothing Industry in Paris 1795–1848'.

Colin Jones is Professor of History at Warwick University. His books include *The Longman Companion to the French Revolution* (1988), *The Charitable Imperative* (1991), *The Cambridge Illustrated History of France* (1993) and (with Laurence Brockliss) *The Medical World of Early Modern France* (1997).

Charlotte Klonk is a Warwick Research Fellow in the Department of History of Art at the University of Warwick. Her publications include 'Science, Art and the Representation of the Natural World', in Roy Porter, ed., *Cambridge History of Science: Eighteenth Century*, 2nd 'Art History: An Interdisciplinary Subject?', in Paul Smith, ed., *Blackwell Companion to Art Theory* (forthcoming).

Sarah Lowengard is a doctoral candidate in the programme in the History of Science and Technology at the State University of New York at Stony Brook. Her dissertation examines connections between changing production methods and scientific theories for colour in the eighteenth and early nineteenth centuries.

Stana Nenadic is Senior Lecturer in Social History at the University of Edinburgh. Her research has focused on the social, economic and cultural life of the middle ranks and business owners since the eighteenth century, mainly with reference to Scotland. Publications include 'Middle Rank Consumers and Domestic Culture in Edinburgh and Glasgow, 1720–1840', *Past and Present* (1994); 'Print Collecting and Popular Culture in Eighteenth-Century Scotland', *History* (1997).

Marcia Pointon is Pilkington Professor of History of Art at the University of Manchester. She has written extensively on British and French art in the eighteenth and nineteenth centuries, on portraiture and on patronage and issues of gender in visual culture. Her recent published works include *Naked Authority: The Body in Western Painting 1830–1908* (1990), *The Body Imaged: The Human Form and Visual Culture since the Renaissance* (1993, edited with Kathleen Adler) and *Hanging the Head: Portraiture and Social Formation in Eighteenth-Century England* (1993). Her most recent book is *Strategies for Showing: Women, Possession and Representation in English Visual Culture 1650–1800* (1997). She is currently engaged on research for a study of the display culture of jewels and jewellery in early modern Europe.

Rebecca Spang is Lecturer in Modern European History at University College, London and researches in the social and cultural history of eighteenth- and nineteenth-century France. Her publications include *The Invention of Restaurant Culture* (forthcoming) and 'Rousseau in the Restaurant', *Common Knowledge* (1996).

Emma Spary is Professor at the Max-Planck-Institut für Wissenschaftsgeschichte, Berlin and a former Warwick Research Fellow. She is currently researching the history of food and the sciences in eighteenth-century France. Her publications include 'The "Nature" of Enlightenment', in *The Sciences in Enlightened Europe*, ed. W. Clark *et al.* (forthcoming) and *Naturalising the Tree of Liberty: French Natural History from Old Regime to Revolution* (forthcoming), and she has jointly edited *Cultures of Natural History* with N. Jardine and J.A. Secord (1996).

PREFACE ◉

Consumers and luxury started as a one-day workshop at Warwick in 1996 on 'Consumption and Culture in Europe, 1650–1850'. The workshop was organised by Maxine Berg and Helen Clifford, then working on an ESRC project on new consumer goods in the eighteenth century, and funded by Warwick's Humanities Research Centre. The workshop was also the first public event of Warwick's recently formed Eighteenth-Century Studies Group, which at that point was an informal group of staff and postgraduate students from across the arts faculties keen to pursue the interdisciplinary study of the eighteenth century. This informal group is now formalised as The Warwick Eighteenth Century Research Centre. The major project of this Centre for its first three years is 'The Luxury Project'.

Our one-day workshop two years ago brought together a strong core of participants from Warwick and several from outside the university, including Rebecca Spang, Neil De Marchi, Marina Bianchi and Marcia Pointon. The workshop did not function as a forum for the presentation of formal papers, but as a conversation seeking to move the existing boundaries on the study of consumption in the eighteenth century out in new directions. We sought to move the focus of the debate beyond the collection of inventories and anachronistic issues of modern consumer culture, and out to new perspectives on social and cultural history. Our conversation was also a practice of our subject itself. We came with ideas on specific topics or objects, very briefly presented, but we moved very quickly to seek connections and cultural context. We discussed the extent to which eighteenth-century conceptions of the market and of luxury and more ordinary consumer objects and spectacles were linked to contemporary debate on civility, sociability and conversation. The market, the price and the consumer object itself, as conveyed by Mandeville, were forms of intimate conversation between strangers. The workshop was a particularly stimulating contact between economists, art historians, historians of science, social and cultural historians, and literary scholars.

A core group of papers, drawing on the interdisciplinary themes and approaches we discovered on that day, was developed out of the workshop. Other topics were identified and papers commissioned. Many of the contributors are particularly grateful to Helen Clifford for her editorial suggestions and for her picture searches on their behalf. Elizabeth Eger and Rita MacKenzie provided timely assistance in the final stages. We thank the Scouloudi Foundation in association with the Institute of Historical Research for an Historical Award in aid of the costs of picture permissions and reproductions. Vanessa Graham at Manchester University Press was enthusiastic and expeditious in her response to our initial proposal of the volume, and Carolyn Hand her assistant was patient and helpful.

Maxine Berg
University of Warwick

@◎ MAXINE BERG AND HELEN CLIFFORD

Introduction

From consumption to consumer culture

This volume initiates an interdisciplinary approach to consumers, the cultural space of their private and public interaction, and the desirable objects and luxury goods they collected and valued. The volume brings together research arising out of material culture, the history of art, economics and economic history, the history of science and cultural history. The essays follow themes of contemporary economic and scientific debates on consumer goods, the styles and methods of collecting, displaying and valuing luxury goods in the seventeenth and eighteenth centuries, and the commercial context of the romanticism and museum culture of the early nineteenth century. More specific emphasis is given to British, French and Dutch consumer culture as conveyed in responses to food and drink, to luxury and fashion goods, and new commodities, collecting and art.

As a major historical issue, the whole subject of the history of early modern and eighteenth-century consumption owes its framework to the collection *Consumption and the World of Goods* edited by John Brewer and Roy Porter.[1] This volume set out the phenomenon of the rise of consumption from the later seventeenth century, investigating into the meaning of possessions, and the development and expansion of literary and cultural consumption. A later volume, *The Consumption of Culture 1600–1800*, edited by Ann Bermingham and John Brewer,[2] focused on art, literature and broader cultural themes. More recent work has dwelt on consumerism as a mentalité informing attitudes to goods, and projected outward to personal relations and political philosophies. Aspects of material culture and sociability have been associated with the bourgeois public sphere and the market for culture. Themes raised some ten years ago in Paul Langford's *A Polite and Commercial People*[3] have been reinvented as histories of culture and pleasure in John Brewer' *The Pleasures of the Imagination*[4] and Roy Porter's and Marie Roberts' *Pleasure in the Eighteenth Century*.[5] The markets for art, reading and print culture, theatre and music are joined to shops, pleasure gardens, shows, spectacles, pleasures of the table and clubs. Porter's and Roberts' edited volume as well as other recent volumes, for example Elizabeth Kowaleski-Wallace's *Consuming Subjects*,[6] have directed attention to literary treatments of the subject and the evidence of literary texts.

Specifically historical accounts are only now appearing in specialist studies of particular luxury goods and their markets – Carolyn Sargentson's *Merchants and Luxury Markets*[7] and Timothy Clayton's *The English Print*.[8] And there are studies of more broadly based consumer goods, notably the clothing trades, as in Daniel Roche's *The Culture of Clothing*[9] or Beverly Lemire's *The English Clothing Trade before the Factory*.[10]

The essays in this volume address very different aspects of consumer culture in various parts of Europe over the period from the seventeenth to the early nineteenth centuries. These include debate over the boundaries between luxury and necessity, and the different settings of private adornment and public display. Some of the essays turn to specific goods or their characteristics, silver, jewellery, new decorative consumer goods made with base metals or other materials and new finishes, high fashion dress, and new colours or means of producing them. These essays focus specifically on the market and class dimensions of consumer culture.

Questions of novelty, imitation, value and taste arise in a preoccupation over the period with the middling ranks. Was their response to the market, objects of possession and display, fashion and luxury an emulation of a pre-existing culture among the elites? We suspect, or in some cases even know this was not the case. But we know very little about the inducements to consumer culture among these variegated and intensely status-conscious groups. Our once fixed categories of a resistant, customary plebeian culture set against a corrupt and hedonistic court culture have broken down. Assumptions of an emulative bourgeois culture leading the way to modern mass consumerism are no longer satisfactory.

We are now at the exciting point of opening up issues over the constraints and possibilities of a relatively broadly based but highly differentiated consumerism in the period surveyed. What things and activities were desired, and what could be and was supplied? What impact did these have on the juxtaposition of elite and middling groups and what was their response? What were the issues as seen by economic, political and scientific commentators?

Perceptions of consumers and luxury

If we turn to contemporary perceptions of consumption, these were frequently expressed as a problem of dividing necessities from luxuries. We look now for the roots of modern consumer society in the emergence of new consumer goods and new consumer practices from the later seventeenth century. But responses to this problem were expressed at the time in terms of an intellectual debate over the political, economic, moral and aesthetic effects of the production and consumption of luxury goods. There was the concern of legislators or of mercantilists trying to decide on sumptuary legislation or on trade policies. And there were the more philosophic aspects of the luxury debates following the challenge posed by Mandeville and rooted in the two contrasting strands of epicurean and augustinian philosophy.

This eighteenth-century luxury debate, thus far but little investigated, has been set out as a problem in the history of political thought, or as a literary and moral issue.[11] At its best it has been developed at the interface between political thought and literature.[12] The contemporary texts themselves, however, took the luxury debate into a discussion of consumer cultures of the middling classes. An association of commerce with consumption took the luxury debates far beyond their customary concerns with the corruption of wealthy elites.[13]

Mandeville made the traditional Augustinian association of luxury with vice, but declared such vice to be a public benefit. He also raised the problem of defining luxury. Luxury was all that was not immediately necessary. There was no greater moral virtue in needs for cleanliness, for comforts of life, decencies and conveniencies.[14] As the luxury debate developed over the century, it was dissociated from a moral framework, and was increasingly seen in terms of economic advantages in the works of Melon, Montesquieu and, although less so, Voltaire.[15] Rousseau once again associated luxury with moral corruption.[16] In the work of Hume and Smith, it became associated with commerce, convenience and consumption, though Hume separated out the 'philosophical' and economic questions. On the one hand luxury was a 'refinement in the gratification of the senses', and on the other it was the incentive to the expansion of commerce.[17] The expansion of commerce would make available to all persons not just the necessaries of life, but the 'conveniences'. It is in questions of convenience and who was doing the consuming that we can see emerging another side of the debate – one concerned less with virtue and vice, moral corruption and good citizenship, idleness and industriousness, and more with the incentives to consume and the consumer practices of broad groups of the population, its middling orders and even its labourers.

Consumer culture and commercial society

The making of that consumer culture not as private vice but as public sociability and as economic benefit was debated throughout the century. Luxury was in a sense deconstructed. Beneath the layers of sumptuousness, excess and indolence, we can find the industry of commercial society. This was associated with the practices of commerce and was set out in Mandeville at two levels. The first is that of two merchants striking a deal: the sugar merchant, Decio, and the West India merchant, Alcander, engage in civility, entertainment and feigned indifference over the discourse of the price. These are the 'innumerable Artifices, by which Buyers and Sellers outwit one another that are daily allowed of and practised among the fairest of Dealers'.[18] The commerce in which both engage during the process of striking a bargain is deeply embedded in a consumer culture involving a country house, coach, dinner, horse riding, conversation and humour.[19] At a second level, that of shopping, Mandeville delights in the entertainment of the 'conversation of a Spruce Mercer, and a Young Lady his Customer that comes to his Shop'. He sets out an account of trade in which a consumer culture of fashion, gesture and conversation establish an emotional relationship not unlike a sexual seduction. Each participant wields a certain power – the mercer has the knowledge of the price; the young lady chooses which shop she goes to. 'When two Persons are so well met, the Conversation must be very agreeable, as well as extremely mannerly, tho' they talk about trifles.'[20] The mercer wields great psychological skill. Here is 'a Man in whom consummate Patience is one of the Mysteries of his Trade ... By Precept, Example and great Application he has learn'd unobserv'd to slide into the inmost recesses of the Soul, sound the Capacity of his Customers, and find out their Blind Side unknown to them'. But whatever his skill in deploying the arts of conversation and fashion, he can lose her custom through such trifles as insufficient flattery, some fault in behaviour or the tying of his neckcloth, or gain it by no more than a handsome demeanour or fashion. The 'reasons some of the Fair Sex have for their choice are often very Whimsical and kept as a great Secret'.[21] Their choices, however, were based in the civility and fashion of consumer culture.

The part taken by consumer culture was also set out in the middle of the century in discussions of the creation of commodities and the means of opening a market for these. It is notable that there was little discussion by the key players in the luxury debates of actual objects. Mandeville referred to buildings, furniture, equipages and clothes.[22] Melon mentioned foodstuffs and raw materials – sugar, coffee, tobacco and silk, and elsewhere delftware and china, rich stuffs, works of gold and silver and foreign laces, and diamonds.[23] But it seems that it was not until Smith that we see luxury goods distinguished – ornamental building, furniture, collections of books, pictures, frivolous jewels and baubles – and separated from expenditure on retainers, a fine table, horses and dogs.[24] Both Smith and Hume, however, connected luxury consumption to the expansion of trade and to the proliferation of wider consumer goods manufacture. Both attributed this positive economic benefit of luxury consumption to behaviour, especially of the middling ranks, and to a wider cultural setting.

Early description of consumer behaviour among the middling ranks is to be found in the works of commercial journalism, projects, dictionaries and encyclopedias which proliferated from the 1720s into the middle of the century. Two of the richest of these discussions were Daniel Defoe's *A Plan of the English Commerce* (1731) and Malachy Postlethwayt's *Britain's Commercial Interest Explained and Improved* (1757). Defoe (1661–1731), prolific pamphleteer, social and economic commentator and novelist, described his country thus:

> But in England, the Country is large, populous, rich, fruitful; the Way of living large, luxurious, vain and expensive, even to a Profusion, the temper of the people gay, ostentatious, vicious, and full of excesses; even criminally so in some Things, and too much encreasing in them all.[25]

Defoe, while denouncing the luxury, vanity and high living of the gentry and aristocracy, found rich rewards in the expenditure of the 'trading, middling sort of people'. He argued that it was on the consumption of manufacturers and shopkeepers, and their large numbers, that home consumption and foreign trade were raised.

> These are the people that carry off the gross of your consumption;
> 'tis for these your markets are kept open late on Saturday nights;
> because they usually receive their week's wages late: . . . these are the
> life of our whole commerce, and all by their multitude . . . their num-
> bers are not hundreds or thousands, or hundreds of thousands, but
> millions . . . by their wages they are able to live plentifully, and it is
> by their expensive, generous, free way of living, that the home con-
> sumption is rais'd to such a bulk, as well of our own, as of foreign
> production . . . [26]

Defoe not only ascribed great consumer power to these groups, but
noticed that they generated a trade in a range of qualities of commodities. If the leading contenders in the luxury debates said little about
actual goods, Defoe revelled in their variety and their description. He
argued that though the rich might take the top quality wines, spices,
coffee and tea, the coarser varieties and the overall bulk of trade in all
of these were taken by the middling and trading people, 'so that these are
the people that are the life of trade'.[27] The gentry might take the finest
hollands, cambrics and muslins, but the middling tradesmen took vast
quantities of linens of other kinds imported from Ireland, France, Russia,
Poland and Germany. To imports of great varieties of linens were added
any number of drugs and dyestuffs: 'brasil, and brasiletta wood, fustic,
logwood, sumach, red-wood, red earth, gauls, madder, woad, indico,
turmerick, cocheneal, cantharides, bark peru, gums of many kinds, civet,
aloes, cassia, turkey drugs, african drugs, east India drugs, rhubarb, sas-
safras, cum allis'.[28]

To these foreign imported luxuries in all their varieties and
qualities, the British had responded by developing their own imitative,
substitute and even entirely new commodities, selling these at home
and abroad. There was the bone lace industry of Buckingham, Bedford,
Berkshire, Oxfordshire and Cambridgeshire, and the wrought iron and
brass manufactures of Birmingham and Sheffield.[29]

> It is not many Years since the best Scissars, the best Knives, and
> the best Razors were made in France, and the like of the fine Watches,
> Tweezars and other small Ware; nothing is more evident in Trade at
> this Time, than that the best Knife Blades, Scissars, Surgeions Instru-
> ments, Watches, Clocks, Jacks and Locks that are in the World,
> and especially Toys and gay Things are made in England, and in Lon-
> don in particular; and our Custom-house Books, will make it appear,
> that we send daily great quantities of wrought Iron and Brass into
> Holland, France, Italy, Venice, and to all Parts of Germany, Poland
> and Muscovy.[30]

Twenty years later Malachy Postlethwayt (1707–67), projector and economic writer, felt no need to justify the connection between middle-rank consumption and trade. He simply asserted that consumption was the source of economic progress, and especially the consumption of common commodities, 'if a nation were to abandon its more common arts for those of less general use, the riches of its trade would dwindle away'.[31] He was much more interested in explaining the sources of this consumption. Real advantages, he argued, accrued to the 'art of seducing, or pleasing to a higher degree the consumer of every kind'. Postlethwayt distinguished different classes of consumer and the facility to produce and to import the widest variety and range of qualities of commodities: 'to tempt and please them all, it is proper to offer them assortments of every kind proportioned to their different abilities in point of purchase'.[32] He then passed on to what it was that 'seduced' and 'tempted' the consumer. These were the 'look of a thing' and 'its cheapness'.

> The luxury of buyers in general is excited by lowness of price. The mechanic's wife will not buy a damask of fifteen shillings a yard; but will have one of eight or nine; she does not trouble herself much about the quality of the silk; but is satisfied with making as fine a shew as a person of higher rank or fortune.[33]

Cheapness was not enough; the 'elegance' of products was also important, and this depended on the 'rivalry and competition among workmen'. High wages and skills were important to the national reputation of commodities: 'if her workmen are not ingenious and skilful they will not be able to hit the taste of foreign purchasers; to tempt them with new inventions, or imitate those of other nations; nor, in short, to satisfy the various humours and caprices of consumers'.[34] Postlethwayt concluded that the wise legislator could not act more prudently than to increase the number of home wants, or the 'quantity consumed by the subject, in order to preserve, at all events, the greatest number possible of manufacturers'.

Postlethwayt's interest in the broad group of consumers and what it was that tempted them to consume opened up the subject of consumer culture. Technological change during the eighteenth century, as well as international trade within Europe and with the East and the New World, created a greater variety of luxury goods at the same time as making them available to much broader groups of the population. This was not the creation of a mass consumer society, but it made available goods of unprecedented variety, distinction and individuality.

Culture, taste and style were aspirations which might be pursued through commodities by the middling ranks as well as the elites. Velvet knee breeches, wigs and silks were not the preserve of metropolitan macaronies, but were glimpsed in the 1770s and 1780s among the calico printers of Bury and the weavers of Bolton in Lancashire.

What was it, however, that tempted and 'seduced' the consumer? Postlethwayt discussed elegance, cheapness and variety. More extended analysis was provided by Adam Smith in his *Lectures on Jurisprudence*[35] in which he set out four characteristics of objects which attracted consumers. These were colour, form, variety or rarity and imitation.[36]

> These four distinctions of colour, form, variety or rarity, and imitation seem to be the foundation of all the minute and, to more thoughtfull persons, frivolous distinctions and preferences in things otherwise equall, which give in the pursuit more distress and uneasiness to mankind than all the others, and to gratify which a thousand arts have been invented.[37]

Smith drew attention to the importance of colour. 'Even colour, the most flimsy and superficial of all distinctions, becomes an object of his regard.'[38] It was colour which set apart precious stones – diamonds, rubies and emeralds – from ordinary pebbles. And the reproduction of such colours in clothing, furnishings and art forms was a vital aspect of the desire for such objects. It was thus that dyestuffs, indigo, turkey red, Prussian or cobalt blue, and nankeen made up some of the important items of European commerce, and a major incentive to taking out patents and the invention of chemical dyestuffs.

Smith recognised that form was just as important to aesthetic sensibilities. Uniformity combined with variety went with ease of comprehension in an object or building: 'a house or building . . . pleases when neither dully uniform nor its parts altogether angular'.[39] Curvilinear figures pleased more than abrupt and irregular angles.

Rarity was another aesthetic value, and one entirely contextual. Precious gems were valued by Europeans for this quality, but the 'savage' nations that bartered them valued the technique of the paste and glass substitutes and the pinchbeck and French plate, using cheaper European materials to produce an even greater glitter.[40]

These qualities of uniformity and variety as well as rarity also lay behind the significance of 'imitation'. 'Imitation' might be seen in the copying of rare materials – as in paste, pinchbeck and French plate – but for European consumers these lacked the quality of rarity, though they might evoke it. But Smith also saw the aesthetic appeal of 'imitation' in terms of objects evoked, but imitated in other forms. The example he used was a Dutch still life painting of ordinary objects, where the 'imitation' in the painting was valued much more than the actual objects. That imitation was also closely related to those other values of 'uniformity' and 'comprehension' or recognition.

Smith turned to a more detailed discussion of this in *The Theory of Moral Sentiments*.[41] In two different chapters, 'The Influence of Custom and Fashion on the Sentiments of Moral Approbation and Disapprobation' and 'The Effect of Utility on the Sentiment of Approbation', he explored those characteristics which lent desirability to objects. Here Smith introduced further qualities which made objects beautiful and desirable. These were custom and fashion on the one hand, and elegance and fitness on the other.[42] In chapter 1 of this volume Neil De Marchi discusses Smith's analysis of 'imitation' and fitness in some depth, and in chapter 2 Maxine Berg relates Smith's analyis of 'imitation' to contemporary ideas of product innovation. We will not, therefore, discuss this quality here further, but focus instead on custom and fashion.

In introducing the importance of custom, Smith set out the re-lationship of objects to each other. 'When two objects have frequently been seen together, the imagination acquires a habit of passing easily from the one to the other . . . Of their own accord they put us in mind of one another, and the attention glides easily along them.' The com-plementarity of two goods increased the attraction of both. Without each other, both goods became awkward.

> We miss something which we expected to find, and the habitual arrangement of our ideas is disturbed by the disappointment. A suit of clothes, for example, seems to want something if they are without the most insignificant ornament which usually accompanies them, and we find a meanness or awkwardness in the absence even of a haunch button.[43]

Fashion was different and was conveyed not just by the object, but by those who possessed or displayed an object. It was a quality endowed by association with the high ranking or the rich. It was man-ners, gestures and style as much as the physical attributes of the object itself which lent it fashion.

> The graceful, the easy, and commanding manners of the great, joined to the usual richness and magnificence of their dress, give a grace to the very form which they happen to bestow upon it. As long as they continue to use this form, it is connected in our imaginations with the

idea of something that is genteel and magnificent . . . As soon as they drop it, it loses all the grace, which it had appeared to possess before, and being now used only by the inferior ranks of people, seems to have something of their meanness and awkwardness.[44]

Fashion thus changed continuously. Smith noticed that with clothes they were outmoded within a year; with furniture within every five or six years. They were therefore 'not made of very durable materials'.[45]

We have thus seen that alongside a contemporary debate on luxury, social and economic writers of the period were investigating the class structures, psychological assumptions and aesthetic values which underlay a widely observed expansion of consumer expenditure. In their attempts to depict and to understand a new consumer culture they provided both rich description and incisive analysis of qualities of variety, individuality and novelty, of the parts played by fashion and custom, and of the aesthetics of design. Recent historical treatments of eighteenth- and early nineteenth-century consumer society have yet to investigate very many of those aspects identified by commentators at the time. The chapters in this volume will, we hope, provide a start in this direction. Over a selected range of objects, experiences and countries, they seek to develop this history of consumer culture.

From Adam Smith to the National Gallery

The first three chapters in this volume explore the conceptual frameworks of consumption through definitions of necessity and luxury. Neil De Marchi challenges the sceptics who have doubted Smith's commitment to his own dictum that 'consumption is the sole end to production'. He deftly argues that Smith made consumerism the central characteristic of his new system of political economy. In doing this Smith reconciled a personal distaste with a rational approbation of luxuries. This reconciliation was achieved, De Marchi suggests, through his concept of fitness, which embraced an admiration for and acknowledgement of fine crafting and dexterity. In goods which incorporate this type of ingenuity, labour endures. They are thus more valuable than the 'horses, dogs and keeping a fine table', in which labour disappears in the act of being performed. Through this concept of fitness a whole series of small bridges were created linking personal ethics, economics and aesthetics.

Colin Jones and Rebecca Spang turn their attention to the most corporeal form of consumption, that of eating and drinking. Their examination of sugar and coffee as foci of debate and demand in France during the Revolution is set against their rejection of recent historical caricatures of the period as one of British boom and French stagnation. Jones and Spang favour Sewell's argument that the issues about subsistence were as much rhetorical as economic, but question his understanding of contemporary ideas about what necessity actually was. They reject the 'miserabilism' of the Braudelian–Labrousse orthodoxy in favour of a picture of a growing and significant group of middling urban consumers. The increasing range and value of consumer goods identified by Roche, Paradilhé-Galbrun and Fairchilds are evidence of a growing commodification of material culture in the form of 'populuxe' objects. Jones and Spang argue that the simple binary logic of 'need' versus 'desire' on which so much thinking about consumption has focused must be complicated. They use examples from contemporary advertisements to show how coffee, sugar and tobacco moved from being exotic products to medicinal substances to common staples, proving that the relationship between luxury and necessity was fluid rather than fixed.

What were the new goods consumed by this group of middling urban consumers? Maxine Berg asks whether they were inexpensive versions of aristocratic luxuries, or genuine novelties. She argues that the history of consumer objects must be set in the context of contemporary debates and ideas, the uses and symbolism of objects in daily life, and their place in the formation of identities of individuals, families and groups. Even the most ordinary objects could convey ingenuity, choice and culture, and be ascribed with values of usefulness and civility. Berg's investigation then moves to questions about the manufacture and sale of these new commodities. Methods of production and marketing were often shared between luxury and semi-luxury goods, using the same patterns and tools, trade cards and catalogues, and demonstrating adaptability across materials and the exploitation of complex networks of manufacture. Costs were cut in the production of semi-luxury goods through imitative processes such as varnishes. As we have seen, Adam Smith knew the aesthetic value of 'imitation'. Imitation was a form of invention, and also a process of adaptation, creating distinctive products adaptable to broader markets. Berg concludes that the contemporary appreciation of novelty, which fuelled the quest for imitation, lifted principles of invention in semi-luxury goods out of an association with baubles and trinkets, and into a desirable category in its own right.

Novelty and imitation are key themes pursued in the specific examples of the tulip craze by Marina Bianchi, and of colours by Sarah Lowengard. In an investigation of tulip mania, which reached its height in Holland between 1634 and 1637, Bianchi explores the endless delight that consumers can gain from novelty, showing that consumers, no differently from producers, can be actively engaged in creating new and newly enjoyable consumption opportunities. Like many new goods of the early modern period tulips came from the East, but in their propagation and mutation they offered endless variations, fuelling a sustained passion that existed both before and after the speculative bubble of the 1630s. As was the case with many other luxury goods, tulips activated a process that was one of both diffusion and multiplication of its novel characteristics, which extended beyond the flowers themselves into their 'counterfeits' produced in paint. But why, Bianchi asks, do we derive so much pleasure from novelty? Deploying research in experimental psychology and economics, Bianchi shows that tulip mania was not a mania or an irrational form of behaviour. Tulips evoked an innovative, learning rationality which shared in microcosm what active consumption is always about: trying to find new pleasurable solutions to the problems of choice by an expanding set of wants.

We have seen the significance Smith attached to the aesthetics of colour. Yet few historians have noticed the impact of colour on the material culture of the eighteenth century, nor the new sources of dyestuffs and techniques of colour making. Colour, like novelty and imitation, evoked both the familiar and the surprising. Sarah Lowengard reminds us that colour is not only an integral part of things, but also has an existence separate from objects. The use of colour establishes links between people, commodities and contemporary social culture because it contributes to definitions of new and old, desirable and mundane. She creates a definition of colour as something simultaneously technical, scientific and experiential. Using four case histories, of Turkey red, nankeen, cudbear and Prussian blue, Lowengard discusses colour in terms of fashion and novelty, and the idea of improvement as a way to consume both fashionable and scientific ideas. Colour was familiar and accessible, and brought the ideas of the philosophers close to everyday experience.

The next chapters turn to ideas about value, and the distinctions between public and private arenas of display. The debate is harnessed to specific categories of luxury commodities, jewellery and precious metalwork. Marcia Pointon takes jewellery, and particulary diamond jewellery, for which there was a fascination in the 1730s, as a conspicuous gauge of luxurious consumption, and as a sign of symbolic worth set within speculative and imaginative discourse. Jewellery operates at transitional points where economic and aesthetic dynamics merge: it is designed for show but often hidden. The hallmarking of jewellery opens questions of regulation and of governance. Using the example of mourning rings, Pointon moves on to questions of identity: who is the consumer – the deceased, the executor or the mourner? Jewellery also marked out private display from the public sphere: night earrings and stay buckles played upon the interdependence of concealment and ostentation, of the seen and the imagined.

Helen Clifford examines aspects of the commerce between people and objects in terms of ideas of value, focusing upon the shifting relationship between priorities of monetary worth, respect for workmanship and personal association. Discussion is centred upon objects made of precious metal, prime indicators of power and status, both in terms of sterling worth, and in their form and workmanship, of taste. Clifford charts a mid-seventeenth-century shift in values and priorities from the standard of the metal to that of workmanship. This laid the ground for the reception of the labour intensive products of the French Rococo style, and the indication of value through an increasingly complex language of taste. Mid-eighteenth-century technologies introduced new materials, notably Sheffield plate, and wider markets.

Excess and fashion were most actively debated over food and clothes. Emma Spary explores the consequences of the transformation of the social meaning of food in France during the first quarter of the nineteenth century. Gastronomic writings provided a major setting at which many different commentators came together in attempts to stabilise the nature and significance of food, taste and consumption. The invention of the science of taste involved the partial assimilation of what had previously seemed two conflicting perspectives. Spary argues that discussion of food became the focus for dissatisfaction with the neoclassical Republic. A science of taste was gradually fashioned which combined the old regime's fascination with the medical and physiological processes of digestion with the new era's obsession with antiquity and lavish displays of wealth.

The other most widely discussed setting for displays of wealth was luxury clothing. Fiona Ffoulkes takes the business of the *marchand de mode* Louis Hippolyte LeRoy as a means to investigate the production of luxury clothing and its consumption in Paris in the first half of the nineteenth century. Between 1792 and 1795 there was no court in Paris and an ostentatious display of luxury in dress was interpreted as a signal of allegiance to the old discredited monarchy. Napoleon, however, recognised the importance of the luxury trades to the economy of France, as well as the power of conspicuous display to strengthen public awareness, at home and abroad, of the assurance and prestige of the new regime. LeRoy, as the milliner to the Empress Josephine and other key figures, was thus at the centre of a transformation in attitude towards high fashion, and the creation of a new cult of the *marchandes de modes*.

If consumption can be viewed as an act of individual imagination, as Colin Campbell and others after him have argued, then it can be connected to a new form of 'hedonistic self-consciousness' that was emerging as a product of romanticism in the early nineteenth century. Stana Nenadic argues that, although critical of the debasing power of the market, popular manifestations of romanticism were intimately tied to modern commercialism. She explores this through the place of Scotland in the 'commerce' of romanticism. One defining characteristic of the romantic movement was the preoccupation with 'expansion', of both emotional range and experience. In response domestic objects and architecture were often designed to evoke the exotic, in terms of place and past. The desire to experience nature in its virgin state stimulated the development of tourism and its attendant commodities, which in the nineteenth century extended to the middle classes. Romanticism also stimulated the rise of modern nationalism. This preoccupation was translated into many different types of consumer objects which lent material substance to romantic identity, as shown in Edinburgh during the building of the largely middle-class New Town. The multiplication of objects within the romantic interior fuelled the phenomenon of mass consumption which was emerging by the second half of the nineteenth century.

Nowhere is the shifting place of class structures in consumer culture more apparent than in the public consumption of art. Charlotte Klonk maps the transformation of the public picture gallery in the first half of the nineteenth century, from market-place to temple of aesthetic contemplation, set apart from the commercial world. Using the debates over the creation of the National Gallery, she shows that its founders continued the tradition of leaving the nation's heritage in the hands of an elite of rich connoisseurs. A utilitarian radical vision of the public importance of art as a contribution to the improvement of home manufactures lost out to a notion of art as a vehicle for moral and social refinement. To an older eighteenth-century debate on the moral worth of art was added a distinctive debate, derived from Germany, over the independence of aesthetic contemplation and social reality. The newly systematised and historicised museum, ordered according to art historical principles, came closer to Ruskin's concept of a temple of treasures for the educated than to the early nineteenth-century radical vision of the museum as a place which would form communal bonds across the different classes and groups of the nation. The consumption of art in the nineteenth-century public picture gallery became intellectually as exclusive as the private collections of the eighteenth century had been physically.

Notes

1   John Brewer and Roy Porter, eds, *Consumption and the World of Goods* (London, 1993).
2   Ann Bermingham and John Brewer, eds, *The Consumption of Culture 1600–1800: Image, Object, Text* (London, 1995).
3   Paul Langford, *A Polite and Commercial People: England 1727–1783* (Oxford, 1989).
4   John Brewer, *The Pleasures of the Imagination: English Culture in the Eighteenth Century* (London, 1997).
5   Roy Porter and Marie Roberts, eds, *Pleasure in the Eighteenth Century* (London, 1996).
6   Elizabeth Kowaleski-Wallace, *Consuming Subjects: Women, Shopping, and Business in the Eighteenth Century* (New York, 1997).
7   Carolyn Sargentson, *Merchants and Luxury Markets* (London, 1996).
8   Timothy Clayton, *The English Print 1688–1802* (New Haven, 1997).
9   Daniel Roche, *The Culture of Clothing: Dress and Fashion in the Ancien Regime* (1989), translated by Jean Birrell (Cambridge, 1994).
10 *The English Clothing Trade before the Factory 1660–1800* (London, 1997). Also see Lemire's earlier *Fashion's Favourite: The Cotton Trade and the Consumer in Britain 1660–1800* (Oxford, 1991).
11 Christopher Berry, *The Idea of Luxury: A Conceptual and Historical Investigation* (Cambridge, 1994); John Sekora, *Luxury: The Concept in Western Thought, Eden to Smollett* (Baltimore, 1977).
12 Edward Hundert, *The Enlightenment's Fable* (Cambridge, 1995).
13 These points were made by Roberta Sassatelli and John Robertson in their contributions to the Warwick Eighteenth-Century Centre Workshop on the Luxury Debates of the Eighteenth Century, University of Warwick, 30 January 1998.
14 Bernard Mandeville, *The Fable of the Bees* (1714), ed. Phillip Harth (Harmondsworth, 1970), Remark L, p. 137.
15 This argument is developed in John Robertson's introduction statement in the Warwick Eighteenth Century Centre's workshop on the Luxury Debates of the Eighteenth Century. See Jean-François Melon, *Of Luxury*, in *A Political Essay upon Commerce, written in French by Monsieur M***, Translated with some Annotations, and remarks by David Bindon, Esq.* (Dublin, 1739), pp. 173–99; Charles Louis de Secondat Montesquieu, *De l'Esprit des lois* (1740), translated by A.M. Cohler (Cambridge, 1989); Voltaire, 'Le Mondain' (1736) and 'Defense du Mondain, ou l'apologie du luxe' (1737), in Louis Moland, ed., *Oeuvres completes de Voltaire*, 52 vols (Paris, 1877), vol. X, pp. 83–93.
16 Jean-Jacques Rousseau, 'Discourse which won the Prize on the Academy of Dijon in the Year 1750, On this Question proposed by that Academy: Whether

16

the Restoration of the Sciences and the Arts contributed to the Purification of Mores', in Donald A. Cress, transl. and ed., *Rousseau: Basic Political Writings* (Indianapolis, 1987), part II, pp. 10–21.

17   David Hume, *Essays Moral, Political and Literary* (1741, 1742) (London, 1903): part II, essay 1, 'Of Commerce', pp. 259–75; essay 2, 'Of Refinement in the Arts', pp. 275–89.

18   Mandeville, *The Fable of the Bees*, remark B, p. 96.

19   *Ibid.*, pp. 96–7.

20   Bernard Mandeville, 'A Search into the Nature of Society', in idem, *The Fable of the Bees*, p. 353.

21   *Ibid.*, p. 355.

22   *Ibid.*, remark L, p. 144.

23   Melon, *Of Luxury*, pp. 1, 3–8.

24   See below, Neil De Marchi, 'Adam Smith's Accommodation of "Altogether Endless" Desires', ch. 1 in this volume.

25   Daniel Defoe, *A Plan for the English Commerce* (London, 1731), p. 144.

26   *Ibid.*, p. 77.

27   *Ibid.*, p. 78.

28   *Ibid.*, p. 166.

29   *Ibid.*, p. 217.

30   *Ibid.*, p. 218.

31   Malachy Postlethwayt, *Britain's Commercial Interest Explained and Improved*, 2 vols (London, 1757), vol. 2, p. 395.

32   *Ibid.*, p. 399.

33   *Ibid.*, p. 403.

34   *Ibid.*, p. 411.

35   Adam Smith, *Lectures on Jurisprudence* (1762–63, 1766), ed. R.L. Meek, D.D. Raphael, P. and G. Stein (Oxford, 1978).

36   See De Marchi, 'Adam Smith's Accommodation'.

37   Smith, *Lectures on Jurisprudence*, p. 337.

38   *Ibid.*

39   *Ibid.*, p. 336.

40   *Ibid.*

41   Adam Smith, *The Theory of Moral Sentiments* (1759, 1790), ed. A.L. McFie and D.D. Raphael (Oxford, 1978).

42   For analysis of Smith's discussion of elegance and fitness see De Marchi, 'Adam Smith's Accommodation'.

43   Smith, *The Theory of Moral Sentiments*, p. 194.

44   *Ibid.*, p. 195.

45   *Ibid.*

PART ONE

Luxury and necessity

Adam Smith's accommodation of 'altogether endless' desires

Suspicion lingers among some students of social history that Adam Smith, percipient critic and remarkable systematiser of the economic events and thought of his age though he was, somehow failed to grasp the significance of one major contemporary development: the spread of consumer goods to 'middling and inferior' households all over Britain.[1] Alternatively (so runs the same line of reasoning, albeit in a different channel), supposing he saw what was occurring, the fact is that he nevertheless resisted admitting that the desire, and the freedom to consume, was of equal importance to the division of labour and productivity, and neglected to give it the same prominence and rigorous analysis in his writings.[2]

There is no doubt that Smith was sceptical about luxuries – possessions beyond strict needs and modest conveniencies. He gave two reasons, one moral and the other rational. First, it is only in the 'middling and inferior stations of life' that the road to virtue is 'very nearly the same' as the road to fortune: '[i]n the superior stations of life the case is unhappily not always the same'.[3] Second, and setting aside the threat to virtue, when we view in an 'abstract and philosophical light' the 'real satisfaction' afforded by most luxuries, they 'will always appear in the highest degree contemptible and trifling'.[4] Smith was not only sceptical towards luxuries in general, but stern in his personal handling of them. On being appointed a Commissioner of Customs for Scotland in January 1778, and discovering that several items of his own clothing fell under prohibited imports, Smith burned them to set an example, even though he believed and advocated strongly that all such restrictions should be abolished for the economic good of the land.[5] Nor was this just a matter of propriety; in his ordering of frivolous items Smith set fine clothes below even 'jewels, baubles, ingenious trinkets of different kinds'.[6]

It is true, then, and not surprising, that one looks in vain in Smith for an excited recognition of the elements of a consumption revolution. There is no extended litany of exotic imports to tantalise and amaze; no pæan to the inventiveness of domestic producers who shaped their own versions of these things or produced new forms from old materials and established, home-grown products; barely a hint of an awareness that the working week may have been voluntarily extended by the poorer classes to gain the wherewithal to buy comforts and conveniencies.[7]

These impressions, however, valid though they are, do not suffice to convict Smith of a bias against consumption. There are good reasons why he wrote about the new consumer culture with reticence. Some of these relate to the circumstance that a lot of the new goods were traded. There were both classification and measurement problems in the trade statistics that hindered detailed discussion: where should truly novel goods be fitted into the customs lists, and what allowance should be made for reporting problems linked to smuggling and other deceptions? Deeper-seated problems were present too in the form of what Smith held to be distortions in the pattern of Britain's trade; these preoccupied him more than did the characteristics of the goods involved, however exotic they might be. For the rest, Smith's focus on growth meant that the single most important issue to him was whether labour is 'productive': creates an extra value, and fixes itself in durable forms, 'in some particular subject or vendible commodity, which lasts for some time at least after that labour is past'.[8] Nothing would have been added to his discussion of this important subject by introducing a description of the kinds and diffusion of new articles of consumption.

Reasons can form bulwarks, but Smith actually crafted a conceptual framework to allow him positively to delight in the fashioning of goods, though without having to relish or seek them as possessions. Central to his construction was the notion of 'fitness', or ingenuity.

I shall begin by addressing in a number of forms the question of whether Smith was really opposed to luxury spending. Then I turn to his preoccupation with growth and his concern about Britain's distorted trade pattern. Finally I shall try to re-position Smith by making fitness central to his thinking. Whether the idea merits quite that place is not to the point; the exercise of placing it at the centre allows us to see Smith on consumption in a new light.

The fuzzy boundary between necessaries and conveniencies

Smith has been charged with having paid mere lip service to the idea that '[c]onsumption is the sole end and purpose of all production', a phrase that occurs but once in the *Wealth of Nations*, at that a full two-thirds of the way through the book,[9] and then only in the context of arguing against governmental interventions which promote monopolies for manufacturers. His well-known, and apparently dismissive, talk about 'trinkets' and 'baubles' is also adduced as proof of a wholly disapproving attitude towards luxury purchases.[10] I suggest instead that these phrases, though they capture accurately enough Smith's personal view that many acquisitions are pointless indulgences, mostly occur in contexts where it is clear that they serve rhetorical purposes and hence disclose nothing about how he viewed consumption or luxury in general. That will be argued in a moment. First, however, I want to examine Smith's attitude to what he referred to as 'conveniencies' and 'amusements', that is, non-necessaries.

If Smith were opposed to luxury consumption we would expect him to make much of the necessaries/luxuries distinction, and to emphasise the former. In fact he treated this boundary as flexible, a flexibility necessitated in part by his own conviction that there is a strong element of custom in what counts as a necessary. Thus, necessaries are 'not only the commodities which are indispensably necessary for the support of life, but whatever the custom of the country renders it indecent for creditable people, even of the lowest order, to be without'. That definition enabled Smith to determine that soap, while not life-supporting, had become a necessity by virtue of a linen shirt's now being required clothing for a 'creditable day-labourer' in much of Europe. It also allowed him to conclude that the use of tea and sugar, though these had spread to the very lowest ranks in both England and Holland, were nonetheless luxuries since it was not considered indecent to live without them. The same could be said of tobacco and spiritous liquors.[11]

Custom, then, more even than nature, determined where the line should be drawn. Was this problematic for Smith? Not according to his own disclaimer. Having defined 'necessary', and thus, by default, 'luxury', he expressly lifted his use of the latter term out of the context of the long-running luxury debate, noting: '[a]ll other things, I call luxuries; without meaning by this appellation, to throw the smallest degree of reproach upon the temperate use of them'.[12] Intemperance was universally condemned and, since excess could be shown to be self-destructive in various ways, no special defence of the qualification 'temperate use' was called for.

None of the foregoing is to say that there were no economic consequences to classifying a good one way or the other, as necessary or as luxury. All excise taxes, for example, tend to reduce demand, and hence the scale of production, and this restricts the scope for division of labour and opens up the possibility that competitiveness will be hurt. But imposts on necessaries drive up wages; the higher wage is invariably passed on to prices, 'always with a considerable overcharge';[13] and, since taxes on necessaries increase a price which already includes taxes on other necessaries, the more necessaries are taxed the greater will be the cost to rich consumers, and the greater the potential damage to sales of luxuries at home and abroad. These were real dangers, but Smith noted that Britain's taxes on necessaries were in fact confined mainly to soap, candles, salt and leather and, though he found some of the rates heavy, they seemed to him less unavoidably injurious to the economy than, say, the Dutch taxes on flour, meal and bread.[14] The tenor of his remarks on this point is that there is no immediate or heavy threat to Britain's economy from the prevailing taxes on necessaries; that being so, nothing of pressing practical importance turned on the necessaries–luxuries distinction.

A digression on fashion goods

But what of that special category of luxury items, the fashion good? Rather than dismiss fashion demands because they were unreasoning and perhaps imprudent, Smith chose instead to represent them as essentially harmless. This falls short of approval, but it is also very far from condemnation. Fashion, he noted in the *Theory of Moral Sentiments*, is 'a particular species' of custom. In matters of fashion, moreover, we take our lead from those of high rank or character. For in dress, whatever the objective merits of the case, '[t]he graceful, the easy, and the commanding manners of the great, joined to the usual richness and magnificence of their dress, give a grace to the very form which they happen to bestow upon it'. Smith extended this observation to furniture, poetry and music. But the common implied argument is that fashion is not 'founded upon reason or nature' but upon 'habit and prejudice'. This would be dangerous if habit and unreason threatened to destroy our sense of beauty and our notions of propriety. But that is not what happens; on this Smith is clear: though these may be 'warpt', they 'cannot be entirely perverted' by habit or education.[15] From this

we can derive that for Smith fashion was a curious but basically innocent phenomenon.

This interpretation is reinforced by the fact that Smith experienced no difficulty in integrating demands that arise from whim, fancy
and fashion in his general analysis of pricing. That was not the reaction of the eminent nineteenth-century Cambridge economist Alfred
Marshall. Marshall, in his *Principles of Economics* (1890), excluded from
the theory of temporary equilibrium pricing old master paintings, rare
coins and other things 'which cannot be "graded" at all'. His reason for
the exclusion was that this class of goods is of little practical importance; but he notes that the influence of fancy may and does cause the
price paid for the same item to alter even between successive auctions,
and the reader can easily infer from the surrounding discussion that
such whimsicality in prices is inconsistent with the existence of a 'true'
equilibrium price.[16] Smith's contemporary, Galiani, who also reflected
on the influence of fashion upon price, quickly gave up, merely noting
that the prices of fashion goods have no upper limit, while describing
fashion itself as *un' afflezione del cerebro, propria alle nazioni europee.*[17]
In eighteenth-century Britain, too, dire consequences were sometimes
predicted from the 'irregular Motions' in price caused by luxury imports
such as paintings whose quality (status as originals) was uncertain, and
which were sold by methods (auctions) calculated to dupe the public
and undermine 'the fair Trader'.[18]

Smith set himself apart from such naysayers, and in fact developed the very model needed to make sense of their fears. In the case
of any novel product, he reasoned, initial costs may be high, partly
because workers must be induced to move from more established industries. Over time, however, costs will settle to the 'average or ordinary'
level, and a price can be set so as to yield the average or ordinary rate
of profit. But where fashion is involved, the demand typically disappears before a new industry can become old and established, so neither
costs nor profits ever do become normal. Even so, Smith showed, the
actual or market price of fashion goods can be explained; it will not just
float as Galiani feared.

Market price, Smith suggested in his lectures on jurisprudence,
will depend on three circumstances: (i) the demand or need; (ii) the
supply relative to the demand; and (iii) the wealth of the demanders.
When supply is less than is demanded, the parties contend, as in an
auction: 'If there be two persons equally in fancy with any thing and
equally earnest to have it, they will bid equally according to their
abilities, whether their desire for it be reasonable or unreasonable. The

richest however will always get it as he is best able to bid high[e]st'.[19] Here we should imagine a pyramid, divided into wealth strata; there are fewer persons at each level of 'fortune', hence as price is bid up, fewer and fewer potential buyers are left. A similar construct was later employed by J.-B. Say.[20] For both Smith and Say this served, not as a modern demand curve, to show the notional amount that would be purchased at different prices, but to illustrate how price may be constrained when demand is price-inelastic.

In this, and other respects, Smith's approach is remarkable. Auctions are the appropriate selling technique for unique items (though not only those), and Smith shows that he understood this: he mentions unique diamonds and clearly saw the link between the auction form and bidding for an item in strictly limited supply. He also stressed the attractiveness to rich buyers of the possibility of owning something rare.[21] For such goods, and for this class of purchasers, price inelasticity is an appropriate assumption. In relation to our concern, which is to construct the contexts in which Smith viewed consumption, it is also worth stressing that he was quite undeterred by the fact that some demands may be 'unreasonable', including those based on 'fictitious' needs. This is yet more confirmation of an ease in accommodating whim, fancy and fashion that was unusual then and since.

Was consumption for Smith truly the sole end for which we labour?

All this notwithstanding, Smith's assertion that consumption is the sole end of production still rings hollow to some. We do at least know, however, from the lectures on jurisprudence, that what is represented in the *Wealth of Nations* as so self-evident as to require no defence, had at one time been considered as part of a larger argument, the shortcomings of the mercantile system.

In the report of the lectures on jurisprudence of 1762–63, Smith urged, against Locke, that the perishability of all goods other than gold and silver does not make them less significant to the wealth of a nation. On the contrary, their very 'consumptib[il]ity' makes them 'of greater real worth' than the precious metals.[22] The assertion is amplified a few pages further on. 'The business of commerce and indust[r]y is to produce the greatest quantity of the necessaries of life for the consumption of the nation ... [which is] the sole benefit of industry. If you do not use them, what is the benefit of the greatest abundance?'[23] Lest we think that by 'necessaries' Smith has in mind only such physical goods as nature or custom has made essential, he immediately widens his ambit to include 'the cultivation of the arts'. He also mentions corn, cloth and wine in a single breath, and answers any who would object that 'wine is merely a superfluity' by saying: 'but it is not more so than pepper, sugar, tea, coffee, tobacco, dying stuffs, drugs, etc., and there is nothing more absurd in desiring to have good wine for our money than any other commodity'.[24] In the report of the lectures of 1763–4 this argument is repeated, only directed this time against Mun.[25]

By making consumptibility the chief characteristic of the new system of political economy, replacing the unsatisfactory mercantile system, Smith gives proof that he was serious about consumption's being the goal for which we labour.

There remains still the matter of his dismissive language. Smith paired '[f]rivolous and useless' at one point, and frivolous was linked with other epithets – 'trinkets', or 'baubles' – at least three times in the *Theory* and the *Wealth* combined.[26] Strikingly, however, he raised no objection to the possibility that demand may know 'no limit or certain boundary';[27] and while he did regard lavishing money on personal adorn-ments and the like probably as a sign 'not only of a trifling, but a base and selfish disposition',[28] here it was the excess that Smith judged, not its object, consumption. I suggest that there is no conflict here, that the dismissive talk was introduced for rhetorical purposes, as a vehicle to drive home quite other points. Examination of the passages involved bears this out.

Thus in the main passage in the *Theory* where Smith discusses frivolous consumption, he is actually arguing that the difficulty and ingenuity of a good's fashioning, and the aptness of a contrivance for the end for which it was devised, are among the chief sources of the pleasure we take in luxuries. Moreover, this plus our love of distinction, he insists, motivates not just trifling purchases but 'the most serious and important pursuits of both private and public life'.[29] These were novel ideas and, it seems likely, strange to at least some of Smith's contem-poraries: Dugald Stewart later dubbed the 'difficulty' aspect of the thesis one of Smith's 'peculiar notions'.[30] For Smith, then, it must have been a concern as to how he could most convincingly present these notions. His answer, plausibly enough, was to make the case for trivial purchases; for goods chosen without any regard for use or conveniency can only have been acquired with something like pleasure in ingenuity or love of distinction operating as a factor on the choice.

Turning to the *Wealth of Nations*, the first of the occurrences there of the derogatory language occurs at the point where Smith asks whether opulence is better promoted by spending beyond needs in the form of retainers, horses, dogs and keeping a fine table, or by spending on ornamental buildings and furniture, collections of books, pictures or statues, and 'things more frivolous, jewels, baubles, ingenious trinkets of different kinds'. The issue might seem to be a fine one, since both lists consist of luxuries and every item is to some extent frivolous. That is just the perception Smith needs; he shows at once that there is one additional characteristic that separates the two lists: whether the labour involved endures. The former kind of spending leaves nothing behind once the labour has been performed, whereas the latter embodies the labour in a durable product.[31]

Durables, because they are just so much embodied labour, can always be bartered for living labour at some future moment, or for products to be consumed. Fresh labour in turn might be used to add to value, thereby increasing the stock of society, in other words its opulence. But neither possibility – adding to stock or to consumption – exists if labour disappears in the act of its being performed. With replacement of or addition to stock, on the other hand, there is at least the possibility of enhancing future consumption, and this point, like so much else that Smith deemed important, is not affected by whether goods are necessaries or not. Given a substantial inheritance of negative presumptions against luxury as counterweight, it is as if Smith deliberately chose to put his argument in a provocative form, showing that it holds even for the most frivolous of durables.

There is a second discussion in the *Wealth*, in which Smith offers a rational reconstruction of the process by which medieval landowners came to cede their political and economic power over their one-time dependants. The nobles were strong when their power was measured in terms of how many retainers and tenants-at-will they controlled; but when foreign commerce and manufactures introduced goods which they might purchase for their own enjoyment exclusively, the nobles in effect found themselves exchanging the loyalty of dependants for consumables no more substantial than 'a pair of diamond buckles perhaps'.[32] Though it is not his immediate point, implicit in this narrative is Smith's earlier distinction between spending on retainers and spending on durable goods. While nobles spent their substance on maintaining a retinue and a fine table, both the political arrangements and total material well-being remained constant. With the switch to spending on durables the political order collapsed but economic growth also became a possibility. For spending on durables maintains productive labour and makes possible an increase in value; spending on menial servants and the like does not. Smith's rhetoric here is also the same: the argument is not less true just because the luxury durables happen to comprise things 'fitter to be the playthings of children than the serious pursuits of men'.[33]

Saving as postponed consumption

This has been ground clearing, but it has already led us to one of Smith's main concerns: the conditions making for sustained (and enhanced) growth. The argument is now familiar, though a complementary point needs to be made: although consumption is the sole end of production, at every point in time there is a choice to be made between saving and spending on consumption. The rate at which stock (capital) grows will reflect the choice made. (In addition, of course, there is an absolute limit to spending on immediate consumption if capital is not to be destroyed.)

Some critics have focused on individual parsimony as if it was antithetical to consumption, but that was not Smith's emphasis. In words that are not quite the same as, but echo fully his assertion that consumption is the sole end, he wrote: '[t]o maintain and augment the stock which may be reserved for immediate consumption, is the sole end and purpose both of fixed and circulating capitals'.[34] The real question, then, is not whether, but at what point in time, we elect to consume. Taking this as established, the advantage of saving is that it offers an opportunity to *add* to one's future consumption possibilities. Moreover, saving does not destroy consumption even in the present, it merely affects what kinds of goods are bought – wage goods, perhaps, rather than diamond buckles. Making allowance for that shift, '[w]hat is saved is as regularly consumed as what is annually spent, and nearly in the same time too; but it is consumed by a different set of people'.[35]

It follows from all this that growth strictly is in the service of consumption. Saving, as we have seen before, merely enables productive labour to be stored temporarily in one or another commodity form, and keeps open the possibility of adding to stock, or consumption, in the future. But the exact form, the precise nature of the goods comprising either saving or stock, does not affect the principle, precisely because stock is fungible. No purpose would have been served had Smith enumerated and celebrated the consumption goods available.

Opulence, agriculture and trade

Smith, it is well known, argued that there is a 'natural' order to growth: the way to increase opulence fastest and most securely is to invest first in the improvement of agriculture, then in manufactures, and lastly in foreign commerce. He constructs several narratives showing how this sequence and its transitions can be varied. I leave these aside, but do wish to emphasise the primacy of agriculture.

One element underpinning the natural order is the notion that the rate of profit declines successively as a society moves from agriculture to manufactures, to trade. The argument here is left incomplete, but part of Smith's rationale is that nature makes a free double contribution towards a surplus in agriculture, labouring 'along with man'[36] as well as bestowing free productive labour in the form of cattle. He also adduces factors that count against manufactures and commerce: uncertainty is heightened outside agriculture by the loss of immediate oversight and control over one's capital and operations, and in long distance trade in particular, by the multiple dangers, vexations and delays common to realising returns in that sphere.[37] These factors gave him an independent defence for the proposition: 'Of all the ways in which a capital can be employed, it is by far the most advantageous to the society' when employed in agriculture.[38]

That proposition itself turns on the amount of productive labour 'supported' by each level of activity in society, and on the total value added at each level. Imagine calculating value added, layer by layer, from the retailer at the top to farmers at the base. The retailer replaces, with a profit, the capital of his supplier, the wholesaler, but is himself the sole productive labourer immediately supported by his capital. The number of productive labourers supported enlarges as we move towards the base. There, farmers put into motion directly both working men and cattle – a far greater number than at any higher level; but farmers, unlike workers in any other sector, must also return not just normal profits but a rent to those who own the land. Smith suggests that this rent is 'seldom less than a fourth, and frequently more than a third of the whole produce'.[39] With such a sizeable proportion of society's revenue generated in agriculture, he could justifiably conclude that whatever interventions discourage agricultural improvement 'are extremely prejudicial to the progress of opulence'.[40]

We have here part of what is needed to advance a second reason why Smith might have been reticent about the new goods available to the British consumer, though more on that in a moment. The first reason, remember, was that nothing is added to our understanding of growth by knowing the particulars of goods. But Smith could reasonably have been expected to be expert in very many of the new goods. For him to have said as little as he did about them therefore seems to call for some additional comment.

As a Commissioner of Customs for Scotland Smith was obliged to know which goods coming from the British colonies in America and the Caribbean were required to be sold in the home country and which could be sold anywhere, subject to certain restrictions on the carrier. He also had to know those affecting goods from India, the Spice Islands, the Far East and European nations, including import prohibitions and the conditions governing declaration and warehousing for re-export. Then there were the details of the rates of import duty applicable to various goods, and those of rebate on exports and re-exports. As the tale of his own clothes suggests, prior to 1778 Smith did not know all these details.

From the works drawn on in preparing the *Wealth of Nations*, however, we may infer that he did know a good deal. Chief among Smith's sources was Henry Saxby's *The British Customs* (1757). Saxby was a customs official, and he gives what must be close to a definitive listing of goods, customs provisions and rates. He lists more than 800 categories for goods 'inwards', and within many of these there were multiple items: over 270 under 'drugs', 33 under 'linnen', and 12 each, for example, under 'buttons' and 'silk'. Under prohibited imports, moreover, Saxby lists: 'Woollen cloths, Laces, Corses, Ribbons, Fringes of silk and thread, Silk twined, Silk in any wise embroidered, Laces of thread, of gold, of silk or gold, Saddles, Stirrops or Harness pertaining to saddles, Spurs, Bosses for bridles, Andirons, Grid-irons, any manner of Locks, Hammers, Pinsons, Fire-tongs, Dripping-pans, Dice, Tennis-balls, Points, Purses, Gloves, Girdles, Harness for girdles of iron, latten, steel, tin, or of alkmine, anything wrought of any tawed leather, and tawed Furs, Buskins, Shoes, Goloches or Corks, Knives, Daggers, Wood knives, Bodkins, Sheers for taylors, Scissors, Razors, Chessmen, Playing-cards, Combs, Pattens, Pack-needles, any Painted wares, Forcers, Caskets, Rings of copper, or of latten-gilt, Chafing-dishes, Hanging candlesticks, Chafing-balls, Sacring-bells, Rings for curtains, Ladles, Scummers, Counterfeit basons, Ewers, Hats, Brushes, Cards for wool . . .'[41]

I have done what Smith did not do, list many of the goods made at home (under protection) and available to consumers. Some of these are mentioned in his writings, but even allowing for an imperfect knowledge prior to his appointment as a Customs Commissioner, Smith must have been aware of many of the items in Saxby's list. A sufficient reason for his reticence in mentioning them, I suggest, lies in the fact that he perceived the trade legislation he was soon to find himself administering to have distorted and destroyed the 'natural balance of industry', that allocation of capital which respected the scale of values added by sector, and hence the natural order for achieving opulence.[42] Artificially elevated rates of profit in protected pursuits had enticed new capital into commerce, hindering thereby 'the improvement of land', while old capital had been withdrawn from other branches of industry. The overall effect was that the available capital at any moment had been prevented 'from maintaining so great a quantity of productive labour as it would otherwise maintain, and from affording so great a revenue to the industrious inhabitants as it would otherwise afford'.[43]

Two illustrations will convey the basis for Smith's concerns. Two of his main preoccupations were what he dubbed 'the over-growth of the colony trade' and the spread of the re-export trade.[44] The former distortion came about because Britain had used its colonies to obtain relatively cheap raw materials and to provide itself with protected markets for domestic manufactures. As to the re-export trade, drawbacks (rebates of import duties) were allowed on the re-exportation of many imported goods, whether from the colonies or from otherwise penalised third countries. Moreover, because of the virtual monopoly Britain had engineered for itself in commodities imported from the colonies, often more was acquired than could be used at home. These surpluses were exported to third countries, and the manufactures obtained in return re-exported to the colonies. In Smith's eyes, all this re-exportation merely gave artificial encouragement to the carrying trade. But capital invested in the carrying trade, being less under 'immediate view and command' than the home trade or than in the purchase of foreign goods for home consumption, its returns were less certain and took longer. In addition, 'no part of [such capital] is necessarily ever brought home',[45] and what does not reside at home employs there absolutely fewer hands.

Still worse effects were identifiable. By so forcing the colony trade and the carrying trade, Britain had less capital to support its own manufactures than would otherwise have been the case and, as noted above, less with which to improve agriculture. And, by concentrating so much of its industry and commerce in the American and Caribbean markets, the whole state of industry and commerce had been made less secure.[46]

Smith's own detailed account of all this fills almost the whole of Book IV of the *Wealth of Nations*. And it is at the very end of that long account, just prior to a chapter devoted to the Physiocratic system, that

he introduces the proposition about consumption being the sole purpose of production. We can now see, from another angle, how deeply
held was this conviction. It was anything but a throwaway concession
to the advocates of consumption; for it defined all that was wrong-
headed about the efforts of those who denied it, the proponents of the
'mercantile system'. Getting that message across took precedence over
glorying in the range and variety of consumer goods that had become
available. For these had only become common at a cost in terms of
foregone opulence and increased insecurity. Others might overlook these
costs, Smith would not.

Fitness

I have portrayed Smith as unable personally to relish acquisitions
beyond the most modest, and sensitive to the moral risk in avidity, yet
rationally convinced that consumption is what gives point to all our
labours. How could he have maintained such a seemingly contradictory
stance? A reconciliation, at least at the conceptual level, as I have
already hinted, is to be found in the notion of fitness.

Fitness basically meant the nicety with which means are fitted to
their ends, objects fashioned to their intended uses. Use or conveniency,
plus order, gives us a sense of propriety and beauty, Smith says in the
Theory of Moral Sentiments.[47] But having acquiesced in this very common view, he at once goes on to say that frequently we appreciate 'the
adjustment of the means' itself more than any intended or actual end.
This was unusual, as he himself was aware, and he gave it relatively
more emphasis than fitness for use, both in the *Theory* and elsewhere.
Thus, towards the end of his extended assessment of drawbacks and
bounties, mostly negative, in the *Wealth of Nations*, Smith came out in
favour of '[p]remiums given by the publick to artists and manufacturers
who excel in their particular occupations'. What such bounties might
do, at little cost, is encourage 'extraordinary dexterity and ingenuity',
but without overturning the natural balance of trades.[48]

This exception to the rule of non-intervention is interesting on
two counts. First, it confirms how much Smith valued fine crafting,
something we also know from his involvement with the Glasgow School
for the Art of Design.[49] Second, he distinguishes between average skill
and extraordinary dexterity and ingenuity. That hints at a further gloss
on fitness, something spelled out in his essay, 'Of the Nature of that
Imitation which takes place in what are called The Imitative Arts'.
Here Smith argues that the reproduction of some prototype existing in

nature may please, quite apart from any beauty or lack thereof in the original, because of the extraordinary ingenuity required to overcome the disparity between two spheres in themselves so different, the world of nature and that of artifice. He illustrates this with reference to two artefacts, a carpet and a picture in which the carpet appears. The image may please because the carpet appears in perspective, and because it captures the carpet's softness and the appearance of its wool pile, even though the painter is constrained to a flat surface. We admire 'the art which surmounts so happily that disparity which Nature had established' between 'an object of one kind . . . [and] an object of a very different kind'.[50]

Smith's introduction of this additional cause of pleasure was not adventitious. It is a theme common to two of his surviving essays, and finds some echo also in his 1756 'Letter' to the *Edinburgh Review*.[51] In the essays he gives examples from painting (the one above) and from the history of systems of astronomy.

The details Smith selected for emphasis in the painting example suggest, misleadingly I believe, that this ingenuity comprises only technical difficulty: the mastery of exact perspective, for instance, and the artifice requisite to conveying solid substances on a plain surface.[52] Indeed, difficulty is what Dugald Stewart understood to be Smith's emphasis, as we have seen. Notwithstanding these appearances, I am inclined to think that for Smith something more was also involved.

The best evidence for this is the language Smith uses both in his essay on the imitative arts and in the more famous essay on the history of astronomy. What we find satisfying about an ingenious representation in painting, or a successful system in natural philosophy, Smith says, is that both move us beyond initial wonder, to that special sort of wonder that elicits our 'admiration', our 'approbation'. In the essay on the history of astronomy those words are reserved for the satisfaction we experience when the mental tumult caused by discordant or disjointed appearances is settled by a hypothesis that creates a chain of 'intermediate, though invisible events' between them.[53]

It is striking that Smith in that context talks of gaps or intervals – disparities, no less – between disjointed objects, and of the imagination as the only 'bridge' that can 'smooth the passage from the one object to the other'.[54] For that is the very same language he employs to account for our appreciation of a convincing painting: the artist in such a case has overcome the 'disparity' between objects of quite different kinds. And that achievement too evokes not just the wonder of ignorance, but 'the still more pleasing satisfaction of science': we are pleased that we 'comprehend, in some measure, how that wonderful effect is produced' by the artist.[55]

If we comprehended fully, then artefacts and systems of natural philosophy would 'carry, as it were, their own explication along with them'.[56] Then technique alone would comprise fitness or ingenuity. But in the case of painting, it seems, we can follow the artist only imperfectly; while in systems in natural philosophy, 'it rarely happens' that we can identify very readily the connecting chain that would soothe our minds, and in just a very few cases do we seem 'to have been really admitted behind the scenes' where all hidden mechanisms are revealed.[57] Technique, then, generally carries us only so far; the ingenuity of the bridging process also involves the ineffable.

In sum, Smith allowed that we take pleasure in fitness in any of three forms: as ingenuity in the fitting of means to an end (the case of useful objects); or, when ingenuity is present but the objects are merely frivolous (and not necessarily beautiful); or, when there is a disparity overcome by mental invention ('The supposition of a chain of … events'), even if we can only partially follow the process. These distinctions mattered greatly. They were Smith's way of bridging different spheres of enquiry. The separation of use from ingenuity allowed him to feel appreciation for useless goods, even if he would not have wished to acquire them for himself. Ingenuity also gave him the luxury of not having to confront directly the moral taint and dangers associated with unnecessary acquisitions for personal amusement. In both these ways Smith found he could retain his moral and personal scepticism about possessions, while delighting in the fashioning of the goods themselves – a form of virtual possession. There is also a link within the strictly economic sphere, between inventiveness and opulence. The premium he wanted paid to workers of extraordinary ingenuity alerts us to this. Finally, since approbation of ingenuity was initially introduced by Smith as an aspect of aesthetics – fitness sustains beauty[58] – we have, by way of fitness or ingenuity, a whole series of small bridges linking personal ethics, economics and aesthetics.[59] This is not to collapse these separate spheres into one; fitness only allowed a determined individual like Smith to claim all three intellectual sites as his own without becoming involved in contradictions.

Conclusion

Prior to Smith's taking a position towards consumption there was a decision he took about the origin of our demands.[60] He sided with

Barbon who, a century earlier, had argued that strict necessities absorb such a tiny fraction of resources for people in most parts of the world that virtually all wants must be adjudged 'wants of the mind'. This at once made 'luxuries' of almost all commodities, and ensured that most values will be affected by fashion and fancy, thereby putting into question the relevance of the terms within which luxury had been debated. Smith accordingly simply set those terms aside. From this point he reasoned on two levels: the personal, from which perspective acquisitions might be judged frivolous and possibly as evidence of a selfish disposition; and the economic, which led to what we might call his analytics of enlightened consuming – the nature and role of saving in achieving opulence; the consequences of consuming now versus later; and other similar issues.

I have focused on reasons why Smith might have been reticent about embracing more openly the new consumer culture. That way of formulating the problem deliberately mixes the two levels. The mixing, however, finds some justification in Smith's own proclivity for, and interest in, bridging gaps. His appreciation of ingenuity, I have argued, enabled him to connect, without loss of coherence, several spheres of intellectual enquiry: the aesthetic, the economic and the ethical. As part of that process of connecting, consumption won rational approval, if not Smith's personal approbation. Smith accommodated 'altogether endless' desires,[61] though it was a distinctly cerebral achievement.

Notes

I am grateful to Marina Bianchi, who has helped me clarify some of the ideas expressed here, and to Istvan Hont, for patiently refusing to accept initial positions that were closer to some of those I now criticise. Maxine Berg, Donald Winch, Judy Klein, and above all John Robertson, have kindly made useful comments and suggestions for improvement, and I thank them.

1   Smith was both more sceptical of system-building in general and less systematic in his own political economy than is often granted. In fact it seems to have mattered less to him that he often left untidy summaries of forces pulling in opposite directions than that he could set down interesting insights in some kind of order. An example of this untidiness is his failure to resolve the tension posed by the dual facts that agriculture is said to have advantages over manufacturing and commerce, and that the scope in that sector for division of labour is probably least. My description in the text is thus meant to express the contemporary and traditional assessment of Smith rather than his actual practice.

2   I have in mind Joyce Appleby, for whom Smith is a central player in a 'puzzle' of silence about consumption: J. Brewer and R. Porter, eds, *Consumption and the World of Goods* (London, 1993), pp. 162, 168, 169, 172; and the welcome

and sophisticated remarks of Jules Lubbock, who re-examines Smith from the perspective of taste, beauty, design and the arts, in *The Tyranny of Taste. The Politics of Architecture and Design in Britain, 1550–1960* (New Haven and London, 1995), ch. 6.

3   A. Smith, *The Theory of Moral Sentiments*, ed. D.D. Raphael and A.L. Macfie, *Works and Correspondence* (Oxford, 1979), vol. I, p. 63.

4   *Ibid.*, p. 183.

5   Letter of Smith to William Eden, 3 January 1780, in A. Smith, *Correspondence of Adam Smith*, ed. E.C. Mossner and I.S. Ross, *Works and Correspondence* (Indianapolis, 1987), vol. VI, pp. 245–6.

6   A. Smith, *An Inquiry into the Nature and Causes of the Wealth of Nations*, ed. R.H. Campbell and A.S. Skinner, *Works and Correspondence*, 2 vols (Oxford, 1976), vol. II, p. 346.

7   This has been argued recently by Hans-Joachim Voth, in studies based on the testimony of witnesses at the Old Bailey. He finds that in the second half of the eighteenth century the working week in London may have expanded by at least a third, and perhaps upwards of two-fifths, a change best understood, he adds, if we assume that individuals wanted the extra income to enable them to make purchases on an expanded scale: see H.-J. Voth, 'Work and the Sirens of Consumption in Eighteenth Century London', in M. Bianchi, ed., *The Active Consumer* (London and New York, 1998). Smith notes only that artificers and soldiers, when liberally paid, are apt to apply themselves excessively: Smith, *Wealth of Nations*, p. 100. Sir James Steuart came closer to Voth's finding: '[a]t present', he suggested, 'there is a demand for the ingenuity of man', and 'men are forced to labour now because they are slaves to their own wants': J. Steuart, *An Inquiry into the Principles of Political Economy* [1767], ed. A. Skinner, 2 vols (Edinburgh and London, 1966), pp. 49, 67.

8   Smith, *Wealth of Nations*, p. 330.

9   *Ibid.*, p. 660, though note the earlier, almost equivalent phrase on p. 283.

10   Lubbock, for example, sees a progressive shift in Smith's thought away from consumption as engine of growth and towards the idea that consumption only keeps things 'ticking over', that savings and fixed capital are the real keys: *The Tyranny of Taste*, pp. 121, 126. Appleby, instead, notes that, while Smith expresses the thought that consumption sustains growth, he cannot extol consumption. The (unstated) implication is that he was either unable to resolve an internal conflict or not entirely serious about consumption's purported centrality. J.O. Appleby, *Economic Thought and Ideology in Seventeenth-Century England* (Princeton, 1978), pp. 172–3, 272–3; and 'Consumption in Early Modern Social Thought', in Brewer and Porter, eds, *Consumption and the World of Goods*, p. 168.

11   Smith, *Wealth of Nations*, pp. 869–74.

12   *Ibid.*, p. 870.

13   *Ibid.*, p. 873.

14   *Ibid.*, pp. 874, 875–6.

15   Smith, *The Theory of Moral Sentiments*, pp. 194–5, 200.

16   A. Marshall, *Principles of Economics* [1890], ninth (variorum) edition, with annotations by C.W. Guillebaud, 2 vols (London, 1961), pp. 331–5.

17   F. Galiani, *Della moneta* [1751], ed. A. Merola (Milan, 1963 (1780 edn)), pp. 51–2.

18   I. Pears, *The Discovery of Painting. The Growth of Interest in the Arts in England, 1680–1768* (New Haven and London, 1988), p. 65.

19 A. Smith, *Lectures on Jurisprudence*, ed. R.L. Meek, D.D. Raphael and P.G. Stein, *Works and Correspondence* (Indianapolis, 1982), vol. V, p. 358.
20 E. Forget, 'Disequilibrium Trade as a Metaphor for Social Disorder in the Work of Jean-Baptiste Say', in N. De Marchi and M.S. Morgan, eds, *Higgling. Transactors and Their Markets in the History of Economics*, Annual Supplement to volume 26, *History of Political Economy* (Durham, NC, and London, 1994), pp. 140–1.
21 Smith, *Wealth of Nations*, pp. 190–1.
22 Smith, *Lectures on Jurisprudence*, p. 381.
23 *Ibid.*, pp. 390–1.
24 *Ibid.*, pp. 391–2.
25 *Ibid.*, p. 508.
26 Smith, *The Theory of Moral Sentiments*, pp. 180–1; *Wealth of Nations*, pp. 346, 418–19, 421.
27 *Ibid.*, p. 181.
28 *Ibid.*, p. 349.
29 Smith, *The Theory of Moral Sentiments*, pp. 181–2.
30 A. Smith, *Essays on Philosophical Subjects (and Miscellaneous Pieces)*, ed. W.P.D. Wightman and J.C. Bryce, The Glasgow Edition of *The Works and Correspondence of Adam Smith* (Indianapolis, 1980), vol. IV, p. 173.
31 Smith, *Wealth of Nations*, pp. 346–7.
32 *Ibid.*, pp. 418–19; cf. *Lectures on Jurisprudence*, p. 261.
33 Smith, *Wealth of Nations*, p. 421.
34 *Ibid.*, p. 283.
35 *Ibid.*, pp. 337–8.
36 *Ibid.*, p. 363.
37 *Ibid.*, pp. 368–9, 426–7.
38 *Ibid.*, p. 364.
39 *Ibid.*
40 Smith, *Lectures on Jurisprudence*, p. 522; cf. *Wealth of Nations*, p. 366.
41 H. Saxby, *The British Customs* (London, 1757), p. 637.
42 Smith, *Wealth of Nations*, pp. 504, 523; cf. 453, 457.
43 *Ibid.*, p. 611.
44 *Ibid.*, p. 597. These concerns are discussed, with particular reference to Scotland, in the valuable editors' introduction to the Glasgow edition of the *Wealth of Nations*: see especially pp. 45–6.
45 *Ibid.*, p. 454.
46 *Ibid.*, pp. 604, 607, 610–11.
47 Smith, *The Theory of Moral Sentiments*, p. 179.
48 Smith, *Wealth of Nations*, p. 523.
49 Lubbock, *The Tyranny of Taste*, p. 220.
50 Smith, *Essays on Philosophical Subjects*, p. 185.
51 *Ibid.*, pp. 242–54.
52 Smith, *The Theory of Moral Sentiments*, p. 179.
53 Smith, *Essays on Philosophical Subjects*, p. 42; cf. pp. 33, 105.
54 *Ibid.*, p. 42.
55 *Ibid.*, p. 185 for painting, and p. 98 for Newton's system.
56 *Ibid.*, p. 185.
57 *Ibid.*, pp. 42–3.
58 Smith, *The Theory of Moral Sentiments*, p. 179.
59 The editors of the Glasgow edition of the *Theory of Moral Sentiments* notice the link between ethics and political economy, but do not extend the chain to

aesthetics, an extension for which I find the evidence in the surviving essays to be compelling.

60   Smith actually devoted a separate discussion to this in the lectures on jurisprudence: *Lectures on Jurisprudence*, pp. 333–7 and 487–8. This is given close attention in N. De Marchi and H.J. Van Miegroet, 'Ingenuity, Preference, and the Pricing of Pictures. The Smith–Reynolds Connection', Duke University, mimeo, 1998.

61   Smith, *Wealth of Nations*, p. 181.

Sans-culottes, sans café, sans tabac: shifting realms of necessity and luxury in eighteenth-century France[1] [2]

In the winters of 1792 and 1793, as the social, political and economic uncertainties occasioned by war and revolution mounted, the working people of Paris took to the streets in vigorous and sometimes violent protest against the rising costs of urban life. Harassing shopkeepers and haranguing anyone who would listen, they demanded that 'honest people' be provided with 'goods of prime necessity': soap and candles, sugar and coffee. When their deputations to the Legislative Assembly and then the Convention met with no response, the frustrated Parisians took measures into their own hands, storming grocers' shops, taking goods by force, and paying their own definitions of 'a fair price'.[2]

These so-called 'sugar rioters' have been important characters in debates about the nature of popular revolution in the French capital. In the now classic account of Albert Soboul, 'hunger' was the 'essential feature' that united these master artisans and little-skilled day labourers into the category known as the 'sans-culotterie' (literally, the 'people without knee breeches').[3] Moved by economic hardship, they were allied against the feudal aristocracy and the merchant bourgeoisie, forming an active and vital part of the revolutionary struggle. Partially mollified by the Montagnard imposition of wage and price controls (the General Maximum) in September 1793, the sans-culottes would see their further demands for social equality eventually founder on the 'fundamental contradiction' between their goals and that of a revolution that was, in Soboul's interpretation, inherently, indeed necessarily, bourgeois.

From Soboul's perspective, the sugar riots were about 'consumption' in its most corporeal sense. People were angry and hungry: because they desperately needed food to put in their mouths, established artisans and youthful apprentices overlooked their other differences and joined together to riot and demand their 'fair share'. In contrast, William Sewell, in his 'The Sans-Culotte Rhetoric of Subsistence', takes exception with the idea that it was the shared socio-economic experience of hunger that shaped the sans-culottes' sense of identity and purpose. Shifting the focus of analysis from material conditions to political culture, Sewell argues that 'subsistence' was as much a concrete category of abstract debate as an issue of daily anguish. Tracing metaphors of 'starvation' and 'blood-drinking' through numerous petitions and speeches, he theorises that popular attention focused on potential food shortages not because they had 'practical effects on consumers', but because they seemed to prove the existence of diabolical counter-revolutionary conspiracies.[4] Since Nature was bountiful and food therefore plentiful, conniving villains had to lurk behind all shortages; following from this assumption, unmasking the Revolution's enemies was best done by talking about shortages. As a political issue, subsistence was a set of tropes and images that had developed during the bread riots of earlier decades; this powerful language remained central to popular political demands throughout the Revolution, even when no real threat of shortages existed. Subsistence, Sewell concludes, was as much a rhetorical structure as an economic one. The grocery riots may have been driven by their own, ideological imperatives – their logic intimately linked, Sewell suggests, to 'the larger discursive armature of terror' – but they were not a reaction to material necessity.[5]

Sewell's overall point – that in order to understand popular activity during the Revolution, we need to see the sans-culottes as defined by political intervention and emotional rhetoric and not by objective social position alone – is persuasive. As he acknowledges, his is an interpretation that does not so much reject Soboul's work as it further complicates the causal relation between experience and ideology. But in his closing paragraph Sewell makes an observation about the eighteenth-century culture of consumption that is, to our minds, misleading. Referring specifically to the riots of winter 1793, he comments on the 'remarkable fact' that popular unrest erupted not over bread, the staff of life (which was sold by bakers rather than grocers), but over 'relatively dispensable consumer goods' such as soap and sugar. 'To me,' he writes, 'this remarkable fact implies that subsistence worries were produced by sans-culotte rhetoric as much as sans-culotte rhetoric was produced by worries about subsistence.'[6]

This final paragraph takes Sewell's argument in an unexpected direction. Overall, his is a nuanced argument, one that explores the interplay of language, imagery and popular urban mentalities in a period of crisis and conflict, and that transcends a mechanistic base-superstructure model in favour of a more genuinely dialectical understanding of cause and effect. But Sewell's remarks about the sugar riots sacrifice subtlety in order to divide the world into two distinct categories: necessity ('the edge of starvation') and luxury ('dispensable consumer goods'). Concluding that no one motivated by 'real hunger' ransacks a grocer's store for sugar, Sewell echoes a point first made two centuries ago by Bertrand Barère and Maximilien Robespierre. The day after the worst riots, in fact, Barère addressed the Convention to denounce the protests as counter-revolutionary rabble rousing, while Robespierre berated the people for their obsession with 'measly merchandise', and enjoined them to rise 'not to gather up pieces of sugar but to overwhelm the brigands'.[7] The two great ideologists of revolutionary government emphasised different points – Barère condemned plots and conspiracies, while Robespierre diagnosed counter-revolutionary self-indulgence – but they both drew, and politicised, a thick dividing line between 'necessity' and 'luxury'. Coffee and sugar, from the perspective of the Committee of Public Safety, could have no properly revolutionary content.

Sewell's remarks effectively endorse and re-inscribe the neat necessity/luxury dichotomy that made Revolutionary Government so rhetorically forceful and so practically impossible. Weakening his own argument, he says that because the bakeries of Paris were full of bread, the people could not really have been hungry. But he thereby misses a key point: the history of the eighteenth century is overwhelmingly a story of the move away from subsistence economies and of the widespread emergence of new, but equally real, hungers. As Marx and Engels – hardly ones to underemphasise material conditions – wrote in *The German Ideology*: 'the satisfaction of the first need . . . leads to new needs; and this production of new needs is the first historical act'.[8] To assume that because people have access to daily bread they therefore cannot feel themselves to be needy is to overlook the supremely historical act which is the creation of needs.

Ample evidence from other food riots indicates that 'hunger rioters' have rarely been people on the verge of starvation.[9] Rather, the eighteenth-century grain riot crowd consisted predominantly of established and self-respecting people, outraged when prices grossly exceeded accepted norms, when grain cost more than it 'ought to'. Sewell is right to say that the sans-culotte movement becomes all the more 'remarkable' when one imagines it driven by demands for coffee and sugar, but he overstates the case when he concludes that subsistence rhetoric had therefore outlived the subsistence crisis. What is most striking is that coffee and sugar had, by 1793, become 'needs' worth rioting about. Of all the things available for purchase (or theft) only some cause large-scale unrest. The sans-culottes denounced restaurateurs who served lavish meals but, as far as we know, they never staged asparagus or shrimp riots. That may have been because the price of asparagus fluctuated much less dramatically than that of white sugar, but it seems more plausible that far fewer people had a strong moral sense of what it ought to cost. In the late eighteenth century, asparagus and shrimp (like 'culottes') were things that the people of Paris could do without. Sugar and coffee – the essential ingredients of the *café au lait* which observers remarked had become the daily breakfast of the urban worker long before 1789 – were clearly not.[10] Though historians of the popular classes have largely ignored it, popular diet had been changing over the eighteenth century – and changing faster than the staple political rhetoric of food entitlement. The sans-culotte of Year II, it appears, could plausibly regard as a subsistence matter his being *sans sucre* or *sans café*.

At the peak of the crisis of Year II, revolutionaries often made it clear that they were involved in a moral struggle, defending the exigencies of collective need against a luxury-loving and selfish nobility. This harsh perspective, with its starkly manichean contrast between good and evil (need and indulgence), was a commonplace of revolutionary speechifying, with a distinguished career both before and after the 1790s. The image of France as a country populated by only two significant groups of actors – the grime-coated *peuple* whose lives of unrelieved drudgery made them look eighty years old when they were actually thirty-five, and rakish *aristos* who appeared youthful and gay until they removed their finery and revealed decrepit skeletons – has had a remarkable tenacity, enduring from British caricatures of Hogarth's time to the social history of the mid to late twentieth century. While French revolutionaries in 1792–94 contrasted the new regime's egalitarian moral economy with the old regime's aristocratic and self-indulgent frivolity in order to highlight historical change, earlier commentators had fixed on a comparable pattern to characterise the national differences between Britain and France. For half a century before the Revolution, debate on both sides of the Channel centred on a systematic contrast between allegedly aristocratic France and the putatively more robust and freer English society. Voltaire pioneered this kind of analysis: his *Lettres philosophiques* (also known, tellingly, as his *Lettres anglaises*) of 1734 singled out England as the home of social mobility, benign public-spiritedness, religious tolerance, material prosperity and open commercialism.[11] Subsequent social critics were fast to pick up his message as they endeavoured to import commercial values into France on the back of English (and, to a lesser extent, Dutch) agricultural and manufacturing technology. Nor were reform-minded Frenchmen the only ones to marvel at England's 'advances'. From mid-century, English travellers routinely criticised French retailers for their appallingly under-developed commercial spirit: William Cole, visiting Paris in 1765, thought most shops 'the poorest gloomy Dungeons you can possibly conceive', and, like many of his compatriots, regarded the French custom of haggling as utterly barbaric, a bastard form of beggary and theft.[12] Agronomist Arthur Young likewise travelled extensively in France, in the years immediately before the Revolution, and did not need the Père Duchesne to tell him that French society was distinguished by the coexistence of privilege and poverty. In his *Travels in France in 1787, 1788 and 1789*, Young repeatedly juxtaposed rare instances of arrogant affluence with images of widespread rural misery. Mary Wollstonecraft, writing in 1794, sketched a similar picture and highlighted the fatal absence of a strong middle ground in French society. For her, as for other British observers, it was the 'cast-like [*sic*] division' of French society that ensured a perpetual pattern of 'servility and voluptuousness', mass impoverishment and elite luxury. Lacking the social 'middle' characteristic of England, France could never achieve the harmonious levels of consumption found across the Channel – as was demonstrated by the fact that the very word 'comfort' was untranslatable and untranslated into the French language.[13]

Breathing the life of caricature into an otherwise potentially sterile discussion of economic developments, political rhetoric and witticism often focused on the most corporeal forms of consumption: eating and drinking. Hogarth and other cartoonists portrayed their fellow Englishmen tucking ravenously into roast beef, which they washed down with ale and followed with noble old puddings so as to produce a heartening stoutness. The French, in contrast, were depicted surviving on a diet of thin soup, frogs, snails and rotting black bread – the only foods allowed them under Catholicism's hypocritical dietary regulations. (English images of French clergymen, by contrast, often showed them fat and decadent.) Throughout the 'Second Hundred Years War' of 1688–1815, then, English patriotism was presented as warmly nourishing and sustaining, a clear victor over the meagre culture and measly cuisine of its main commercial and military rival.[14]

Much recent comparative scholarship on eighteenth-century French and English socio-economic developments has often shown little inclination to depart from this cartoon. Harold Perkin, for example, has helped to harden the caricature into an orthodoxy by arguing that England's precocious industrialisation owed much to the size and solidity of its middling groups. In spite of a historiographical tradition which, in the wake of the work of E.P. Thompson, has placed emphasis on social division, conflict and the uneven distribution of wealth in eighteenth-century England,[15] for Perkin and numerous others, the gentle slope of England's social pyramid allowed industry-encouraging patterns of emulative consumption, while the steep gradation of society in France and other Continental states produced in contrast 'a small class of luxury consumers' and 'a large mass of consumption-resisting peasants'.[16]

Such an account is not merely the product of British francophobia, for Perkin's conclusions fit surprisingly well with the essentially miserabilist – if we can call them that – assumptions about eighteenth-century French economic growth that have been almost universally accepted by historians since World War II. Under the powerful influence of Ernest Labrousse and Fernand Braudel, an exceptionally wide range of scholars has endorsed a picture of British boom and French stagnation. Thanks, at least in part, to the eminent positions Labrousse and Braudel occupied in post-war French academic politics, even historians on both sides of the acrimonious 'Jacobino-Marxist' vs 'Revisionist' debate over the origins of the Revolution have agreed that the French economy of the eighteenth century was in a sorry state. Supplementing their account during the 1960s with a demographic analysis that appeared to elaborate and strengthen their argument, Labrousse and Braudel expounded their views at greatest length in their 1970 volume of the *Histoire économique et sociale de la France* (today a work of near canonical status).[17] Painstaking composition and correlation of serial sources allowed Labrousse to conclude that between the 1720s and the eve of the Revolution, while land rents and tithes boomed, agricultural prices rose by some 62 per cent and nominal wages merely by 26 per cent – suggesting a fall of between 15 and 25 per cent in purchasing power for those needing to purchase their foodstuffs.[18] This was a pattern of development from which a happy few benefited, but, since population growth outpaced economic expansion, it also entailed the long-term pauperisation of the mass of the population.

Labrousse organised his history of the economy around the concept of 'demand', and he anchored this notion in the rhetoric of imperative, observable, empirical necessity. For Labrousse, need and demand were not complex problems debated within societies, but brute issues of simple, mathematical reality: more people (France's population rose by a third in the period under study) required more food than an archaic economy could provide. Throughout the eighteenth century, the seigneurial rentier class profited from developments without investing in economic growth. At the other end of the spectrum, low and inelastic demand for manufactured products had ruinous effects on business – high bread prices consequent on bad harvests, for example, caused disastrous slumps in demand for manufactured products by the popular masses who were intent merely on not starving or not going to the wall. The countryside was moreover always in command – urbanisation rates were slow, with only one French person in five a town-dweller even by 1789. Survival rather than improvement – or even change – seems thus to have characterised the life of the mass of the population. 'No new product, colonial or metropolitan', Labrousse tells us, of the eighteenth century in general, 'perceptibly modified popular styles of living'.[19] On clothing, he remarks, 'people pass, from one generation to the next, clothing of everlasting drugget. The role of fashion is virtually nil. In cloth as in cut, popular dress remained traditional'. Overall, he states, his work is based on the 'postulate of general fixity in consumed qualities': 'nothing can more recall the appearance of a worker or peasant in 1734 than a worker or peasant in 1789'.[20]

This view of an economy irremediably rural, weak and unable to break through structural constraints on growth, and of a society in which, while a few prospered, much of the population was locked in a timeless fixity and an elemental struggle for survival – an outlook which Louis Cullen recently characterised as 'depression history of the 1930s'[21] – has been buttressed by much outstanding scholarship on the structure of Ancien Régime society. Olwen Hufton's work on the poor, for example, has given the distinct impression that, while the luxury-loving elite prospered, a majority of the population in the eighteenth century were literally on or below the breadline and engaged in a daily struggle to bring bread to their dinner-table.[22] Nor has Fernand Braudel's interest in consumption – as demonstrated in his *Capitalism and Material Life* – shifted the assumption of a basic bipolarity in French society, for he highlighted the relative imperviousness to changes in fashion in most localities in the world and most social groupings below the very highest elites before the late eighteenth century.[23]

The middling groups of French society located between the impoverished many and the noble-dominated elite have thus until relatively recently suffered neglect at the hands of historians more anxious to focus their analyses on the ranks of the poor or else on the luxury-loving elite.[24] This neglect is grounded – sometimes unconsciously – in Physiocratic analyses of the late eighteenth century, with their condemnation of the 'sterility' located in trade and manufacturing.[25] Arguing that agriculture was the source of any true wealth, the Physiocrats agonised over the grain trade (that *locus classicus* of 'necessity') while ignoring, if not outright attacking, other forms of commerce. Their emphasis was hardly unique: bread clearly acted as a major cultural marker in Ancien Régime France, where the daily ingestion of white loaves was the single greatest indicator of modest normality, continuity and fidelity. As Steven Kaplan has shown, the country was massively 'bread-centred' (or 'panocentric'),[26] and the French had as many names for different types of bread as the Eskimos for snow and the Bedouins for sand. Panegyric panocentrism has an almost uninterrupted legacy in France (and among Francophiles); it is this, perhaps more than any other single factor, that has permitted generations of historians to accept largely uncritically Mary Wollstonecraft's characterisation of pre-Revolutionary France as a society where 'servility and voluptuousness' were strangely juxtaposed but never mediated.

Braudelo–Labroussian orthodoxy has proved a hard nut to crack, and many historians show no stomach for the task. In a recent account, for example, Peter Jones, while highlighting Labrousse's relative neglect of institutional factors of economic development, gives the French scholar a pretty clean bill of health.[27] Early attempts by David Landes as long ago as 1950 to undermine Labrousse's model on the grounds that prices are a poor proxy for production and that elasticities in supply and demand are not symmetrical, especially where consumption goods are concerned, failed to make much impression.[28] And it is now over thirty years, moreover, since François Crouzet launched a head-on assault on many of the 'miserabilist' presuppositions behind Labrousse's work. Crouzet's work still commands a good deal of respect. Utilising what quantitative measures were available to him, he showed a French economy making more determined economic progress on many fronts than the 'First Industrial Nation' across the Channel. Though in this article and in subsequent comments, Crouzet stressed the need to set comparisons within the context of structural differences between the economies of the two states, his anti-miserabilism undermined some Labroussian certainties, not least over the question of demand.[29] Even if there were, he pointed out, a long-term fall in real wages after the 1760s, the concomitant rise in feudal rents and agricultural profits must have acted to counter any erosion of demand, by bringing extra income from these sources into numerous hands (including those of the wealthy peasantry), and boosting trade and manufacturing.[30] David Weir's recent reworking and supplementing of Labrousse's figures has had an even more devastating effect: for him, rapid growth in rents, improving markets and relatively constant real wages formed the master-story of the eighteenth-century economy. His figures suggest rough stability in worker purchasing power – a 7 per cent drop in real wages is his worst-case scenario, a figure which bears up pretty well when set against European – including English – comparators (Mary Wollstonecraft, please note).[31]

Michael Sonenscher has further challenged Labroussian assumptions about the extent to which a putative fall in real wages triggered an overall fall in demand from another angle. Labrousse's figures for wage rates massively underestimate, he argues, the extent to which the wage was a bargain subject to a range of complicating influences. Official wage tariffs used by Labrousse may have shown relative stability over several decades, but these were invariably only an imperfect guide to what actually changed hands on the ground once one took into account overtime arrangements, payment in kind, increases due to production in difficult circumstances, and so on. To this must be added a 'kaleidoscopic undergrowth of credit' far more extensive than Labrousse appears to have imagined, and an increase in coinage available which almost certainly acted to extend demand within the economy.[32]

Weir's and Sonenscher's critiques – which are applicable in rural as well as urban contexts – are all the more telling when the domestic arrangements of the labouring classes and peasantry are taken into account. Labrousse's arguments about consumer demand were structured by the concept of a family budget largely, sometimes exclusively, devoted to essential foodstuffs. Yet the wage rates on which he was drawing applied primarily to single, unmarried men – men who specifically endeavoured to *give up* wage labour once they became master artisans and married. It is hardly surprising that a picture of necessitous parsimony emerges from calculations juxtaposing the official wage rate for a young, single man with the imagined expenses of a family of five. (Labrousse admits that his dreary figures do not apply to workers living alone or even to those based in towns.)[33] Moreover, when we consider the extent of female employment in the eighteenth century (in domestic outwork and domestic service in particular), we recognise how fantastical a creature Labrousse's 'real wage' must have been. This is all the more the case if we accept Jan de Vries's 'industrious revolution' hypothesis, whereby household members in eighteenth-century western Europe chose to work harder, with wives and children joining adult males in money-making activities which would allow them greater purchasing power in the new world of goods.[34] At all events, to make rigid comparisons between wage levels and prices without taking into account the actual behaviour of the varied types of domestic unit or the availability of work to all family members is gravely to simplify and distort any worthwhile analysis of earning power and demand in this era of proto-industrialisation.[35]

Labrousse's model thus signally underestimates the diversity of worker and peasant households, the complexity of the family earning cycles and the extent of female engagement in the labour-market. The official day-wage on which Labrousse's calculations are made was not the rock-solid arithmetically precise yardstick Labrousse envisaged but a 'cipher'[36] – maybe we could say a fiction? – which bore an unstable and somewhat arbitrary relationship to the alleged signifier of actual earnings. With these caveats in mind, it becomes possible to propose a more generous estimation of the evolution of the volume and nature of demand over the course of the eighteenth century which shifts France out from under the shadow of allegedly more socially advanced England.[37] This should be contextualised of course in the light of the very real and unavoidable presence of widespread urban and rural poverty of a kind, moreover, which was cruelly exposed by short-term oscillations in food prices: even if we reject as too extreme the ambient 'miserabilism' of the Braudelo–Labroussian orthodoxy, it is not our aim to deny the existence of widespread misery and suffering within eighteenth-century French society. But things were not as pervasively bad for most of the population for most of the time, as Labrousse and his followers have seemed to claim. And even if Labrousse's model is taken to give a rough and ready approximation of the overall rhythm and tempo of economic development, it does not do justice to the enormous variations around the arithmetic mean – nor to the changing meanings of luxury and necessity.

Investigation of other source materials can help indicate just how significant that variation was. Evidence from the marriage dowries of individuals from lower-class groups is particularly eloquent: supporting David Weir's critique of Labrousse, studies show that the size of these dowries rose with relative steadiness over the century, with little sign of the decline in popular living standards regarded as axiomatic by the miserabilists.[38] And while the dowry record suggests a less gloomy picture of consumption patterns, comparable data from post-mortem inventories point even more emphatically in the same direction. Although there are problems about the latter source as an indicator of trends of wealth,[39] another feature about them highlights the need to complicate the Labroussian model of demand and consumption: namely the growth in the range and value of consumer goods. Here, the work of Daniel Roche, Annik Pardailhé-Galabrun and Cissie Fairchilds on eighteenth-century Paris has been of paramount importance.[40] Fairchilds has systematically compared the presence of a number of consumer objects in lower-class inventories in the years 1725 and 1785 in Paris, and shows a pattern of consumption pretty far removed from the realm of brutish necessity implicit in the Labroussian account. 'Furniture novelties' (chests of drawers, bookcases, tea-tables, secretaries, etc.) had been found in 20 per cent of inventories in 1725; 79.7 per cent of 1785 inventories included them. Other noteworthy rises included jewellery (49.2 to 78.1 per cent), gold watches (5.1 to 54.7 per cent), umbrellas (10.2 to 31.3 per cent), fans (5.1 to 34.4 per cent), snuffboxes (6.8 to 32.8 per cent), tea and coffee accessories (18.6 to 45.3 per cent) and books (29.8 to 43.8 per cent).[41] Fairchilds' work has been important too in showing the extent to which the growing commodification of material culture was conducted in the form of what she calls 'populuxe' objects – imitations of luxury items once largely confined to the aristocracy. Using cheaper raw materials and streamlined production techniques, manufacturers responded to the demands of social emulation with – for example – paste jewellery, rows of book-spines to fill empty shelves, artificial flowers and fruit, papier mâché (rather than wood or metal) accoutrements such as snuffboxes and caskets, and rabbit-fur (rather than beaver) hats.[42] *Pace* Labrousse,[43] the households and the personal appearances of ordinary town-dwellers changed drastically in the last decades of the Ancien Régime. Analysing the consumer goods in the possession of the sorts of artisans, shopkeepers, servants and petty officials who would later form the core of revolutionary popular radicalism, Daniel Roche demonstrates that such individuals were acutely fashion conscious, and that their wardrobes actually indicate a marked preference for knee-breeches over straight trousers![44] Thus prior to the extraordinarily socially deflationist period of the Terror, it would appear, sans-culottes could no more do without culottes than they could sugar or coffee.

Two key issues emerge from this discussion. First, there is the vital empirical point that many French people in the eighteenth century simply had much more stuff in their possessions than has previously been imagined. A population in which one-third of households owns a coffeepot or tea set is not the same, of course, as one in which nearly everyone does. Yet the general scale and intensity of the consumer phenomenon are fairly unequivocal. Nor was this merely a Parisian phenomenon: though equally extensive inventory analyses have yet to be conducted for the provinces, the record begins to look broadly similar.[45] France is habitually represented as a peasant-based society in contrast to England, yet though the French urban population which formed the bedrock of consumer demand did not grow as rapidly as that in England's over the eighteenth century, at the century's end there were still one-third more town-dwellers in France than in England.[46] In sum, the French economy of the eighteenth century can no longer be summarily described as a regime of suffering peasants and indolent aristocrats. Neither the fabulously wealthy nor the miserably poor have any use for papier mâché *chinoiserie* or 'beaver' hats made of rabbit. Rather, these are the sorts of goods that alert us to the existence of a growing and significant group of middling urban consumers.

Listing and enumerating widely diffused populuxe commodities can be amusing and enlightening, but it is also, eventually, limited. An account emphasising that half of the households in pre-Revolutionary Paris owned gold watches and books, while four-fifths included jewellery and 'furniture novelties', merely replaces Labrousse's dour statistics with Fairchild's (or Roche's) more optimistic ones. 'The best would be to count', wrote Braudel in *Civilisation and Capitalism*, and the powerful legacy of this and many similar statements has too often prompted historians simply to substitute one numericalism for another.[47] Nor has this impulse been specific to economic history: historians of reading and literacy have counted volumes in-octavo and those in-quarto, and struggled to estimate circulation figures; historians of diet have attempted to calculate whether boarding-school boys in the Ancien Régime were receiving their daily minimum requirements of calcium, protein and iron.[48] Yet an overbearing need to count can affect our research habits and shape our perceptions in ways we do not always consider: we know so much about bread precisely because it was a topic of state control. Hence it has remained far more visible in the archival record and far more susceptible to being counted, but as long as we focus on bread alone we allow our historical questions to be dictated by eighteenth-century preoccupations and categories of administrative police.[49] While efforts to distinguish honest necessity from indolent waste were central to eighteenth-century writing on luxury, we are not obliged to accept these categories as givens. Indeed, the historical specificity of this debate argues for a more nuanced interrogation of these very concepts.

Labrousse and Braudel's definition of 'the necessary' – like that of the Physiocrats whom they echoed – was polemical. They needed to define 'necessity' in a particular fashion in order to make their calculations and research meaningful. Olwen Hufton conceded that it was 'artificial to use wheat prices alone as the measure of living standards', but she went ahead and did so anyway, since wheat *mercuriales* were the one set of sources susceptible to extensive serial analysis.[50] It goes almost without saying that we have learned much from this approach, but it is not evident that we must remain tied to this vision. Average grain prices can no more tell us how coffee or sugar transmuted from luxury into necessity than textile production figures can tell us why Marie Antoinette dressed up like a shepherdess.

This, then, is the second, more theoretical, point to emerge from the discussion: the simple binary logic of 'need' versus 'desire' – on which so much thinking about consumption still depends – must be complicated. For as more goods circulate, more things become necessities – and more still become the focus of want and desire, shifting the contours of notions of right and entitlement in more materialistic, even 'luxurious' directions. One means of entry into that nether world between old luxuries and new necessities, between having and wanting and between possession and desire, is to explore the under-researched eighteenth-century world of advertisement – a medium which can highlight not merely the growth and changing patterns of consumer demand but also illuminate the techniques and methods utilised by entrepreneurs to create demand and to stimulate desire. From the 1750s, urban France was covered by a dense network of advertising newssheets (the *Affiches*) which grew progressively larger, fatter and more numerous as more and more 'necessary' announcements had to be made.[51] The editor of the *Affiches de Lyon* was not unusual in promising to include in his paper 'everything that concerns trade and that bears the traits of utility' and he was equally typical in his expansive definition of 'utility'. Covering every kind of property (land, office, seigneuries), all manner of commodities (from books, scientific instruments, jewellery and silverware through to rat poison, waterproof shoes, patent medicines and piles of horse manure) and an extremely wide array of services (domestic service, business cards, food and drink, medical attention), little except for explicit political commentary escaped the *affichiste*'s definition of 'utility'. With their advertisements for 'best quality turtles', or 'embroidered black silk for ladies' shoes', they remind us that 'usefulness' and 'necessity' are not categories that exist independently of history and culture.

'Necessity' is perhaps most often invoked in discussions of food and nutrition, but even here it would be ridiculously reductive to assimilate all non-'luxury' foods and drinks to the realm of raw necessity. In twentieth-century Trinidad, for instance, people consider sweetened soft drinks a 'basic necessity' and it is extremely rare to see anyone drinking water.[52] The majority of eighteenth-century Europeans (including almost all French people) knew that potatoes were unfit for human consumption; they would have scoffed at the notion that a potato famine could cause mass starvation.[53] In an Ancien Régime that was overwhelmingly and officially Catholic, the eating of non-meat foods on Fridays and during Lent was not a taste or craving but an absolute need – one that might be met with lentils, eggs or pistachio-truffle-fish pâté but that remained a necessity nevertheless.[54] The cook-caterer or tavernkeeper who did much of his business in veal, mutton and pork was not invited or enticed but required by law to sell only *maigre* on fast days, and had any contravening pheasant, rabbit or veal quickly confiscated.[55] The Encyclopedists rejected that religious definition of need as contrived superstition – pointing, like so many cultural materialists *avant la lettre*, to the functional wisdom of a ritual calendar that kept animals alive for breeding. They also noted the physical benefits of springtime abstinence, thereby highlighting the emerging interest in questions of mental health and corporeal well-being among the population in general.

Friandises médicamenteuses – medicinal dainties – were in fact among the most assiduously advertised commodities in the late Ancien Régime.[56] The eighteenth century's booming medical market-place, characterised by an expanding and diversifying use of medical and pseudo-medical goods and services, clearly redefined necessity and luxury in increasingly scientific, rather than moral, terms. More medical practitioners and new medical specialisms; the extensive commercialisation of proprietary medicines and drugs; the appearance of new medical institutions such as private madhouses, childbirth facilities and clinics for the treatment of venereal diseases[57] – all contributed to, and in turn were made possible by, medical science's definition of a panoply of new needs and imperatives. Medicine, in all its avatars (reputable and not so reputable), identified necessities which few had hitherto even imagined. Pierre Pomme, perhaps the most famous medical man of his day, insisted that a diet of white foods, ten hours of daily baths, and a steady supply of ice cubes were all absolutely required in order 'to defeat the many-headed hydra' of convulsive vapours.[58] Dr Joseph Raulin, former Inspector General of Mineral Waters, told patients suffering with phthysie that 'in your condition, you may only permit yourself a few light, easily digested foods, and those in very small quantities'.[59] In prescriptions and proscriptions, a patient's conduct and behaviour – no matter how extraordinary – were determined by scientifically defined necessity, and not by whim or desire.

Medicinal goods were prescribed as necessities, but they were often promoted as (semi)luxuries – as populuxe products in fact. As likely to be incorporated into regimes of leisure as into daily work habits, the dictates of eighteenth-century medical science had profound effects now rarely considered or acknowledged: the first restaurateurs opened shop in the 1760s, making it their business to serve specifically 'restorative' bouillons; manufacturers of cosmetics, under attack from physicians, retaliated by touting their products' natural ingredients so successfully that the wearing of make-up became increasingly acceptable – even into a Revolution habitually antagonistic to cosmetics as 'unnatural' and 'untransparent'. (Robespierre, it will be remembered, powdered his hair throughout the Terror.)[60]

As the example of quasi-therapeutic restaurateurs suggests, medicinal products were available from a range of retailers on the fringes of, or often frankly outside the core of, the orthodox medical community. *Médecin du roi* Sénac, for example, licensed the pastry-cook, Bezou, to sell his cough-calming marshmallows; while at the Hôtel d'Auvergne on the rue Saint Honoré, fresh tortoises 'of the quality necessary for medicinal bouillons' could be acquired throughout the year.[61] Gosset *père*, grocer-distiller-confectioner near the Pont Saint Michel, sold his 'admirable cologne water, excellent for cases of apoplexy, vapours, migraines, colic, and other ills' alongside twenty-seven liqueurs and forty-five sorts of flavoured and scented oils.[62] His fourteen varieties of ratafia included common favourites such as peach, raspberry and carnation, but also the more specific 'cassis pectoral' and 'noix stomachale'. He sold boxes of bonbons 'for baptisms' and Breton gruel 'for chest maladies'. If a consumptive Parisian needed gruel for his chest, he just as clearly required sweets for a newborn's family.

Outlining a doctrine that might be called 'therapeutic individualism', eighteenth-century medicine emphasised that one person's meat could be another's poison, and one person's luxury, another's necessity. Widely available medical advice literature, such as Le Bègue de Presle's *Le Conservateur de la Santé*, painted a terrifying picture of the dangers posed by a host of actions – eating food that is too hot, eating food that is too cold, eating without drinking, and drinking without eating are only a few of the dozens of 'dangers' he outlined – but it stressed that effects did not so much inhere in specific foods or practices as they depended on the relation between behaviour and individual.[63]

This kind of individualised therapeutics addressed to the medical consumer was correlated with another highly noticeable trait within the advertising world, namely the tendency to use health issues as a means of selling goods and services. Merchants and shopkeepers soon realised they could expand the market for their products (and incidentally add to them the veneer of science) if they added the phrase *de santé* to their goods. Advertiser-sheets offered their readers *corps de santé* (body corsets), *bains de santé* (health-giving baths), *tables de santé* (bed-trays for food and medicines) and *poeles de santé* (smoke-free braziers). In the food area, there was – for example – *farine de santé* (potato flour), *thé de santé*, *chocolat de santé* and much else besides.[64] The phrase *de santé* tacked on to a commodity that might otherwise be considered a luxury thus was ample justification for its purchase. A *moutarde de santé* ('health mustard') used as a remedy for chilblains was offered by vinegar-maker Jean-Baptiste Maille: he gave it away gratis to help the poor (who were encouraged to bring their own pots) throughout the winter. But this arch-entrepreneur was also a generalist of genius: he stocked his elegant shop with more than two hundred further varieties of mustard and vinegar, each with its own amazing properties. Thus there was a vinegar to redden cheeks and one to whiten skin; a vinegar to whiten teeth and one to darken white hairs, as well as the 'Four Thieves Vinegar' to be used against airborne contagions.[65]

The increased importance attached to questions of health individualised and relativised provision while justifying the passage of erstwhile luxuries into the realm of necessity – a transformation evident, as we have seen, at every level of commodity exchange. Just as substances like Maille's mustards and vinegars were marketed to a popular audience in terms of health, beauty and general well-being, so coffee, sugar and tobacco all followed similar trajectories into the French diet, moving from exotic products to medicinal substances to common staples in the course of the late seventeenth and eighteenth centuries. Sugar had been used throughout the Middle Ages as a preservative, in medicines and as the key ingredient in elaborate pieces of semi-edible table decoration, but the growth of Caribbean sugarplanting colonies had generalised its use and lowered its cost. As Labrousse showed, the cheapest grains around which popular diet revolved were the most subject to long-term price rises and short-term price fluctuations. Conversely, one-time luxuries such as sugar experienced a long-term decline in market price across the eighteenth century.

Sugar's status as food, medicine or dangerous drug still provoked scholarly debate in the early eighteenth century, but all the learned commentary was unlikely to slow production in the West Indian colonies. While sugar consumption in France may not have expanded quite so dramatically as it did in England (and this point is hardly settled), Bernardin de Saint-Pierre nonetheless blamed it for immiserating both Africa and America, and the enduring conflict in the 'Second Hundred Years War' (1688–1815) between England and France often came to revolve around the fortunes of the 'Sugar Islands', which as a royal decree in 1767 put it, formed 'the kingdom's most important branch of commerce'.[66] Sugar became so common that by the late 1770s, Parisian pastry-cooks specifically emphasised that some few of their most specialised delicacies were made *without* sugar – an exception that in many ways substantiates Claude Fischler's claim that the 1780s and 1790s in France were 'plutôt saccharophile'.[67]

Coffee, introduced into France in the late seventeenth century, had been the subject of immediate fascination and controversy as well. Its beneficial and harmful side effects were debated in medical schools and polite society; Madame de Sévigné wondered whether she was to 'take it as if it were a medicine?'.[68] Already in 1692, Louis XIV granted tax farmers the exclusive right of selling coffee, on the assumption that funds raised would help pay the costs of 'the current war'.[69] The monopoly proved difficult to enforce and eventually lapsed; coffee drinking continued on the uprise. Suggestions that its growing popularity contributed to falling wine sales (and thereby further immiserated the peasantry) are unsubstantiated: a marked rise in coffee drinking in the 1760s actually coincided with the golden age of the wine industry, as Labrousse notes.[70] Though both sugar and coffee had been, at points in the past, luxury goods available only to a tiny fraction of the population, by the end of the eighteenth century, their status had changed considerably. They had become common, daily items, things it was difficult to imagine life without. What, after all, could be more Parisian than a café, and what is more necessary for the running of a café than coffee and sugar? Prior to 1789, two and a half million pounds of the former and six and a half million pounds of the latter had been consumed in the city each year.[71] Although it is true – as Gwynne Lewis has pointed out to us[72] – that it would be difficult to imagine the average *portefaix* from the Faubourg Saint-Marcel nipping up to the

Rue Saint-Honoré to buy fresh tortoise for lunch, it had become commonplace for even such figures from the lowlier strata of the popular classes as these to consume sugar and coffee in their morning *café au lait* without much sense – in normal times at least – that these were 'luxury' commodities.

It is important, then, not to lose sight of the degree to which the libidinous outreach of the consumerist market had transformed popular attitudes and political outlooks before the Terror.[73] The fluid definition of 'necessity' over and against 'luxury' was evident in the political posturing of February 1792, when the General Assembly of Section Croix Rouge announced that its members had all sworn to forgo coffee and sugar and invited all other patriots to do likewise. The gallant sans-culottes could heroically give up these 'luxuries' only because other, less 'patriotic' citizens viewed them as necessities. Georges Thomas Brémontier, *négociant* in Rouen and deputy from the Seine Inférieure, spoke in the Legislative Assembly to commend them on the privation 'that shows how truly they merit their liberty'; their vow met 'hardy applause' and was printed for circulation to all the departments.[74] But congratulating the men of Croix Rouge for their sacrifice in some ways only complicated the picture: if coffee and sugar were luxuries, then where was the virtue of doing without them? And, conversely, if they really were necessities, how long could Parisians be expected to survive without them? Several days earlier, another deputation, this one of artisans from the Faubourg Saint-Antoine, had made it clear that sugar was irrelevant to their revolutionary struggle. 'As citizens of the Faubourg Saint-Antoine', their spokesman proudly proclaimed, 'we leave it to women, children, and the elderly to cry over sugar. The *vainqueurs de la Bastille* do not fight for bonbons . . .' Asserting, almost threatening, that the 'savage nature' of their district 'loves only iron and liberty', the men from the faubourg made it clear that they had no physical wants but weaponry.[75] Were sans-culottes planning to eat their pikes? Their fierce renunciatory appeal was less an attack on commodities hitherto unknown to the lower classes than a hyperbolic attempt to forge a new kind of heroic republican austerity.

When the men of Section Croix Rouge renounced sugar and coffee (rather unconvincingly in our view), then, they were doing as much to enforce gender divisions as to lessen economic dependency on faraway islands (with which the infant Republic would soon be deprived of contact by British blockade). Yet if sugar and coffee could be shrugged off as the luxuries of the ladies, another colonial product – tobacco – could not be so easily abandoned. Tobacco too had made the transition from exotic luxury and medical debating-point through to popular necessity. Snuff might be aristocratic – the ornate snuffbox was a luxury Enlightenment art-form – but pipe tobacco was irredeemably popular: there had been over a thousand outlets in Paris even in the early eighteenth century, and consumption expanded considerably in the following decades.[76] Distributed gratis to serving soldiers from the time of Louis XIV, the substance was thorough-goingly masculine. As thorough-goingly masculine, in fact, as that ultra male chauvinist and arch-sans-culotte, Hébert's semi-eponymous Père Duchesne, who was normally depicted brandishing a pipe. By a deliciously consumerist irony, Hébert's radical followers were accused by the Revolutionary Tribunal in March 1794 of having confiscated sugar and coffee from private individuals: such 'gastronomic pillage' could only be viewed as both unmanly and unRevolutionary.[77]

As this final example of the gendered nature of the consumption of colonial commodities illustrated, the relationship between luxury and necessity was fluid rather than fixed, even for those who bought into the regnant austerity of the Terror. In such a context, the General Maximum of September 1793 – that shibboleth of overt consumer renunciation – could not fail to be a shimmeringly indeterminate document. A set of wage and price controls which stands as a snapshot of what Revolutionary Government regarded as prime necessities, the Maximum, when scratched, does not chart the grim and tedious obsessions with bread so often taken as emblematic of French life under the Terror. Rather – covering some twenty groupings of 'goods of prime necessity', ranging through firewood, fabric, clothing, candles, whalesperm, camel-hair and tortoise-shells through to manifold butters, cheeses, honeys, wines, eau-de-vie, anchovies, almonds and figs plus nearly a score of kinds of coffee (plus *cacaos divers*), half a dozen sugars and as many types of tobaccos, it evokes a cornucopia of cockagne desire, living proof that Mary Wollstonecraft's accusation of the French oscillation between 'servility' and 'voluptuousness' had been triumphantly transcended.[78]

Grand Ciceronian speeches, moral exhortations and even political programmes might work in the register of republico-manichean binaries, but the realities of the market-place remained altogether more pantheistic. A whole host of household necessities were, like household gods, specific and local. Society – notwithstanding Labroussian notions of economic fixity and popular immiseration, and despite the sporadically atavistic and loudly anti-consumerist tastes of popular and Jacobin radicalism – was still marked by vibrant commercialism and strong commodity production. English satirists like Gillray might portray the Terrorists gorging themselves on guillotined bodies and basted babies in a way which suggested that the French had passed beyond the bounds of civility and market transaction. Yet the Revolution, even in its most Rousseauian moments, had helped create new needs and new consumer goods. The Bastille had not simply been torn down, let it be remembered, it was also commodified and packaged in material metamorphoses as jewellery, diceboxes, snuffboxes, paperweights and inkpots, while the books, engravings, buttons and brooches its image graced were legion.[79] The *Journal de la mode et du goût français* began publishing in 1790, citing the Revolution's 'inconceivable rapidity' as the force responsible for changing hat and dress styles.[80] In the Ancien Régime, ribbon may have been a vital part of any servant's livery but after 1793 a tricolour cockade (of ribbon or leather) was a required, government-mandated part of every citizen's wardrobe. The wearing of cosmetics might have been frowned on as aristocratic decadence, but even radical newspapers carried advertisements for 'vegetable rouge' throughout the 1790s.[81] And – assuming that they had formerly not eschewed knee-breeches[82] – sans-culottes still needed to purchase the straight trousers which were the uniform of the fashionable popular radical. Just as, in this ultra socially deflationary era, life was unthinkable for Maximilien Robespierre without hair-powder, so the truest of sans-culottes might find it possible to imagine life *sans sucre*, but almost impossible to manage *sans tabac*.

Despite their best attempts to look and sound like Athenians and Romans, the French found it altogether more difficult than their Classical forebears to draw a hard-and-fast line between the realms of necessity and luxury. One can scarcely blame them for that. For they were living in a world where more and more items transmuted from one category to the other, where, even in the tough times of Year II, discourses of virtuous republican austerity provided only a deceptive guide to a transformed realm of popular expectations.

Notes

1   We wish to thank Maxine Berg, Gwynne Lewis, Morag Martin, Michael Sonenscher and Dror Wahrman for their help and advice on this chapter.

2   G. Rudé, *The Crowd in the French Revolution* (Oxford, 1959), pp. 114–19.

3   A. Soboul, *The Parisian Sans-Culottes and the French Revolution, 1793–1794*, trans. G. Lewis (Oxford, 1964), quotation from p. 42.

4   W.H. Sewell, Jr, 'The Sans-Culotte Rhetoric of Subsistence', in K.M. Baker, ed., *The Terror*, vol. 4 of *The French Revolution and the Creation of Modern*

Political Culture (Oxford 1994), pp. 249–70, quotation from p. 257. Sewell's is not, of course, the only critique of Soboul's account, much of which has been repeatedly attacked and massively undermined by critics. See, for example, R.M. Andrews, 'Social Structures, Political Elites and Ideology in Revolutionary Paris, 1792–4: A Critical Evaluation of Albert Soboul's *Les Sans-culottes parisiens en l'an II', Journal of Social History*, 19 (1985–86); M. Sonenscher, 'The Sans-Culottes of Year II: Rethinking the Language of Labour in Revolutionary France', *Social History*, 9 (1984).

5 Sewell, 'The Sans-Culotte Rhetoric', p. 261.

6 *Ibid.*, p. 267.

7 Barère in Conv. 26 Feb. 1793, *Archives parlementaires*, vol. 59, p. 272; Robespierre quoted in A. Soboul, *The French Revolution*, trans. A. Forrest and C. Jones (New York, 1975), p. 295.

8 *The German Ideology*, ed. C.J. Arthur (London, 1974), p. 49.

9 E.P. Thompson, 'The Moral Economy of the English Crowd in the Eighteenth Century', *Past and Present*, 50 (1971), pp. 76–136; L. Tilly, 'Food Entitlement, Famine, and Conflict', *The Journal of Interdisciplinary History*, 14:2 (1983), pp. 333–49; J. Bohstedt, *Riots and Community Politics in England and Wales, 1790–1810* (Cambridge, MA, 1983). Comparable arguments have been made about south-east Asia in the early twentieth century and the so-called 'IMF riots' of the 1970s and 1980s. See J.C. Scott, *The Moral Economy of the Peasant* (New Haven, 1976) and J. Walton and D. Seddon, *Free Markets and Food Riots* (Oxford, 1994).

10 Yet 75,000 pounds of shrimp were consumed in Paris each year: A.-L. Lavoisier, *De la richesse territoriale*, reprint edn, ed. J.C. Perrot (Paris, 1988), pp. 141ff.

11 For Voltaire, cf. J. Grieder, *Anglomania in France, 1740–89: Fact, Fiction and Political Discourse* (Geneva, 1985).

12 W. Cole, *A Journal of My Journey to Paris in the Year 1765*, ed. F.G. Stokes (London, 1931), p. 50. Cole's prejudices did not prevent him from being entranced by the up-market shopping to be found on the Rue Saint-Honoré: see *ibid.*, p. 233.

13 M. Wollstonecraft, *An Historical and Moral View of the Origins of the French Revolution and the Effect It Has Produced in Europe* (London, 1794), vol. I, pp. 511 and vii. Perhaps she was being a little harsh: on the eve of the Revolution, social commentator Louis-Sébastien Mercier talked about *'luxe de commodité et d'aisance'* – though, characteristically, he maintained that it was a commodity more to be found in London, while Paris in contrast displayed a more aristocratic and, in Mercier's eyes, morally reprehensible *'luxe d'ostentation'*: L.S. Mercier, *Tableau de Paris*, 12 vols (Amsterdam, 1782–88), esp. vol. VII, p. 285. See too, on very much these contrastive lines, Mercier's posthumously published *Parallèle entre Paris et Londres*. And cf. A. Young, *Travels in France in the Years 1787, 1788 and 1789*, ed. C.M. Maxwell (Cambridge, 1929).

14 D. Jarrett, *England in the Age of Hogarth* (St. Albans, 1974), pp. 23–6, 180; R. Paulson, *Hogarth: His Life, Art, and Times* (New Haven, 1971); M. Duffy, ed., *The Englishman and the Foreigner* (London, 1981). See too C.M. Maxwell, *The English Traveller in France, 1698–1815* (London, 1932); J. Black, *Natural and Necessary Enemies: Anglo-French Relations in the Eighteenth Century* (London, 1986); and, for the formation of English patriotism, L. Colley, *Britons: Forging the Nation, 1707–1837* (London, 1992).

15 Besides E.P. Thomson's *œuvre* – notably *The Making of the English Working Class* (London, 1963); *Whigs and Hunters: The Origins of the Black Act* (London,

1975); *Customs in Common* (London, 1991) – see his and others' essays in D. Hay, *Albion's Fatal Tree: Crime and Society in Eighteenth-Century England* (London, 1975); P. Linebagh, *The London Hanged: Crime and Civil Society in the Eighteenth Century* (London, 1991); and R. Wells, *Insurrection: The British Experience* (Gloucester, 1983). Stressing inequality in English society from a completely different angle, see J. Cannon, *Aristocratic Century: The Peerage of Eighteenth-Century England* (Cambridge, 1984).

16 H. Perkin, *The Origins of Modern English Society* (London, 1969), p. 91. The same contrast is found in the canonical N. McKendrick, J. Plumb and J. Brewer, *The Birth of a Consumer Society: The Commercialization of Eighteenth-Century England* (London, 1982). Cf. too J. Appleby, 'Consumption in Early Modern Social Thought', in J. Brewer and R. Porter, eds, *Consumption and the World of Goods* (London, 1993), esp. p. 169.

17 C.E. Labrousse, *Esquisse du mouvement des prix et des revenus en France au XVIIIe siècle,* 2 vols (Paris, 1933); idem, *La Crise de l'économie française à la fin de l'Ancien Régime et au début de la Révolution* (Paris, 1944); idem and F. Braudel, eds, *Histoire économique et sociale de la France. ii. 1660–1789* (Paris, 1970). Labrousse's conclusions were accepted largely uncritically in both the Jacobino-Marxist tradition represented by Georges Lefebvre and Albert Soboul and by the Anglo-American 'Revisionist' school of Alfred Cobban, William Doyle, etc.

18 These figures are drawn from the 1970 updating of Labrousse's original thesis. In general there is remarkably little change in the broad lines of the interpretation and in the range of statistics behind them between 1931/44 and 1970.

19 *Esquisse*, p. 572. In the same work (p. 571), Labrousse claims that commodities regarded as non-luxury items in 1910 such as oil, rice, sugar and coffee were 'unknown or negligible' in the eighteenth century: yet see pp. 53–4.

20 *Ibid.*, pp. 572–3.

21 L.M. Cullen, 'History, Economic Crises and Revolution: Understanding Eighteenth-Century France', *Economic History Review*, 46 (1993). Cullen's criticisms of Labrousse for underestimating the extent of internal trade and for characterising the French economy as 'dualist' with one, largely rural half sunk in relative torpor while the other more commercial, geographically peripheral and outward-looking half was more dynamic, are most pertinent to our argument in this chapter.

22 O. Hufton, *The Poor of Eighteenth-Century France, 1750–89* (Oxford, 1970). At the other end of the social spectrum, work on the nobility has tended to eclipse middling groups. See esp. G. Chaussinand-Nogaret, *The French Nobility in the Eighteenth Century: From Feudalism to Enlightenment* (Cambridge, 1985). The latter has had a greater influence on Anglo-American than on French scholarship, partly as a result of the embracing of its contentious theses by arch-Revisionist William Doyle (who translated the work into English) and by S. Schama, *Citizens: A Chronicle of the French Revolution* (London, 1989).

23 F. Braudel, *Capitalism and Material Life. I. The Structures of Everyday Life*, Eng. trans. (London, 1992).

24 There are, however, encouraging signs of an awareness of the gaps: for example, Michael Sonenscher identifies artisans, the middling sort and the petite bourgeoisie as 'the least-known component of French society of the seventeenth and eighteenth centuries' (*Work and Wages. Natural Law, Politics and the Eighteenth-Century French Trades* (Cambridge, 1989), p. 3); while David Garrioch comments on 'how little we know about the Paris middle classes' (*The Formation of the Parisian Bourgeoisie, 1690–1830* (London, 1996), p. 2).

25 The Physiocratic influence is strongly felt in the highly influential H. Luthy, *La Banque protestante en France de la Révocation de l'Édit de Nantes à la Révolution*, 2 vols, (Paris, 1959, 1961), esp. vol. II, ch. 1. For Physiocracy more generally, see E. Fox-Genovese, *The Origins of Physiocracy* (Ithaca, NY, 1976). The emergence of historical demography – whose family reconstitution techniques could best be practised on rural parishes – was a contributory factor in the priority French historians accorded the countryside and the consequent disfavour of urban history down to the 1970s at least: since then, see esp. G. Duby, ed., *Histoire de la France urbaine*, 5 vols (Paris 1980–85); J.C. Perrot, *Genèse d'une ville moderne: Caen au XVIIIe siècle* (Paris, 1975); B. Lepetit, *The Pre-Industrial Urban System: France, 1740–1840*, Eng. trans. (Cambridge, 1994).

26 See S.L. Kaplan, *The Bakers of Paris and the Bread Question 1700–75* (Durham, NC, 1996), esp. pp. 23–60.

27 P.M. Jones, *Reform and Revolution in France: The Politics of Transition, 1774–91* (Cambridge, 1995): see esp. pp. 81–8. Jones ignores the devastating critique of Labrousse's position by David Weir, 'Les Crises économiques et les origines de la Révolution française', *Annales. Économies, Sociétés. Civilisations*, 46 (1991), on which we draw here, and may have gone to press too early to take on board the strictures of Cullen's 'History, Economic Crises and Revolution'.

28 D. Landes, 'The Statistical Study of French Crises', *Journal of Economic History*, 10 (1950). Landes argues that a rise in farm prices could stimulate rather than deaden demand for manufactured goods, initially at least.

29 F. Crouzet, 'England and France in the Eighteenth Century: A Comparative Analysis of Two Economic Growths', in R.M. Hartwell, ed., *The Causes of the Industrial Revolution in England* (London, 1967). It is reprinted in his *De la Supériorité de l'Angleterre sur la France: L'Économique et l'imaginaire, XVIIe–XXe siècles* (Paris, 1985: Eng. trans. as *Britain Ascendant: Comparative Studies in Franco-British Economic History* (Cambridge, 1990)), along with a number of other related articles and commentaries.

30 *De la Supériorité*, p. 41.

31 Weir, 'Les Crises économiques', esp. pp. 920–1. Weir is particularly severe on the weakness of the serial sources Labrousse had at his disposal for wage trends. The article should be read alongside the more general analytical issues raised in Cullen, 'History, Economic Crises and Revolution'.

32 Sonenscher, *Work and Wages*, esp. pp. 134, 174ff., 197ff. See too P. Hoffman, G. Postel-Vinay and J.L. Rosenthal, 'Redistribution and Long-Term Private Debt in Paris, 1660–1726', *Journal of Economic History*, 55 (1995), pp. 256–89.

33 *Esquisse*, pp. 585ff. (and esp. p. 595 n.). Labrousse made some later concessions to the presence of female employment, but without altering the basic thrust of his arguments: see *Histoire économique et sociale*, esp. pp. 487ff. and (in a section authored by Pierre Léon), pp. 655ff.

34 For the 'industrious revolution', see J. de Vries, 'Between Purchasing Power and the World of Goods: Understanding the Household Economy in Early Modern Europe', in Brewer and Porter, eds, *Consumption and the World of Goods*, esp. pp. 103ff.

35 *Ibid.* For an introduction to both sectors of female employment, see G.L. Gullickson, *Spinners and Weavers: Rural Industry and the Sexual Division of Labor in a French Village, 1750–1850* (Cambridge, 1986); and C. Fairchilds, *Domestic Enemies: Servants and their Masters in Old Régime France* (Baltimore, MD, 1984).

36 Sonenscher, *Work and Wages*, p. 174.

37   Ironically, one of the foundations on which French 'retardation' has been
     based, namely the speed and extent of England's Industrial Revolution, has
     been much challenged of late. See, for example, the discussion in C. Jones,
     'Bourgeois Revolution Revivified: 1789 and Social Change', in C. Lucas, ed.,
     Rewriting the French Revolution (Oxford, 1991).

38   Sonenscher, *Work and Wages*, pp. 175–6; M. Garden, *Lyon et les Lyonnais au*
     XVIIIe siècle (Paris, 1970), p. 339.

39   Pre-deathbed gifts, for example, are not recorded.

40   D. Roche, *The People of Paris: An Essay in Popular Culture in the Eighteenth*
     Century, Eng. trans. (Leamington Spa, 1987); idem, *The Culture of Clothing:*
     Dress and Fashion in the Ancien Régime, Eng. trans. (Cambridge, 1994); idem,
     La France des Lumières (Paris, 1995); A. Pardailhé-Galabrun, *The Birth of*
     Intimacy: Private and Domestic Life in Early Modern Paris, Eng. trans. (London,
     1991); C. Fairchilds, 'The Production and Marketing of Populuxe Goods in
     Eighteenth-Century Paris', in Brewer and Porter, eds, *Consumption and the*
     World of Goods; idem, 'Marketing the Counter-Reformation: Religious Objects
     and Consumerism in Early Modern France', in C. Adams, J.R. Censer and L.J.
     Graham, eds, *Visions and Revisions of Eighteenth-Century France* (Philadelphia,
     1997).

41   Fairchilds, 'Populuxe Goods', p. 230.

42   *Ibid.*; C. Todd, 'French Advertising in the Eighteenth Century', *Studies on*
     Voltaire and the Eighteenth Century, 266 (1989), p. 534; Sonenscher, *Work and*
     Wages, pp. 199–200; and, more generally, idem, *The Hatters of Eighteenth-*
     Century France (Berkeley, 1987).

43   See above, p. 43 and n. 19.

44   Roche, *The People of Paris*, p. 189.

45   See now, for the broader, extra-Parisian perspectives, D. Roche, *Histoire des*
     choses banales: Naissance de la consommation, XVIIe–XIXe siècle (Paris, 1997);
     and, for an extraordinary (and ultimately unsuccessful) attempt to fit Rochean
     material into a Labroussian mould, B. Garnot, *La Culture matérielle en France*
     aux XVIe, XVIIe et XVIIIe siècles (Paris, 1995).

46   E.A. Wrigley, 'Urban Growth and Agricultural Change: England and the
     Continent in the Early Modern Period', *Journal of Interdisciplinary History*, 15
     (1985), p. 688: England's total urban population grew over the century from
     0.85 millions to 2.38 millions; France's from 2.54 to 3.22 millions.

47   F. Braudel, *Civilisation matérielle, économie et capitalisme*, XVe–XVIIIe siècles
     (Paris, 1979), vol. II, p. 33.

48   For a review of the quantifying impulse in histories of literature, see R. Darnton,
     The Literary Underground of the Old Regime (Cambridge, MA, 1982), esp.
     ch. 6. W. Frijhoff and D. Julia, 'The Diet in Boarding Schools at the End of
     the Ancien Régime', in R. Forster and O. Ranum, eds, *Food and Drink in*
     History (Baltimore, 1979), pp. 73–85; see also R.J. Bernard, 'Peasant Diet in
     Eighteenth-Century Gévaudan', in E. Forster and R. Forster, eds, *European Diet*
     from Pre-Industrial to Modern Times (New York, 1976), pp. 19–46.

49   Kaplan, *The Bakers of Paris, passim.*

50   O. Hufton, 'Social Conflict and the Grain Supply in Eighteenth-Century
     France', in R. Rotberg and T. Rabb, eds, *Hunger and History* (Cambridge,
     1985), pp. 104–33, quotation from p. 107.

51   C. Jones, 'The Great Chain of Buying: Medical Advertisement, the Bourgeois
     Public Sphere and the Origins of the French Revolution', *American Historical*
     Review, 103 (1996); idem and L. Brockliss, *The Medical World of Early Modern*

France (Oxford, 1997), esp. ch. 10; R. Spang, 'Rousseau in the Restaurant', *Common Knowledge* (Spring 1996); idem, *Restaurant Cultures* (Cambridge, MA, forthcoming); G. Feyel, 'La Presse provinciale française dans la seconde moitié du XVIIIe siècle: géographie d'un réseau', *Revue historique* (1984).

52　D. Miller, *Capitalism: An Ethnographic Approach* (New York, 1997), ch. 4.

53　There is a considerable literature on the introduction of the potato into Europe: see R. Salaman, *The History and Social Influence of the Potato* (Cambridge, 1949); Béatrice Fink, 'L'avènement de la pomme de terre', *Dix-huitième siècle*, 15 (1983), pp. 19–32; M. Morineau, 'The Potato in the Eighteenth Century', in Forster and Ranum, *Food and Drink in History*, pp. 17–36.

54　*Affiches de Paris*, 28 Feb. 1757: Bouin *pâtissier-traiteur*, rue des Déchargeurs (boudin maigre, pistachios, truffles, fish, etc.).

55　Archives Nationales, Y 12801–12811.

56　As is noted in J.C. Bonnet, 'Les Problèmes alimentaires dans la presse de 1768', in J. Varloot and P. Jansen, eds, *L'Année 1768 à travers la presse traitée par ordinateur* (Paris, 1981).

57　Brockliss and Jones, *Medical World of Early Modern France*, esp. chs 10–12.

58　P. Pomme, *Traité des affections vaporeuses des deux sexes* (Lyon, 1769), vol. I, p. 60.

59　J. Raulin, *Traité de la phthisie pulmonaire* (Paris, 1782), p. 211.

60　Spang, 'Rousseau in the Restaurant', pp. 92–108; idem, *Restaurant Cultures*; M. Martin, 'Inventing Beauty: The Medical Regulation of Cosmetics in France, 1772–1791', unpublished paper (kindly communicated by the author).

61　*Affiches de Paris*, 14 Jan. 1765; 18 Feb. 1765; 22 April 1765; 21 Dec. 1766.

62　*Affiches de Paris*, 20 Dec. 1770.

63　A.G. Le Bègue de Presle, *Le Conservateur de la santé* (Paris, 1763).

64　Jones, 'The Great Chain of Buying', p. 28.

65　E.g. *Affiches de Paris*, 24 Dec. 1770; 24 Jan. 1774. Cf. M. Martin, '*Il n'y a que Maille qui m'aille*: Advertisement and the Development of Consumerism in Eighteenth-Century France', *Proceedings of the Western Society for French History* (1996).

66　Arrêt of 29 July 1767, cited in R.L. Stein, *The French Sugar Business in the Eighteenth Century* (Baton Rouge and London, 1988), p. 93. Cf. C. Fischler, *L'Homnivore* (Paris, 1990), p. 294; and, for Britain, S. Mintz, *Sweetness and Power* (New York, 1985).

67　Fischler, *L'Homnivore*, p. 295.

68　Letter of 16 Feb. 1680, quoted in J. Leclant, 'Coffee and Cafés in Paris, 1644–1693,' in Forster and Ranum, *Food and Drink in History*, pp. 86–97, quotation from p. 92.

69　Royal Edict of January 1692, quoted in *ibid.*, p. 97. The war in question was the War of the League of Augsburg (1689–97).

70　Labrousse, *La Crise*, p. 607.

71　Lavoisier, *De le Richesse territoriale*, pp. 141ff.

72　Private communication.

73　The links between burgeoning consumerism and changes in political attitudes have been particularly fruitfully explored by T. Breen in his studies of Anglo-American relations in the late eighteenth century: see esp. his 'Narrative of Commercial Life: Consumption, Ideology and Community on the Eve of the American Revolution', *William and Mary Quarterly*, 3rd ser., 50 (1993); and 'The Meaning of Things: Consumption and Ideology in the Eighteenth Century', in Brewer and Porter, eds, *Consumption and the World of Goods*.

74 *Archives parlementaires,* vol. 38, pp. 3–4.

75 *Ibid.,* vol. 37, p. 686 (26 Jan. 1792). Cf. the comments of a police spy in Paris in January 1794 who struck a similar note: 'dragees and drolleries made out of sugar are not of prime necessity for republicans' (but what of their wives?): P. Caron, *Paris pendant la Terreur,* 6 vols (Paris, 1910–43), vol. II, p. 212.

76 J. Goodman, *Tobacco in History: The Culture of Dependence* (London, 1993), pp. 61ff.

77 Caron, *Paris pendant la Terreur,* vol. V, p. 212 (30 March 1794). For 'gastronomic pillage', see R. Cobb, *The People's Armies* (London, 1987), p. 491.

78 See above, p. 41. Cf. Roche, *Histoire des choses banales,* pp. 40ff.

79 Jones, 'Bourgeois Revolution Revivified', pp. 69–70. The Musée Carnavalet in Paris has on display a wonderful array of such memorabilia.

80 *Journal de la mode et du goût français,* 5 Sept., 1790.

81 J. Harris, 'The Red Cap of Liberty: A Study of Dress Worn by French Revolutionary Partisans, 1789–94', *Eighteenth-Century Studies* (1981); A. Ribeiro, *Fashion in the French Revolution* (London, 1988); M. Martin, 'Consuming Beauty: The Commerce of Cosmetics in France', University of California, Irvine, PhD dissertation (in process).

82 See above, p. 47.

New commodities, luxuries and their consumers in eighteenth-century England

New commodities available to a broader spectrum of the population were one of the distinguishing features of the later seventeenth and the eighteenth centuries. Foreign and domestically produced decorative goods, clothing and household wares were frequently denounced by moral and economic commentators as luxuries, and they were certainly desired as such by their new consumers. Yet new products and their consumers have not been given a significant place in histories of the British economy and industrialisation during the eighteenth and early nineteenth centuries.

Since Neil McKendrick in 1983 claimed a consumer revolution which preceded and accompanied the industrial revolution, a group of quantitative economic historians gave little credance to an independent role for demand in generating economic growth. Increasing incomes or prior economic growth have been regarded as responsible for rising demand.[1] The impact of export demand, of agricultural improvement and demographic growth have been investigated and found wanting as potential props to the demand-led theories.[2] Other possibilities, such as changes in the distribution of income or shifts in time use between leisure or production for self-sufficiency towards market production and consumption, have also been discounted. Some have argued for changes in the distribution of income towards groups more likely to consume manufactured products. But it is claimed that the spending power released very likely went to luxuries and imports. Likewise, a shift in time use, it has been argued, in the absence of pre-existing increases in resources or changes in the organisation or technologies of industry, would only lead to unemployment elsewhere, and thus dampen overall demand.[3]

An investigation of the role of demand factors and consumer-goods industries has been held back by economic historians basing their analyses in neoclassical economic theory. They have accepted arguments that supply creates its own demand; that unless an economy had significant underemployed resources and unemployed labour, demand simply could not initiate economic expansion. Economic historians could thus not think the impossible, and left the investigation of consumption aside. Instead they focused on growth rates and on the technologies of a limited range of well-known industries.

There is much more to the cases made for income distribution and time use than has been allowed by economic historians. The 'luxuries' and imports bought by those groups who consumed manufactured products had important demonstration effects and spawned a whole series of new technologically progressive industries. Changes in time use indicated not just changes in industrial organisation and coercion, but aspirations and behaviour over households, objects and the material culture of ordinary people. These issues needed investigation by economic historians, but instead they were bypassed and the economy presented as a bleak and colourless engine of growth stoked by bodies and bread.

It has been social and cultural historians who have taken up McKendrick's challenge to explore the flowering of material culture in early modern and eighteenth-century Europe. Social historians have investigated not just this material culture, but the possessions of a range of social groups, mainly through inventories and diaries.[4] This was an expansion of goods not just for elite consumption, but much more significantly for middling and bourgeois consumption. Its impact could not be simply dismissed as that of the luxury expenditure of a small and insignificant elite. Likewise historians have questioned the uniformity of plebeian consumption. Hans Medick's classic statement that plebeian culture is a market phenomenon challenged both the old market/custom divide and the simple correspondence between standards of living or real wages and the consumption of manufactured goods or luxuries. Medick argued that plebeian producers invested a large part of their usually modest monetary income in consumption, fashions and drinking culture.[5] Following Bourdieu, Medick argued that this behaviour provided a form of 'symbolic capital' which interacted with wider plebeian culture.

Attention is now turning from quantitative indicators of consumer items and anthropological explanations towards the language of
desire and the meaning attached by groups and individuals to particular
objects and practices. Jan de Vries very recently and Elizabeth Gilboy
in the 1930s assessed the impact of desires and wants for new commodities. In de Vries's 'industrious revolution', the desires for new commodities pushed individual (especially women's) and family behaviour
patterns away from self-sufficiency towards market-oriented production
and consumption. For Elizabeth Gilboy, the new wants provided 'one
of the most active forces leading to changes in standards of consumption'. The new commodities led those with a surplus 'to try this and
that, and finally to include many new articles in their customary standard of life'. The new commodities also attracted those without the
requisite surplus; they worked harder to get the surplus or skimped on
necessities.[6]

What were these new commodities that inspired these shifts in
behaviour among ordinary people and the rise of a new material culture
among the middling groups? To some extent they were exotic foods
and drink, especially tea, chocolate and coffee. They were new textile
fabrics, especially printed calicoes imported initially from India, then
manufactured at home. They were also useful and decorative objects,
light furnishings, ceramics and glass, metalwares, and clocks and watches.
These were among the new household goods (including clocks, prints,
earthenware, cutlery, equipment for drinking tea and coffee, furnishings and window curtains) which stand out in the later seventeenth
and eighteenth centuries as spreading rapidly in the consumption of
the middling sort.[7] They were products of new industries of the eighteenth century. They had many similarities to traditional luxury ware,
but they were not produced simply for an elite. Nor were they mass-
produced standardised ware, or even precursors to this. They were a
new kind of commodity, the special and decorative commodity within
the means of the middling class, and closely attuned to aspirations of
quality and individuality.

These new commodities were perceived by their consumers as
luxuries; they were sometimes substitutes for elite luxury goods, but
more often they were new products inspired by exotic, foreign or
classical associations. We must turn to look at the new things owned
by the middling classes, from ordinary tradespeople to more comfortable merchants and manufacturers. What distinguished their possessions from those of the rich? What meanings can we attribute to these

objects? It is first important to emphasise that these goods were luxuries to their consumers; response to them was part of the wider luxury debates during the period. In writing about them we need to go beyond issues of modern consumer culture to seek the specific cultural contexts of objects, possessions and display. The luxury possessions of the wealthy during the Renaissance, for example, were displayed in domestic settings, in rituals of civility such as dining and in collections. In the mid-fifteenth century Cardinal Gonzaga was famed for his collection of treasures and the opulence which marked him as a figure of magnificence and authority.[8] Consumption for the wealthy of the Renaissance and later was a demonstration of taste. Objects were valued not just for the quality of the materials in them, but also for an appreciation of their craftsmanship. Luxury objects denoted a refinement of a sense of taste and expressed civility. As Goldthwaite has argued, taste was extended to new kinds of objects; it was a way of 'transforming these objects into high culture'. The values attached to an object like maiolica extended 'from standards of personal comportment at table to literary erudition displayed by its painted decoration'. Such objects made for a new elite, not just of wealth, but of taste and refinement.[9]

The goods of the wealthy and the ordinary carried signs and indicated status as much in the eighteenth century as in the medieval period. In an example from the medieval period, Martha Howell has argued for the inhabitants of late medieval Douai that it was 'in their capacity to crystallize value'; that objects became more than the money they could buy.

> When collected in households and draped on bodies, when carefully labelled and described in wills, these goods seemed to escape commerce . . . When Douaisiens labelled their objects, when they attached them to their persons and to the persons of others in their social network, when they 'fixed' their movables, they seemed to remove their property from the world of movables.[10]

Their goods became markers and stabilisers of social hierarchy. For women consumers in the medieval period and in the eighteenth century, possessions were also marked with familial, friendship and emotive values, and sought out, described and bequeathed in this light.[11]

What of the new commodities of the eighteenth century? What was their attraction to their consumers? On the one hand these were commodities conveying a new appreciation of 'decency' and 'utility' in middle-class domestic environments. On the other, they were novelties, fashion goods and new things. They included new luxury and semi-luxury clothes, light furnishings and ornaments. These commodities were not simply replacements of goods formerly made at home. They were special items of personal or household adornment in distinctive materials and styles; their materials were frequently just as new, and the things made with them evoked the exotic. The new materials were lightweight cottons instead of silks, earthenwares instead of porcelain, flint and cut glass, metal alloys and finishes such as gilt and silver plate, stamped brassware, japanned tinware and papier mâché, ormolu and cut steel instead of gold and silver.

The way for the introduction of these new goods was paved during the seventeenth and early eighteenth centuries by Asian imported manufactures, which for the first time were imported in quantities and at prices which made them available to a broad, but discerning middle class. Indian calicoes, Chinese porcelain and Japanese lacquers transformed the visual culture of Europe; some of these were fine luxury products, but most of those bought in were decent high quality semi-luxuries available in a range of patterns, styles, qualities and prices. They could thus appeal to markets ranging from the middling orders of metropolis and province to elite consumers. They undermined the uniformity and clear social hierarchies previously imposed by sumptuary legislation, and made individuality and variety an option to much broader parts of society. Asian producers had an amazing capacity to satisfy this new market, which was not only growing rapidly, but diverse. Their success was to challenge European states and manufacturers to initiate their own brands of semi-luxury commodities.[12]

Earlier ways of approaching these semi-luxury commodities have been to see them as mimicking luxury ware or mass consumer goods; thus they have been termed 'populuxe goods' or 'ordinary things'. John Styles pointed out the inapplicability of terms such as 'consumer revolution' and 'mass production' to the reality of eighteenth-century products and their methods of production. Both these terms spring from the Fordism of the early twentieth century, a system focused on production of large volumes in a very limited number of varieties, and deploying automated production lines, interchangeable parts and unskilled labour. What distinguished both manufacture and consumption in the eighteenth century, by contrast, was the possibilities created of great range of output alongside standardised products. This diversity met desires for individuality, self-differentiation and luxury by means of visual diversity.[13]

Were these products the 'populuxe goods' described by Cissie Fairchilds as the 'inexpensive versions of aristocratic luxuries like fans, snuff boxes and umbrellas which added a touch of class to the life of journeyman or domestic servant'? Fairchilds follows the production and consumption of populuxe versions of stockings, umbrellas and fans, arguing that their accessibility to lower-class consumers was made possible by illegal subcontracting outside the guild and by peddling instead of luxuriously appointed shops. She furthermore claims a distinctive character to French lower-class consumption. The lower classes sought to ape the aristocracy, in contrast to those of England who spent extra income on useful household goods. She accounts for this contrast by the decline of sumptuary legislation in the early eighteenth century, followed by a breakdown of traditional acceptance of the hierarchical social order after the second half of the century. These arguments, however, contain assumptions about luxury production, peddling and the consumer behaviour of the English lower classes which have since been challenged.[14] The idea of 'aping the aristocracy' also needs to be interrogated. Were these goods really only cheaper copies of goods already available to the aristocracy, or were they genuine novelties sought out initially by urban middling groups? If they were versions of aristocratic possessions, was their possession mere emulation, or challenge to social hierarchies, or even theatre? There still remains a case to be made to see the new commodities as a form of luxury, but not just a cheap copy of aristocratic luxury.

The new commodities need to be set in a broader context of the social responses and symbolism of the multiplication of consumer objects, once relatively rare, through much broader parts of the population. As Daniel Roche has recently argued, this was not simply an aspect of the history of material life, as formerly approached by the Annales, focused on a model of economic man.[15] A history of consumer objects must be set in the context of contemporary debates and ideas, the uses and symbolism of objects in daily life, and their place in the identities of individuals, families and groups. Even the most ordinary objects could convey ingenuity, choice and culture.[16] The division between ordinary and luxury consumption was, furthermore, as much about a shift in ideas over the course of the eighteenth century as it was about the proliferation of consumer objects. Luxury, once associated with the preservation of social hierarchies, and its limitations with Christian economic ethics, became associated with the expansion of markets, wealth and economic growth. But this too faced a critique of sterility, and of a redistribution of income in favour of the elites. Attitudes to commodities and to excess grew more relative, and a new ambivalence to luxury focused on baubles, trinkets and trivial things.[17] Adam Smith in *The Wealth of Nations* expressed a sense of the enormity of a passion for individual and selfish possession of a 'pair of diamond buckles'. He condemned the behaviour of the great proprietors who 'to gratify their childish vanity', had sold their land and relinquished their feudal privileges in return for 'trinkets and baubles, fitter to be the play-things of children than the serious pursuits of men'. The result, however, was an unintentional revolution of the 'greatest importance to publick happiness'. But he also saw the beneficent results of such vanities and trinkets. A regular government in the countryside replaced arbitrary aristocratic rule.[18] The 'trinkets and baubles' were not, after all, harmful, merely 'frivolous and useless', and they gratified the 'most childish, the meanest and the most sordid of all vanities'.[19] Some years earlier, in *The Theory of Moral Sentiments*, Smith had tried to understand the desire for such trinkets:

> How many people ruin themselves by laying out money on trinkets of frivolous utility? What pleases these lovers of toys is not so much the utility, as the aptness of the machines which are fitted to promote it. All their pockets are stuffed with little conveniences. They contrive new pockets, unknown in the clothes of other people, in order to carry a greater number.

The desire for such trinkets was like that for wealth and greatness. Neither kind of luxury could prevent exposure to fear, sorrow, danger and death. But both had the effect of rousing and keeping 'in continual motion' the industry of mankind.[20]

New consumer goods as semi-luxuries

The desire for trinkets and baubles went much deeper than the passion for a pair of diamond buckles. It generated a large range of new consumer goods which gratified vanities and appealed to a display of modernism and innovation among those who possessed them. The new consumer goods I discuss here, decorative metalwares, ceramics and glass, light furnishings and clocks and watches, were semi-luxuries. They were frequently ascribed with values of usefulness, civility and ingenuity. They were not so expensive that only the elites could afford them, though they may also have been bought by the elites. And they were not so common that they counted among the possessions of the labouring classes. They were items considered worth saving for. Their producers spanned two worlds. They were located partly in the world of metropolitan luxuries – among the gold- and silversmiths, fine furniture makers and colonial finishing trades. But they were also part of the world of provincial manufacturing regions – watch and clock part makers, fine tool and steel filemakers in the industrial villages of south Lancashire; they were the toymakers and japanners of Birmingham along with the flint glass makers and glasscutters of Stourbridge; the potters of Staffordshire, Liverpool, Leeds and Bristol, and the cutlers and plated ware makers of Sheffield.

There were close complementarities in the consumption of these goods, the marketing strategies of their producers, and in the actual production processes. Their modernism, their new materials, the ingenuities of their design or total product innovation were marked out. A wide variety of goods displaying such qualities were frequently associated with one another. The trade cards and newspaper advertisements of toy-makers, jewellers, silversmiths, and china sellers indicated that many of these goods were sold together. Trade cards produced in the 1720s and 1730s sought to display the wide range of commodities on offer by any individual manufacturer or shopkeeper (Plate 1). Cartouches were designed as mirror or picture frames or clock cases whose scrolling brackets supported candlesticks, teapots and ceramics. Later in the century taste was conveyed by classical imagery; the products conveyed as complementary to antique dress and architecture.[21]

Newspaper advertisements also showed this complementary marketing. Joseph Farror's cheap warehouse, advertised in 1796, offered tea, coffee, chocolate and cocoa, useful and ornamental chinaware – Nankeen, Worcester and Derby ware – and Stourbridge glassware.[22] William Goods advertised his toy warehouse in 1798 as selling foreign and English toys, cutlery, hardware, perfumery, etc. John Clarke called himself 'Perfumer, Cutler and Toyman', and from his Bull Street shop sold perfume 'selected from the first houses of London' and the 'greatest assortment of toys that has ever been seen in any shop in London'.[23] Child and Walker, describing themselves as 'Cabinet Makers and Upholsterers', opened a shop in Wolverhampton to sell a 'genteel assortment of Wilton, Scotch and other carpets, blankets, quilts . . . bed furniture of all kinds, window curtains . . . and an elegant assortment of pier, dressing and swing looking glasses, four poster . . . and other bedsteads, all kinds of mahogany and other cabinet goods, paper hangings, and all kinds of mahogany tables'.[24]

The trade catalogues of brassware manufacturers, potters, glass- and silversmiths showed that many of their products were designed using either similar patterns or specifically to complement each other. Several catalogues contained designs and products for plated ware and glass, or for silver and plated ware and ceramics.[25] A Birmingham

MARY ROLLASON & SON'S
CHINA, GLASS & EARTHENWARE WAREHOUSE,
———— Steel House Lane, Birmingham. ————
MANUFACTURERS of CUT GLASS, LUSTRES, FANCY LAMPS &c.&c.

1 Mary Rollason, china and glass seller, trade card

catalogue owned by Samuel Rowland Fisher advertised brass furniture ware alongside rococo watch frames and stands (Plate 2). Benjamin Hadley's catalogue advertised tea and coffee urns and candlesticks with glass stands, bottles and pitchers, and James Whitehead's catalogue set out earthenware designs with those for plated ware.[26]

The patterns of consumption of middling consumers also indicate the significance of these kinds of goods in special possessions. Decorative furnishings, as well as tea utensils, chests, trays, tables and silver teaspoons and tongs, were particularly singled out for description and bequest in the texts of the wills left by the middling orders, and especially the women during the eighteenth century. These furnishings

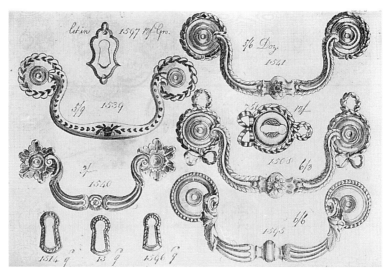

2 Brass furniture handles

were frequently small and associated with specific best rooms; they often featured new luxury materials or finishes such as mahogany, cane or enamel and lacquer, or new luxury goods such as tea tables and pier glasses. Some of these furnishings were bequeathed in individual legacies together with china and silverware. Tea china, described by colour, finish and origin, was bequeathed along with a range of silver novelties: coffee and teapots and spoons, pepper castors and buckles, snuffboxes, silver spoons, tea tongs, salvers, sauce pans, ladles, cups and tankards.[27] If we look at the commodities specifically mentioned in bequests, and therefore accorded some special significance apart from possessions as indicated in probate inventories, we see the following pattern among the tradespeople and middling orders of two of England's industrial towns (Table 1).

Among some of the individuals earmarking specific goods in their bequests we find Elizabeth Lynes, the widow of a metalworker with no real property and little cash to pass on. But she left her daughter the great 'oval' table and the little square table in the house along with the table in the summer house and six cane chairs. She left another daughter a silver snuffbox.[28] Other Birmingham and Sheffield widows left silver spoons to younger relations as a form of family keepsake. New silver items – cups, spoons, pepper castors, tea tongs, cream sauce pans, tankards, castors, salvers, ladles and tumblers – were apportioned among younger male and female relations.[29]

Table 1   Types of goods left in wills: analysis by gender of testator, Birmingham and Sheffield, 1700–1800 (%)*

	Birmingham		Sheffield	
	men	women	men	women
apparel	15.64	26.98	7.21	25.64
furniture	17.77	19.84	22.14	28.85
glassware	0.24	0.79	1.06	1.92
household goods	40.52	18.25	24.61	20.51
jewellery	4.74	16.67	1.76	9.62
books	3.32	3.97	1.41	0.64
linen	14.22	21.43	10.72	19.23
china	5.69	6.35	2.11	5.13
ornaments	1.90	1.59	0.53	0.00
plate	1.66	8.73	5.62	6.41
utensils	12.08	5.56	3.69	0.64
silver	12.08	15.08	6.68	15.39
pewter	1.42	3.97	0.35	0.00
brassware	0.95	3.17	0.53	0.00
clocks	0.00	3.17	0.35	1.92

* This refers to the testators who left this type of goods in their wills, taken as a percentage of those testators who left goods at all.
Sample: Testators who left goods in their wills: 422 male metalworkers from Birmingham, 126 women of all trades from Birmingham; 569 male metalworkers from Sheffield and 156 women of all trades from Sheffield: period 1700–1800.
Source: Analysis of testatory documents of metalworkers and women in Birmingham and Sheffield, 1700–1800. The documents are in the Diocesan Record Office, The Friary, Lichfield and in the Borthwick Institute of Historical Research, University of York.

Complementary innovation

There were also close complementarities in innovation across many of these new commodities. Patent records indicate close associations. James Keeling, a Staffordshire potter, in 1796 patented a substitute for lead for glazing and enamelling earthenware, porcelain and chinaware, and also stated this was useful in the making of glass and enamel.[30] John Richter in 1770 patented a method of inlaying scagliola or plaster on marble and metals.[31] Stephen Bedford in 1759 patented a method of impressing in imitation of engraving upon varnish laid on copper, iron, paper and other bodies, to be used in coach panels, snuffboxes, and other merchandise and devices.[32] Similarly, John Pickering, a London gilt toymaker, in 1769 patented a method of chasing in gold, silver and other metals, coffin furniture, ornaments for coaches, chariots, sedans and other carriages, cabinetwork and domestic furniture.[33] John Skidmore, a Clerkenwell stove gratemaker, in 1786 patented a process for ornamenting china and earthenware with foil stones, Bristol stones, paste and all sorts of pinched glass, sapped glass, and every other stone, glass and composition used in or applicable to the jewellery trade.[34] Joseph Jacob, a London coachmaker, in 1774 patented his process of ornamenting carriages, sedan chairs, building, furniture, musical instruments and books.[35] And finally, Obadiah Westwood, a Birmingham buttonmaker, not to be outdone, in 1796 registered a patent for making or manufacturing tea and other trays, waiters, card pans, caddies, dressing boxes, bottle stands, coat, breast, vest, sleeve and other buttons, frames for pictures and looking glasses and other things; mouldings, cornices and ornaments for rooms, ceilings, chimney pieces, doors, panels and various other purposes.[36]

Inventors were clearly aware of the variety of products across ranges of goods classes to which their ingenuity applied. The manufacturers of these commodities were similarly closely networked. The networking among producers of metal goods and ceramics, or among furniture makers and clockmakers, was not something new, but had long-established precedents in the luxury trades. Michael Sonenscher in his work on the Paris luxury trades demonstrates the wide impact of the Martin japanning firm. He argues that the hallmark of Parisian design from the later seventeenth century was the versatility with which designs could be adapted to multiple materials and products.[37] A comparable place was occupied in London at the end of the eighteenth century and the early nineteenth century by Benjamin Vulliamy. Known as a firm of luxury clock- and watchmakers, it also advertised ornamental plate, silver, ornamental work in metal and the sale of diamonds and pearls. 'They were prepared to supply their customers with anything from a chimney-piece to a door handle, from a piano to a button.' Few of these items, even the clocks, were produced by Vulliamy, but instead were subcontracted out and divided up.[38] The Vulliamy order book for silver indicates the complexities of the subcontracting involved in the production of any single item. A pair of terrines and stands made for one individual involved sending various parts of the work out to eleven different craftspeople, several of whom completed various jobs at different stages of the process of production. Each job was separately priced, and the item costed accordingly.[39]

The extensive networks and subcontracting arrangements deployed by such luxury producers were built upon by Matthew Boulton and Josiah Wedgwood, the two greatest factory masters and producers of both semi-luxury and ornamental luxury ware in the eighteenth century. There was first the very close interaction in product development and techniques between Boulton and Wedgwood themselves. They shadowed each other closely, trading steel, plated and ormolu mounts and cameos and seals. Wedgwood's celebrated engine-turning lathe was developed in close consultation with Matthew Boulton and with the Liverpool watch- and toolmaker John Wyke.[40]

Boulton employed over 600 workers at his new Soho factory soon after it was built in 1766. He developed specialist teams under heads of department, luring away silversmiths, chasers, braziers and coppersmiths from other masters in Birmingham, Sheffield and London.[41] In one dispute with Birmingham's other large-scale toy manufacturer, John Taylor, he accused Taylor and his agent of enticing away three of his articled servants, and admitted that in retaliation he had lured away one of Taylor's workers. Boulton hoped they had balanced accounts, and could then 'proceed hereafter on more gentleman like plans . . . than the shabby custom of secretly seducing each others' servants'.[42] Towards the end of the century he was again in a similar dispute with Robert Cadmore and Company, the Sheffield plater and silversmith.[43] But he was also deeply embedded in a region of specialised toy, jewellery, instrument makers, glasscutters and japanners. He subcontracted work to them, and drew on them to fulfil orders for specialist goods.[44] Sometimes he paid an annual sum to retain the services of a particular subcontractor, such as William Mossop, who was paid £150 a year, to be paid by piece, profit share or annual payment, to engrave Boulton's dies.[45] He subcontracted work much further afield, such as that put out to George Howlette, the Coventry watch- and clockmaker, and to Thomas Bradbury, the Sheffield plate manufacturer.[46] In some cases he used these connections to take over these manufacturers. Francis Butcher was producing platina buttons for Boulton in 1769, but by 1788 Butcher was 'out of business' and applying to Boulton for employment.[47] Peter Capper offered in 1767 to resign his lacquered gilt and plate manufactory to Boulton the following year, and in the same year Boulton bought out Gimblett's of Shaw Hill which made boxes, toothpick cases, tortoiseshell links, buckles and other goods.[48]

Wedgwood was also heavily dependent on a network of specialist producers spanning the industrial regions and the metropolis. He subcontracted enamel and gold work, engraving, mounting, painting, repairing, and the finishing of a range of articles including cameos, display cases, seals, silverware, toys, cutlery, trays and writing boxes. James Archer of Birmingham supplied him with polished bezels for seals in 1774; Henry Clay, the Birmingham japanner, did work on tea caddies and trays for Wedgwood between 1776 and 1808; Cooper & Glover did painting for him in 1777, and Henry Copestake set bracelets and mounted seals in 1785–87. William Dawson did enamelling in 1792, and Charles Dickin engraving in 1788–89. Robert Honeybone of Stourbridge and Hancock and Shepherd supplied glassware between 1792 and 1801. Hoskins & Grant supplied casts and moulds in 1779. Thomas Hyde, the goldsmith, and William Johnson did finishing and repairing in 1781 and 1784. Samuel Pemberton of Birmingham mounted seals and cameos, and Joseph Pearson, also of Birmingham, supplied buttons and masonic devices. Nathaniel and Mary Pollard set rings, seals, bracelets and lockets between 1774 amd 1788, and William Smith, again of Birmingham, worked on seals, buttons, gilt frames and bracelets from 1773–76. John Sadler & Guy Green, the Liverpool potters, decorated Wedgwood ware from 1764–76, and Michael Tijon of Greek Street gilded and beaded ware in London from 1800–2. William Utten of Chelsea provided metal mounting for gems, and Thomas Warner of Birmingham provided gun metal and gilt figures from 1775–76.[49] Wedgwood also bought ware from other Burslem potters and, like Boulton, when faced with competition from them, simply bought them out or took them over.[50]

Invention as imitation

The extensive networks among producers both of fine luxury ware and of more modest semi-luxury goods provided conduits for information flows, and opportunities for extensive product development, for adaptation, new finishes and for techniques substituting new methods or materials, but also for mimicking a product or design. Michael Montias has explored the characteristics of product innovation for the art market, explaining that such innovation created totally new products or goods whose characteristics were significantly different from those of the past. Product innovations such as the rise of realistic landscape painting in Holland in the seventeenth century were, however, also accompanied by process innovations which increased the painter's productivity. A context was provided for the imitation of the product and new processes by an expanding anonymous market.[51] This analysis also contributes to understanding the invention of new semi-luxury goods in the eighteenth century. Central to this type of invention was a process of imitation, deploying the design principles, finishes and associations of fine luxury ware and exotic materials across new things, or producing similar goods out of new materials which mimicked the older luxury ware, but were also widely perceived to be quite different products.

There is a sense in which much of the focus of invention during the eighteenth century was directed towards this process of imitation. This is particularly clear in the projects and premiums of the Society for Arts, Manufactures and Commerce (known as the Society of Arts), and in patents taken out during the period. The premiums offered by the Society and the letters applying for these especially emphasised the invention of substitutes for goods and materials brought from abroad; the countries which featured prominently were France and China. The foundation of the Society of Arts in 1754 was based in creating an English style in manufactures, and in establishing an appropriate national commercial identity. The Society was anticipated in 1745 by the Anti-Gallican Association, founded 'to promote British Manufactures, to extend the commerce of England, to discourage the introduction of French modes and oppose the importation of French commodities'. William Shipley, the Society's founder, argued that 'riches were the strength, and arts and sciences the ornaments of nations'. Shipley's proposals, like many contemporary patents and projects included introducing manufactures which would 'employ great numbers of the poor, which seems the only way of lessening the swarms of thieves and beggars throughout the kingdom, and relieving parishes from the burden they labour under . . .'. The focus on establishing native or colonial sources of raw material supplies and manufactures in luxury and other consumer manufactures was paramount. The first premiums were offered for finding a British source of cobalt and for cultivating madder.[52]

The Society of Arts was different from other projects in its aim to combine design and the fine arts together with the mechanical and commercial arts. It offered premiums 'for the most ingenious and best fancied Designs proper for Weavers, Embroiderers and Calico Printers' as well as cabinetmakers and coachmakers, and for manufacturers of iron, brass, china, earthenware, or 'any other Mechanic Trade that requires Taste'.[53] Shortly after, the premiums were also offered for engraving, mezzotinting, etching, gem-engraving, cameo-cutting and modelling, bronze-casting, mechanical drawing, and architectural and furniture designs. The close association encouraged by the Society between the Polite Arts and Manufactures was evident among a membership of approximately 2,000 in the 1760s, made up of a small number of aristocrats and clergymen, and an equal proportion of gentlemen and a large contingent from the middling classes including professionals, merchants, manufacturers and those with occupations from the Polite Arts.[54]

Not only the premiums offered, but the extensive correspondence of the Society with projectors and inventors, conveys the great concern over discovering means of producing fine consumer goods to substitute for imports. The focus was placed on deploying British resources in art, design and taste as well as native materials and skills to the task of creating both luxury and semi-luxury ware as well as useful invention. The use of cheaper and more available materials, many of them inventions in their own right, was seen as a way of creating new ornamental goods; these were both substitutes for foreign luxuries and at the same time modern novelties. They combined the arts of imitation with the science of invention.

One such product was varnish. This was an imitation product, first of the oriental lacquered furnishings imported into Europe in the seventeenth and eighteenth centuries, and subsequently of those from Venice and varnishes substituted for lacquer. The Society offered premiums, seeking to bypass the Martin japanning process in Paris; other premiums were suggested for seeking substitute raw materials in British colonial territories which 'would produce a varnish the same as the japan and eastern varnish'.[55] Premiums were offered in 1758 and 1763 for the 'greatest improvement in Varnish to answer the end of that of "Martin's" at Paris, the Properties of which are, the being hard, transparent, of a light Colour, capable of receiving the finest Polish, and not apt to crack'. The conditions for claiming the premium were onerous. Each candidate had to produce a quart of the varnish and a panel of wood as large as a coach door, 'painted with the finest ground of white, blue, green, pompadour and red, finished with the same varnish, so as to proof against a hot sun, frost or wet; to be left with the Society six months at least in order to ascertain its merit'.[56] The advertisement elicited a number of enquiries and applications, many from Birmingham. John and Ann Gardner from Moor Street, Birmingham, both sent specimens of different oil and copal-oil varnishes.[57] Stephen Bedford claimed his success in making varnishes like those of the Martins in Paris, but on copper and especially paper.[58] Others claimed access to the secret Martin recipes.[59] The success of efforts to imitate the Martin japanning process was revealed in the extensive patenting activity in the process, and twenty patents for japanning processes and varnishes were registered between 1757 and 1825.[60] By 1782 the *Transactions* of the Society of Arts was confident enough of its success to state, 'The beauty and durability of the varnish invented and used by M. Martin of Paris, and for which large sums of money were annually sent out of these kingdoms, induced the Society to offer premiums for discovering the method of making the like here; and the high perfection to which our workmen are now arrived in that art, evinces that those premiums have had a happy effect.'[61]

In the process of seeking inventions to imitate the expensive oriental, Parisian and Venetian luxury product, the Society of Arts helped to generate a whole new industry and attendant patents drawing in the use of new materials and objects. Instead of a technique used on wood, furnishings and coach panels, new forms of varnish were developed for use on papier mâché and tin-plated ware; these in turn were used on all manner of small items, from tea trays and canisters to vases, buttons and buckles as well as larger coach panels. In the process of imitating an imported luxury process, British producers invented a new process and distinctive japanned-ware products.

Other imitative and substitute processes were encouraged by the Society. There was paper for engraving needed to equal that from France with premiums offered in 1784 and 1787.[62] There were premiums offered in 1784 and 1785 for methods of bronzing copper medals, 'equal to that practised in France', and one in 1791 for making bar-iron from coked pig iron, 'equal in quality to the best Iron imported from Sweden or Russia, and as fit for converting into steel'.[63] More premiums were offered for a method of making white copper, 'in the same perfection as that brought from China or Japan', and for the best method of melting English brass into plates, 'so as to render it equally clean and capable of receiving as fine a polish as the best imported from Hamburg or Holland'.[64]

Applicants to the Society also stressed their success in imitating foreign imports. One pointed out a form of cheap borax in England 'as good as that which comes from China and Venice'.[65] Potters and enamellers tried out methods of using substitute ores found in Britain to improve on imported delftware and to produce a better native porcelain. A Birmingham correspondent speculated on the impact of the discovery of a source of cobalt in Fife. A substitute for the cobalt of Saxony, this might be manufactured into smalt, zafter, arsenic, orpiment, etc., and used in glassworks, potteries, in painting, japanning, enamelling and bleaching.[66] Other potters experimented with a native type of blue tile to substitute for those of Holland. These would 'save many thousand pounds a year to this nation which the Dutch now secure for that commodity'.[67] A Bristol potter wrote in 1766 of his attempts over the past fifty years to imitate and 'if possible equal the Dutch blew stone ware for which such great sums have been and are annually sent out of this kingdom'.[68]

While import substitution appeared to be the first priority of invention, the imitation to which inventors and projectors aspired was also a process of adaptation, of finding cheaper methods and sources of supply and of creating distinctive products adaptable to broader markets for semi-luxuries. 'Imitation' was also a key word of an important group of patents taken out in the period 1627–1825, with most concentrated during the eighteenth century. In a selected set of patents for this period, those covering the group of metalwares, glass, ceramics, furniture and clocks and watches, as well as more general finishing techniques on a range of consumer goods, 'imitation' was one of the main reasons given for new products and finishing processes. Patents from this subgroup of total patents specifically mentioning imitation are included in Table 2. A number of patents imitated classical or Renaissance arts, such as Wedgwood's patent in 1769 for ornamenting earthenware to imitate encaustic painting, or Robert Redrich and Thomas Jones's patent in 1724 for 'staining, spotting, veining and clouding on earthenware to imitate marble, porphyry and other stones, and tortoiseshell'.[69]

The 'imitation' so closely associated with the novelties of the luxury and semi-luxury trades was also a process of recreating arts and manufactures on ancient principles. The ideas on creativity held by Wedgwood and Boulton were said to aim at 'emulation and quotation from the most admired sources, and the creation of new combinations of old ornaments'.[70] This has been associated with the fashion for the culture of classical antiquity in the later eighteenth century, associated both with the impact of the Grand Tour and with a fusion of modernity and classicism. It was much more likely, however, that the 'imitation' of luxury and semi-luxury consumer goods was closely bound up with contemporary perceptions of art in the middle of the eighteenth century. Here, as Matthew Craske has argued, originality was not associated with novelty. Novelty had a pejorative sense, associated with the 'fickle appetites of the public, and the effects of petty consumer demand'. Craske argues that from the 1760s 'originality' in the world of art was increasingly associated with 'imitation', that is an 'inventive' combination or reinterpretation of traditional principles. This gave social and academic respectability to novelty, as a means of distinguishing particular artists at a time of glutted public art markets.[71]

Table 2   Patents specifying imitations, UK, 1627–1825

	pre-1750	1751–75	1776–1800	1801–25	total
Metal imitations for buttons and shoe buckles	0	0	5	0	5
Plating and tinning	2	2	4	8	16
Imitation and ornamentation for ceramics	1	1	3	3	8
Imitation inlaying or stamping on marble, metals and varnish	0	4	1	1	6
Stamping and printing on cloth – imitations	2	0	3	0	5
Stove ornaments or plated, enamel or lapis lazuli	0	0	1	1	2
Glass imitation	1	0	0	1	2
Paper ornaments resembling wood carvings	0	1	1	0	2
Imitation of marble	0	0	1	0	1

Source: Patents selected on core consumer industries from Bennet Woodcroft, *Subject Matter Index of Patents of Invention from March 2, 1617 to October 1, 1852*, Patent Office (London, 1857).

This close association between the new and the familiar offered a route to innovation in consumer goods manufacture. This route lifted principles of invention in semi-luxury goods out of an association with 'baubles' and trinkets, and copies in base materials of already existing luxury goods. Instead innovation was developed in finishes, in the adaptation of design principles in different goods, and in the development of an interrelatedness of commodities. At the same time a fundamental connection was claimed in the 'imitation' of ancient arts and artefacts.

The principles of 'imitation' followed in the production of new semi-luxury commodities were not those of twentieth-century mass consumer wares identified with cheap versions of elite craft-produced luxury ware. Their novelty was their 'imitation' of ancient or exotic principles and designs, their new production methods and materials, and their creative adaptation of these across complementary commodities. Their novelty was also perceived in their reception as 'luxuries' both to the rich and to a newly expanded, but infinitely hierarchical, middling order.

Notes

1   See N. McKendrick, J. Brewer and J.H. Plumb, *The Birth of a Consumer Society* (London, 1983); D.N. McCloskey, '1780–1860: A Survey', in R. Floud and D.N. McCloskey, eds, *The Economic History of Britain Since 1700*, 2nd edn (Cambridge, 1981), vol. I, *1700–1860*, pp. 242–70; J. Mokyr, 'Demand vs. Supply in the Industrial Revolution', in idem, ed., *The Economics of the Industrial Revolution* (London, 1985), pp. 97–118.

2   R.P. Thomas, 'Overseas Trade and Empire, 1700–1860', in Floud and McCloskey, *Economic History of Britain*, 1st edn, vol. I, pp. 87–102; P.K. O'Brien, 'Agriculture and the Home Market for English Industry 1660–1820', *English Historical Review*, 100 (1985), pp. 773–800; Mokyr, 'Demand vs. Supply', p. 101.

3   These cases were made in D.E.C. Eversley, 'The Home Market and Economic Growth in England 1750–1780', in E.L. Jones and G.E. Mingay, eds, *Land, Labour and Population in the Industrial Revolution* (London, 1966), pp. 209–52; in O. Saito, 'Labour Supply Behaviour of the Poor in the English Industrial Revolution', *Journal of European Economic History*, 10 (1981), pp. 633–52; and more recently in Jan de Vries, 'Between Purchasing Power and the World of Goods: Understanding the Household Economy in Early Modern Europe', in J. Brewer and R. Porter, eds, *Consumption and the World of Goods* (London, 1993), pp. 85–133. Their significance as explanations have been dismissed by Mokyr, 'Demand vs. Supply', pp. 101 and 107–9.

4   L. Weatherill, *Consumer Behaviour and Material Culture in Britain 1660–1760* (London, 1988; new edn, London, 1996); C. Shammas, *The Pre-Industrial Consumer in England and America* (Oxford, 1990); see also the essays in Brewer and Porter, *Consumption and the World of Goods*.

5   H. Medick, 'Plebeian Culture in the Transition to Capitalism', in R. Samuel and G. Stedman Jones, eds, *Culture, Ideology and Politics* (London, 1982), pp. 84–112, esp. 89–91.

6   De Vries, 'From Purchasing Power to the World of Goods', p. 118; E. Gilboy, 'Demand as a Factor in the Industrial Revolution' (1932), reprinted in R.M. Hartwell, ed., *The Causes of the Industrial Revolution in England* (London, 1967), pp. 121–38.

7   J. Styles, 'Manufacturing, Consumption and Design in Eighteenth-Century England', in Brewer and Porter, *Consumption and the World of Goods*, p. 537.

8   L. Jardine, *Worldly Goods* (London, 1996), p. 69.

9   R. Goldthwaite, *Wealth and the Demand for Art in Italy 1400–1600* (Baltimore and London, 1993), p. 249.

10   M. Howell, 'Fixing Movables: Gifts by Testament in Late Medieval Douai', *Past and Present*, 150 (1996), pp. 3–45, p. 39; also see D. Owen Hughes, 'Distinguishing Signs: Ear-rings, Jews and Franciscan Rhetoric in the Italian Renaissance City', *Past and Present*, 112 (1986), pp. 3–57.

11 See A. Vickery, 'Women and the World of Goods: A Lancashire Consumer and Her Possessions', in Brewer and Porter, *Consumption and the World of Goods*, pp. 274–305; M. Howell, 'Fixing Movables', esp. pp. 35–40; M. Berg, 'Women's Consumption and the Industrial Classes', *Journal of Social History*, 30, 2, pp. 415–34.

12 See M. Berg, 'Manufacturing the Orient: Asian Commodities and European Industry 1500–1800', *Proceedings of the Istituto Internazionale di Storia Economica 'F. Datini'*, 29 (Prato, 1998); J.E. Wills, 'European Consumption and Asian Production in the Seventeenth and Eighteenth Centuries', in Brewer and Porter, *Consumption and the World of Goods*, pp. 133–47.

13 Styles, 'Manufacturing, Consumption and Design in Eighteenth-Century England', pp. 527–54, esp. 529–30, 540.

14 See M. Sonenscher, *Work and Wages in Eighteenth-Century France* (Cambridge, 1989), pp. 210–43; Medick, 'Plebeian Culture'; B. Lemire, *Fashion's Favourite* (Oxford, 1991), pp. 43–77; L. Fontaine, *History of Pedlars in Europe* (Cambridge, 1996), pp. 183–6.

15 D. Roche, *Histoire des choses banales. Naisssance de la consommation dans les sociétés traditionnelles (xvii–xix siècle)* (Paris, 1997), p. 13.

16 *Ibid.*, p. 15.

17 *Ibid.*, pp. 88–90.

18 A. Smith, *An Inquiry into the Nature and Causes of the Wealth of Nations*, III, iv, (1776), 2 vols (Oxford, 1976), vol. I, pp. 421, 422.

19 *Ibid.*, p. 419.

20 A. Smith, *The Theory of Moral Sentiments* (1759), ed. D.D. Raphael and A.L. McFie (Oxford, 1976), Book IV, ch. 1, pp. 180, 183.

21 See M. Berg and H. Clifford, 'Commerce and the Commodity: Graphic Display and Selling New Consumer Goods in Eighteenth-Century England', in M. North and D. Ormrod, *Markets for Art 1400–1800* (Alckshot, 1998).

22 *Aris's Birmingham Gazette*, 3 October 1796.

23 *Aris's Birmingham Gazette*, 4 June 1798.

24 *Aris's Birmingham Gazette*, 20 November 1798.

25 *Catalogue of Tea Urns, Coffee Urns, Candlesticks, Trays, Goblets, Shaving Basins and other Metal Objects* (*c.* 1790), Sheffield, in the Winterthur Library.

26 See *Catalogue of Candelabra, Escutcheons, etc.* (*c.* 1790), Birmingham? in the Winterthur Library; *Catalogue of Benjamin Hadley* (1815), Birmingham, in the Winterthur Library; James Whitehead (1798), *Designs for Sundry Articles of Earthenware: At the same manufactory may be had, a great variety of other articles, both useful and ornamental, as well as printed, painted & enamelled; as likewise dry bodies, such as Egyptian, black, jasper etc.*, Birmingham (printed by Thomas Person), in the Winterthur Library.

27 M. Berg, 'Women's Consumption and the Industrial Classes of Eighteenth-Century England', *Journal of Social History*, 30 (1996), pp. 415–34, esp. pp. 425–6.

28 Lichfield Joint Record Office, Elizabeth Lynes (3 August 1739).

29 Lichfield Joint Records Office, Prudence Bryan (1703), Sarah Birch (1794), Ann Wright (1773). Borthwick Institute, Dorothy Ridgweay (1775).

30 B. Woodcroft, *Subject Matter Index of Patents of Invention*, Patent Office (London, 1857).

31 Patent 978, 28 December 1770.

32 Patent 920, 7 March 1769.

33 Patent 737, 10 February 1759.

34   Patent 1552, 5 August 1786.

35   Patent 1065, 14 February 1774.

36   Patent 1576, 14 December 1796.

37   Sonenscher, *Work and Wages in Eighteenth-Century France*, pp. 210–43.

38   See G. de Bellaigue, 'The Vulliamys and France', *Furniture History* (1967), pp. 45–53; also see Public Records Office, Chancery Masters Exhibits, C. 104/58 Part 1. Vulliamy (Order Book for Silver) and Vulliamy (Beckford as a Client). Both sets of papers indicate extensive networks of subcontracting in the manufacture of high luxury goods.

39   Chancery Masters Exhibits, Public Record Office, C.104/58 Part 1. Vulliamy (Order Book for Silver).

40   See Matthew Boulton and James Watt Papers, Boulton and Watt Letter Books, vol. 2, Index to outgoing Letters 1775–1800; Matthew Boulton Papers 114, 116, 118, Boulton and Fothergill Journals. These journals provide great detail of sales and supply networks.

41   E. Delieb and M. Roberts, *The Great Silver Manufactory* (London, 1971), p. 37. See pp. 126–8 for lists of heads of department and apprentices, and others working with Boulton.

42   Matthew Boulton Papers, Letter Book D, 1768–1773, no. 136, Letter to John Taylor, 23 July 1769.

43   Matthew Boulton, Assay Office Papers, R2/299, October 1799.

44   See Matthew Boulton Assay Office correspondence. P. de Grave to Matthew Boulton, 28 October 1795, asking Boulton to procure small knives and scissors, and a list of tools from Messrs Hunt & Cliffe. Matthew Boulton Papers 307, Boulton and Fothergill correspondence, Fothergill to Matthew Boulton, 4 April 1771, mentions several independent craftspeople, including Morriset, William Farr, Bradbury, Caldecott, Wright and Harrison doing specialist work on commission for Boulton and Fothergill. They included a swordsmith, burnisher, gilder, clockmaker, a finisher and other toymakers.

45   Matthew Boulton, Assay Office Papers, M2/243, 1 July 1791, Boulton to William Mossop.

46   Matthew Boulton, Assay Office Papers, H3/109, George Houletter to Boulton, 1792.

47   Matthew Boulton, Assay Office Papers, B6/83, September 1769, Butcher to Boulton; B6/84, November 1788, Butcher to Boulton.

48   Matthew Boulton, Assay Office Papers, E/28A, Boulton to J.H. Ebbinghaus, 1767; E1/30B, Boulton to Ebbinghaus, 1767.

49   The Wedgwood Archives, University of Keele. Business letters, orders and some memoranda and accounts, mainly relating to ware.

50   *Ibid.* Also see R. Reilly, *Wedgwood* (London, 1992).

51   M. Montias, 'Cost and Value in Seventeenth-Century Dutch Art', *Art History*, 10 (1987), pp. 455–66, esp. 456, 459–61.

52   D.G.C. Allan, *William Shipley Founder of the Royal Society of Arts* (London, 1968), pp. 16, 46, 51.

53   D.G.C. Allan, 'Artists and the Society in the Eighteenth Century', in D.G. Allan and J.L. Abbott, *The Virtuoso Tribe of Arts & Sciences. Studies in the Eighteenth Century Work and Membership of the London Society of Arts* (Athens, GA, and London, 1992), pp. 91–119, esp. 103.

54   Allan, 'Artists and the Society', p. 95.

55   [Royal] Society of Arts Guard Books, vol. 5 (94), n.d. [1760].

56 *Ibid.*

57 *Ibid.*, vol. 5 (135), 5 and 28 February 1758 and vol. 3 (143), 11 March 1758.

58 *Ibid.*, vol. 4 (50), 29 March 1759.

59 *Ibid.*, vol. 11 (9), 6 September 1764.

60 Woodcroft, *Subject Matter Index*.

61 *Transactions of the Society, Instituted at London for the Encouragement of Arts, Manufactures and Commerce*, with the premiums offered in the Year 1783, vol. 1 (London, 1783), p. 20.

62 *Transactions of the Society . . . of Arts, Manufactures and Commerce* (1783), vol. 1, pp. 201, 231.

63 *Transactions of the Society of Arts*, 1785, p. 318; 1791, p. 284.

64 *Premiums Offered by the Society Instituted at London, for the Encouragement of Arts, Manufactures and Commerce* (London, 1768–75), pp. 18, 24.

65 [Royal] Society of Arts Guard Books, vol. 7 (143), n.d. [1763].

66 *Ibid.*, vol. 2 (32), 24 April 1760.

67 *Ibid.*, vol. 11 (108), 3 December 1766.

68 Guard Books, vol. 11, 3 December 1766.

69 B. Woodcroft, *Subject Matter Index of Patents*: Weckwood, 0939, 16 Nov. 1769; Redrich and Jones, 0461, 28 Jan. 1724.

70 H. Young, *The Genius of Wedgwood* (London, 1995), p. 13; A. Forty, *Objects of Desire: Design and Society 1750–1980* (London, 1986), pp. 13–16.

71 M. Craske, *Art in Europe 1700–1830: A History of the Visual Arts in an Era of Unprecedented Urban Economic Growth* (Oxford, 1997), pp. 28–39.

PART TWO

Novelty and imitation

In the name of the tulip. Why speculation?

One of many satirical prints published in Holland in 1637 shows an oversized fool's cap as the place where the trade in tulip bulbs is carried on (Plate 3). After the collapse of prices in early February of that year, which brought to an end the speculation in bulbs that had started a few years earlier, tulips came to symbolise the vices of greed, vanity and ambition that the increasing demand for new goods in general seemed to stimulate. Yet despite the harm the speculation had caused, and the public disdain for indulging in the consumption of a 'useless' flower, the demand for tulips did not show signs of decline even after the speculation. Why was that so?

In the following, I will take the story of the tulip to illustrate the endless delight that consumers can gain from novelty. Tulips existed in an almost infinite array of colours and colour combinations. To possess and to cultivate them seemed to give access to a world of constant change and wonder. It was also a non-forbidden access: tulips were easy to cultivate and were sold at very many different prices, from low to extraordinarily high.

The story of the tulip will also show that consumers, like producers, can be actively engaged in creating new, and newly enjoyable, consumption opportunities. Why and how novelty is pleasant, and why it has such a relevant place in consumption, I shall address in the second part of the chapter. This will help explain the creative strategies producer-consumers adopt in order to increase novelty and variety. The novelty that tulips seemed to deliver as a gift from nature was soon multiplied by improved cultivation skills. But tulips only became a

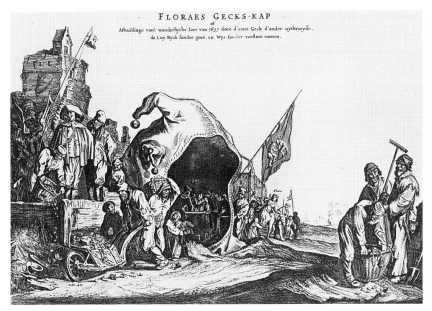

3 Cornelius Danckerts after Pieter Nolpe, *Floraes Gecks-kap*

completely 'manufactured' product when they started to be reproduced in engravings and prints, and in the free compositions of still lifes. Abstracted from the accidents of their natural life, the novelty which comes from combination was fully exploited in these first flower compositions.

Tulips: 'of colour very divers and variable'[1]

Like many new goods of the early modern period, tulips came from the East. They are mentioned in Europe as early as 1555.[2] In that year Ogier de Busbecq, Ambassador of the Emperor Ferdinand I at the court of Suleiman the Magnificent in Constantinople, and collector of ancient manuscripts and naturalia, brought back to Vienna seeds and probably bulbs of an exotic flower, the 'tulipan'.[3] Originally from central Asia, tulips had long been cultivated in the gardens of the Turkish court[4] and had become a cult object amongst the people. Spring festivals were held in their honour and a profusion of tulips with their bright colours and long needle-pointed petals could be seen decorating miniatures, ceramics and tapestries.[5] Just a few years after Busbecq's return the first tulip could be seen in a German garden, resplendent 'like a red lily', as described and first illustrated by Konrad Gesner in his *De Hortis Germaniae Liber* (1561).[6] The fame of the flower spread rapidly. In 1562 there is mention of a shipment of tulip bulbs sent from Constantinople to the port of Antwerp. From Flanders they soon reached Holland, and in 1578 England. There is no known record of this flower in France before 1608.

From the beginning tulips in Europe were a sensation. Carolus Clusius, professor of botany and prefect of the *hortus botanicus* since 1593 at Leiden, possessed many varieties. The letters he received from other botanists, from florists, merchants and even from clergymen, asking and offering to bargain for some of the foreign bulbs, attest to the very particular favour enjoyed by this flower.[7] Soon, however, the tulip's popularity went beyond the restricted circle of botanists and amateur horticulturalists and reached even the population at large, the rarest varieties always commanding very high prices and inducing cunning to obtain them.[8]

It was in moderate Holland, however, that tulips became a national passion and where there occurred one of the first recorded speculative bubbles, the so-called 'tulip mania'. The speculation, which affected the tulip trade between the years 1634 and 1637, nonetheless was only froth on a market where profits and volume had surged for two decades. By the time the speculation was at its height, in the first few days of February 1637, hundreds of varieties of tulip were already cultivated in Holland. Their array of colours was infinitely varied; even those that were plain-coloured had edges of a contrasting colour, while basic colours could also be shot with stripes, veins and flames. The rarest and most desired were the last, the flamed variants, and names were given to them that reflected their flamboyant appearance: Beautiful Helena, Bride of Haarlem, Harlequin, Miracle, along with real and fictitious Generals, Admirals and Princes. One in particular had always been the most prized and highly priced, the beautiful Semper Augustus, having white petals and small ruby veins running to the top of the bluish chalice (Plate 4).[9]

The proliferation of varieties was the result of many changes that had intervened in the production and marketing of the tulip since its first introduction in Holland. Professional growers had replaced the botanist and the horticulturalist, and had started to produce for a larger market. Tulips were no longer sold only by large units (beds) or as expensive single bulbs, but also by the basket and the pound.[10] This in turn opened the possibility of attracting many more buyers by differentiating quality and price, with the rarest varieties at the top of the market and more common and plain ones like the Switsers at the

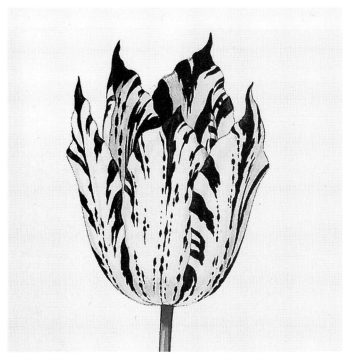

4 Pieter Holsteyn de Jonge, *Semper Augustus* (detail)

bottom. By the 1630s the demand had increased strongly and reached every segment of the market. Tulips were easy to grow and to propagate and anybody with a little patch of land could cultivate them. A steady increase in prices, and the profit opportunities this offered, added an extra incentive to cultivators.

By the end of 1634 speculators had joined the market[11] and the exchanging of contracts for future delivery became a general practice.[12] The creation of a futures market allowed tulip bulbs to be traded all year round, whereas spot contracts were impossible in winter and spring when the bulbs lay in the ground. Futures trading quickly became feverish, and from December 1634 to February 1637 the recorded prices of bulbs increased ten to fifteen times.[13] This implied that the most expensive varieties were now sold for several thousand guilders (one thousand guilders corresponded to more than 800 times the daily wage of a master carpenter in Holland).[14] Even the more common varieties became objects of speculation and showed strong increases in prices towards the end of this period.[15] All sorts of goods, from tools of trade to paintings, were given in exchange for bulbs and sometimes the property pledged could be considerable.[16]

After the collapse, tulips continued to enjoy a large popularity. A century later the best new varieties were still sold at relatively high prices, though none as high as during the speculative years. Only in the nineteenth century did the passion for tulips show signs of exhaustion.[17]

The speculative game which unmade so many quickly made fortunes has captured the attention of analysts the most, especially among economists. The extravagance of the prices reached by the rarest bulbs seems to justify the conviction that this was an episode of collective insanity.[18] It was perceived in the same way by the contemporary moralists and preachers who made the tulip out to be a symbol of sinful excess.[19] Focusing on the madness of the speculation, however, obscures a more important element of the story, that tulips were an object of desire much earlier than the speculation, and remained so long after the speculation ended.[20] Why was it the tulip that inspired such sustained passion?

The botanical gardens

Collecting rare flowers was part of that desire for the new, the rare and the precious that filled the cabinets of curiosities in sixteenth- and seventeenth-century Europe. In the second half of the sixteenth century the first botanical gardens were created, initially in Italy (Padua in 1545 and Bologna in 1547), and later in Belgium, Germany and Holland. These first gardens were linked to the universities, but private botanical gardens soon came into existence, among them the famous garden of Pieter van Coudemberghe which was one of the marvels of Antwerp.[21] New plants, herbs and flowers were actively traded, collected and studied. The until then undisputed authority of the ancient botanical texts of Dioscorides and Pliny began to be challenged, as new scientific interest was aroused, new classificatory devices emerged and illustrations became much more precise.

Tulips shared with other exotic flowers, imported from Greece, Spain, Africa and America, the same aura of new scientific botanical curiosity. For a while also their medical properties were tested, in Germany. Yet tulips had additional advantages over other flowers (and over the other exotic goods as well). In the first place, they could be easily reproduced and multiplied by the simple splitting off of a bulb's outgrowths, which could increase bulb propagation by 100 to 150 per cent a year.[22] This allowed the supply to expand beyond the limited

demand set by connoisseurs. More importantly, tulip bulbs could produce multiple new varieties which bore only a faint resemblance to
their botanical ancestors.[23] Alone among the more modest bulbous
flowers known at the time such as snowdrops, crocuses and scillas,
tulips are unicoloured or bordered if cultivated from seeds, but become
surprisingly multicoloured if cultivated from bulbs. After a certain
period of cultivation, in fact, the bulb of the tulip 'breaks' and gives rise
to a different colour configuration. This was thought to happen spon-
taneously, though, as has become known only more recently, a mosaic
virus tends to attack the bulb. This 'breaking' gave rise to the most
prized variants: those with flamed or striped streamers of red or purple
against a background of white, or of red or violet against yellow; and
petals with ruffled or pleated edges.

It was these variations, these seemingly miraculous mutations, as
well as their reproducibility, that made tulips a general and irresistible
object of desire. To cultivate tulips seemed to open up a Pandora's
box, a process of discovery in which the unexpected and the beautiful
combined. Tulips had the enviable property of promising the constantly
new, with as yet unseen colour combinations arising and vying to
capture the interest of the consumer, even before the old favourites had
become too widely known.

There was a downside: new variants could disappear since
diseased bulbs tended to disintegrate. And even the healthiest bloom
was ephemeral and its beauty only fugitive. Could tulips somehow be
made more permanent? Artists solved this problem. They extended the
life of tulips through representations, and pretty soon the tulips of
illustrations and prints, of aquarelles and still lifes, came to stand in for
the still somewhat exclusive, chancy and evanescent real thing.[24]

'Counterfeit' flowers

Depictions of new plants and their flowers arose in numbers as soon
as discoveries occurred, and exchange and cultivation were begun. The
crude illustrations in the earliest herbariums were of limited scientific
or aesthetic value, but new botany required representations to be precise, true to life. The first botanical books by Dodonaeus, his student
Clusius, and Lobelius in the second half of the sixteenth century, made
extensive use of the new printing techniques and skills in woodcutting
and engraving, and were meticulously and beautifully illustrated.[25] But
it was the skills of the painter, not the engraver, that were used to
illustrate the tulip growers' catalogues. Both painters and engravers,

however, had, and shared with naturalists and amateurs, a keen scientific interest. It was from a shared culture of seeing, with the microscopic precision made possible by new instruments, and an 'attentive eye' that Dutch and Flemish flower still lifes first took their inspiration and pride.[26]

We do not know just when, though it was towards the end of the sixteenth century, that the first bouquet of flowers was composed and painted. By the first decade of the seventeenth century, however, floral still life had already been successfully established as a genre in The Hague (Jacques de Gheyn II, b.1565), in Antwerp (Jan Breugel the elder, b.1568), in Middelburg (Ambrosius Bosschaert the elder, b.1573), in Amsterdam (Roelandt Savery, b.1576) and soon thereafter in Utrecht, Haarlem, Delft and Dordrecht.[27]

In Frankfurt, too, trade centre for flowers and plants as well as books, and workplace for many Flemish painters, we can trace early examples of flower paintings. In a large canvas of 1595 by Lucas van Valckenborch representing *Spring*, three still lifes of flowers separated by two female figures can be seen. One of the three still lifes, placed on a simple rustic table, is a perfect example of the Breugel–Bosschaert style of flower composition. In a Renaissance metal vase a profusion of flowers of every season is symmetrically displayed, a crown imperial at the top and tulips, anemones, narcissi, irises, roses, lilies and other flowers, each reproduced with minute care and botanical precision.[28]

Tulips were placed in eye-catching, even dominant, positions in the early floral paintings, long before the speculation started. They appear in their unending variety of colours – reds, lilacs, yellows – and are captured from every aspect: open, closed, half closed, from below and from above, looking straight into the flower. Moreover, mixed with, and contrasted to all the other common and less common flowers, the singularity of the tulip could be both accentuated and made part of a recognisable, structured order.

It is not difficult, then, to explain why floral still lifes had become in such a short time a specialised, and remunerative, art.[29] Greatly desired flowers that, like the tulips, were rare or impossible for most people to possess, could be seen in one single painting defying time and place. There was an additional element, however, which made these paintings particularly enjoyable and successful. The fact was that the same theme, a simple bouquet of flowers in a bowl, in a vase or in a glass, could be treated in many different ways, giving the flowers themselves an appearance that was constantly new, surprising, stimulating. Playing on the compositional freedom of flower arrangements, on their

contrasts and similarities, on different hierarchies and saliences, new
undetected characteristics and connections could be discovered, both
within a painting and between different paintings. The technique of
execution, too, enhanced the possibility for the painter to exploit to
the full, and innovatively, the combinatory properties inherent in flower
compositions. If Jan Breugel the elder often painted after nature,
patiently waiting for each different flower to bloom, Bosschaert worked
with the help of studies, of sketches and drawings. In this way the
original sketched flower could be 're-used', unaltered, in multiple paintings, without losing its 'freshness' though appearing to be always different because each setting was different. An example is Bosschaert's
beautiful little bouquet by a window (1619) in the Einar Perman
collection in Stockholm. This free and natural composition, which
appears even fresher against the luminous blue sky and the vanishing
landscape, not only follows the strict symmetrical rules that Bosschaert
applies in each of his compositions, but, by Bol's count, out of the nine
main flowers represented, seven are replicas of flowers already in other
Bosschaert works.[30]

These miniature collections of flowers – every painting a cabinet
in itself – offered, then, the excitement and pleasure that every collection offers, that of discovering a set which can be expanded at pleasure
without losing, indeed actually enhancing, its novelty.[31]

As was the case with many other 'luxury' goods, tulips activated
a process that was one of both diffusion and multiplication of its novel
characteristics. Novelty played a decisive role, as seems to be the case
in consumption in general. This aspect, however, is often downplayed,
especially in the writings of economists. There are reasons for the importance of novelty and its selective neglect.

Novelty

Novelty can be defined as something different from what we have
already experienced. The degree of this difference may be very high,
as when something is new relative to everything we have experienced
before, or low, when something represents only a recombination of
known experiences. Time, too, is an important dimension. Something
can be new relative to a recent experience or to one more distant in
time. Expectations, on the other hand, form a dimension of surprise.
Something is more or less surprising in so far as it is less or more
expected. Though novelty and surprise can appear together and reinforce each other, this need not be the case. Something new might

not be unexpected and vice versa, something surprising might not be new. We can act upon these different dimensions of newness and surprise in such a way as to reduce or enhance novelty. Increasing exposure to a new event, or shortening the time between its repetitions, reduces novelty. All procedures of ordering, classifying and developing routines do the same by creating spatial, temporal and hierarchical relations which increase predictability and regularity. On the other hand, all those activities which develop already experienced events into new combinations and patterns increase novelty. Correspondingly, increasing the level of complexity of certain tasks or their uncertainty can add stimulus and surprise to something already known.[32]

These distinctions in fact summarise strategies for reducing and increasing novelty seen in the previous discussion of tulips. Tulips were absolutely new to Europeans. To use them first as a botanical specimen and then as an ornamental flower in private gardens started a process that reduced their novelty by creating classificatory rules, by making the different varieties both recognisable and reproducible, as well as more available and predictable through cultivation. At the same time this process implied that new distinctive properties were identified which made tulips difficult to assimilate to the already known bulbous species. Additionally, as we have seen, there was constant experimentation with new varieties, in spite of efforts to protect the rarest ones from imitation. The result was that the process of acquiring and collecting this flower was never closed: there was always a new variety to be discovered and to be assimilated. Some of these new varieties maintained their status for decades, even centuries, though most were replaced and disappeared, more or less rapidly, in a sequence of elimination and renewal that is seemingly endless.[33]

The artistic creation of flower paintings, as well as their collection, reveals the same strategies for controlling and producing novelty. The rule of order that frames a whole collection of flowers within a single painting collapses into unity the differences of many gardens and the distance of many seasons. At the same time these are highly complex paintings which to hold the viewer's attention, and the artist's as well; both must be constantly alert. They do this by multiplying the views of the objects represented, by creating unexpected differences and similarities among them, by restricting or expanding the set, as when the painting is focused on a single flower, when it includes fruit still lifes, a glimpse of some items of the furniture or architectural elements introduce an unexpected source of light, and so on. As Svetlana Alpers has remarked, in Dutch art fragments are prized.[34]

But the process just described is also none other than a process of learning and of acquiring knowledge. Knowledge proceeds by imposing a set for reference purposes, a unified, abstract order of understanding which makes the object at stake both definable and manageable. Once made more 'familiar', the aim is to break the original set giving rise to fresh observations, combinations and solutions.

Nevertheless, in the process of creating novelty, as in knowledge, there is something else, and the story of tulips reveals what the missing element is. Seventeenth-century moralists saw it and denounced what they saw: tulips, like any novelty, can become an absorbing passion. The unstated and unaddressed question then is: if innovation, the creation of novelty, is the result of learning, why is it also pleasurable?

The pleasure of novelty

The economic theory of choice has always had, though especially in its beginnings, a strong hedonistic element. Rational economic action is driven by the maximisation of utility and pleasure, and the minimisation of pain and costs.[35] Behaviourism and experimental psychology, too, have followed a hedonistic approach, in terms of stimulus–reward–enforcement. Yet in both cases the role that novelty plays in determining the pleasantness of a situation has been little investigated.[36] There are exceptions, however. In the field of economics, Tibor Scitovsky has forcefully and convincingly insisted on the importance of novelty in the organisation of economic choices and decisions.[37] He relies for evidence on some findings of experimental psychobiological research. These findings are related to the pioneering work of D.E. Berlyne in the 1960s and 1970s and are very important to the link I want to draw between novelty and pleasure in consumption.

Berlyne's research showed that novelty, together with surprise, uncertainty, complexity and ambiguity, can be viewed as the stimulus components of a situation (its arousal potential). They are also sources of pleasure, but each only within limits. Thus the stimulus provided by novelty, for example, is perceived as pleasant for degrees which are neither too high nor too low: too low a degree of novelty is boring, too high a degree is threatening. Therefore, as the stimulus potential of a situation increases, so too does its pleasantness; but pleasure also reaches a maximum and thereafter declines (an inverted U-shaped curve, the Wundt curve, represents these functional properties).

These results are intuitively appealing and straightforward, but their consequences for rules of choice are not. For they suggest that the processes of choosing and deciding also involve search, and search, moreover, that is potentially without end. The ambivalent relation of novelty with pleasure provides motivations and drives for endogenous actions and change, even when the external circumstances remain unchanged. If a situation is perceived as too repetitive and predictable, corrective actions will be taken which tend to increase arousal potential by increasing novelty, complexity, and so on. The reverse will occur if the situation is perceived as too unfamiliar and upsetting. Yet, even when successful, these corrective strategies will never discover a resting point or equilibrium. Simply repeating the same successful strategy will erode the pleasurable effects. An unfamiliar situation will become too familiar, and vice versa. Constant new strategies or permanent change are called for.

This brief discussion helps us to understand why the presence of novel goods and of the innovative strategies which brought them into existence and use are so important and yet so difficult to handle in terms of traditional economic modelling. In economic models choice is represented as a maximisation procedure subject to given constraints. The constraints include the subject's preferences as well as prices, the budget, time, knowledge and available goods. But these are the very same things one acts upon when looking for novelty and variety. Configuring them in such a way as to allow for an equilibrium solution to be found, and positing that this equilibrium will be stable in the absence of exogenous change in the external conditions, takes no account of the implications just identified, namely that the creation of novelty is, and has to be, endogenous for it to yield pleasure.

The Dutch passion for tulips, or for any of the many new goods that constantly appear on the market, is therefore either placed among those forms of behaviour – the irrational – which are beyond the reach of economic analysis, or, if they are included, their novelty is denied.

In the case of tulips the speculative bubble which accompanied them for a brief period in Holland has become paradigmatic of the irrationality and mania which make fashion goods intractable in economic terms. Recently some economists have begun to reduce speculative manias to 'rational bubbles', and bursts of fashion to rational 'cascades'. For Garber, for example, the rapid increases in price of the new varieties of bulb, and the subsequent decline, was a perfectly normal phenomenon. The price pattern is typical of every new good, including new flower varieties, when they appear on the market.[38] The data are too scant to allow such a strong conclusion in the case of the seventeenth-century tulips, but even if we had complete information which bore out the pattern, what Garber fails to explain is why novelty, variety and rarity should command high prices in the first place. Tulips were the least 'necessary' sort of goods. Why should such an irrelevant novelty be so highly prized; why should the possession of tulips have so 'deranged' consumption choices?[39] And why did the popularity of tulips last so long? Answers to these questions are available in the factors we have discussed, but they require us to go beyond the inadequate dichotomy, rational versus irrational. Though each single variety of tulip might have faded in popularity, yet the chief characteristic of tulips, that they allowed for new varieties constantly to be experimented with and produced, meant that tulips could continue to be stimulating and to command high prices in their new variant forms. Tulips remained attractive because they were both recognisable and new, both predictable and surprising.

In brief, the tulip mania was not a mania; neither was it an irrational form of behaviour. The novelty and variety of tulips suffice to explain the excitement and pleasure that collecting them provided. Yet neither was it rational in the sense of economic rationality: simply an optimal response under given preferences and constraints. For tulips evoked an innovative, learning rationality which showed in microcosm what active consumption is *always* about: trying to find new pleasurable solutions to the problems of choice posed by an expanding set of wants.

Notes

1   The phrase comes from the English edition (1578) of Dodonaeus' *Herbal*, quoted by L.J. Bol, *The Bosschaert Dynasty. Painters of Flowers and Fruit* (Leigh-on-Sea, 1960), p. 16.
2   In the first of Ogier de Busbecq's 'Turkish letters' from Vienna to his humanist friend Nikolas van Indeveldt: *Botany in the Low Countries (end of the 15th century – ca.1650)*, Plantin-Moretus Museum, Exhibition Catalogue (Antwerp, 1993), p. 14.
3   Some claim the botanist Clusius to have been the first to receive and to cultivate Turkish tulips: *ibid.*, p. 17.
4   Though chiefly in a species with long narrow-pointed petals known as *Tulipa acuminata*, Needle tulips: S. Segal, *Tulips by Anthony Claesz* (Maastricht, 1987).
5   As they can be seen in *Turquie. Au nom de la Tulipe*, Exhibition Catalogue (Thonon-les-Bains, Haute-Savoie, 1993).
6   W. Blunt, *Tulipomania* (Harmondsworth, 1950), pp. 7–8.
7   In one of these letters the author begs for 'two, three or four of his beautifully coloured tulips, indeed if it were only one . . .' (quoted in Bol, *The Bosschaert Dynasty*, p. 17). Clusius' reluctance to give bulbs away had an unhappy ending: eventually unknown thieves emptied his tulip garden, after which he never again cultivated this flower.

8   Anecdotes abound. In France a young man was happy to receive for his bride's dowry the bulb of a rare tulip called appropriately 'Mariage de ma fille', while another one willingly exchanged his brewery for a bulb named 'Tulipe brasserie': see Blunt, *Tulipomania*.

9   As described in the beautiful tales by H. Zbigniew, *Still Life with a Bridle. Essays and Apocryphas* (London, 1994), p. 5. Very few Semper Augustus bulbs were available in any one season, and their prices could reach astonishing heights even decades prior to the speculative peak: a bulb sold for fl.1,000 in 1623, one went for fl.1,200 in 1624, and a year later an owner refused offers of fl.2,000 and fl.3,000: see E.H. Krelage, *Bloemenspeculatie in Nederland* (Amsterdam, 1942), pp. 33–4.

10   S. Schama, *The Embarrassment of Riches. An Interpretation of Dutch Culture in the Golden Age* (Berkeley, 1988), p. 351; N.W. Posthumus, 'Tulip Mania', *Journal of Economic and Business History*, 1 (May 1928–29), p. 438.

11   The speculators were not professional growers but outsiders; many were weavers, but there were also spinners, cobblers, bakers and other small traders: Posthumus, 'Tulip Mania', p. 442.

12   Though non-spot contracts are recorded before that date, see, for example, N.W. Posthumus, 'De Speculatie in Tulpen in de Jaaren 1636 en 1637 (II)', *Economisch-Historisch Jaarboek*, 13 (1927), pp. 1–85, doc. no. 3.

13   Krelage, *Bloemenspeculatie in Nederland*.

14   See J. De Vries and A. Van der Woude, eds, *Nederland 1500–1815. De Eerste Ronde van Moderne Economische Groei* (Amsterdam, 1995), chart 12.1, p. 705.

15   An Admiral van Eyck bulb weighing 80 aces (1 ace = $\frac{1}{20}$ gram) sold at 80 guilders in December 1634, but by February 1637 a bulb of 214 aces fetched 1,045 guilders. Even the common Switsers went from a price per ace of 0.0059 guilders on 2 January 1637 to a price of 0.1074 per ace on 9 February: P.M. Garber, 'Who put the Mania in the Tulipmania?', in E.N. White, ed., *Crashes and Panics: The Lessons from History* (Homewood, IL, 1990), pp. 24 and 27). A list of sixty-eight tulip varieties and their prices from an auction in Alkmaar on 5 February 1637 shows that the average price paid per bulb was 784 guilders. Other bulbs were sold for 3,000 guilders or more: an Admiral Enkhuijsen and a small outgrowth sold for 5,200 guilders: Posthumus, 'De Speculatie in Tulpen in de Jaaren 1636 en 1637 (I)', *Economisch-Historisch Jaarboek*, 12 (1926), pp. 3–99, esp. 96–7.

16   See the famous Dialogues between Waermondt and Gaergoed on the Rise and Decline of Flora (1637), in *ibid.*, pp. 21–94, and Schama, *The Embarrassment of Riches*, p. 358: one Viceroy bulb, highly valued for its purple veins on a white petal, was said to have sold for 2 loads of wheat, 4 loads of rye, 4 fat oxen, 8 fat pigs, 12 fat sheep, 2 hogsheads of wine, 4 barrels of 8-florin beer, 2 barrels of butter, 1,000lbs of cheese, a complete bed, a suit of clothes and a silver beaker, totalling 2,500 guilders. But one bulb of the rare Semper Augustus reached more than four times that sum.

17   P.M. Garber, 'Tulipmania', *Journal of Political Economy*, 97:3 (1989), pp. 535–80.

18   The economist Garber goes in the opposite direction and tries to show that the pricing pattern observed in the years of the speculation was not different from what happens in modern markets when a prized new variety is developed. After an initial period of high prices, the prices of new varieties of bulb fall to their reproduction costs in less than 30 years: P.M. Garber, 'Famous First Bubbles', *Journal of Economic Perspectives*, 14:2 (1990), pp. 35–54, esp. 38.

Garber, nevertheless, fails to explain why new varieties should command high prices in the first place. More on this point later.

19 A century later, when the popularity of double hyacinths seemed to threaten a recurrence of the mania, many of the satirical prints of the 1630s were reproduced: see Schama, *The Embarrassment of Riches*, p. 365.

20 Evidence for this exists in two forms. First, contracts dating from 1612, 1626 and 1633, and a legal proceeding from 1616, all show prices for specific bulbs in the range of fl.24 to fl.60: Posthumus, 'De Speculatie in Tulpen in de Jaaren 1636 en 1637 (II)', pp. 1–85, doc. nos 3, 5; 'De Speculatie in Tulpen in de Jaaren 1636 en 1637 (III)', *Economisch-Historisch Jaarboek*, 18 (1934), pp. 229–40, doc. nos 1, 2. Second, sales in the first decade of the eighteenth century show single bulbs, of novel varieties, selling for prices ranging from fl.10 to fl.358: Krelage, *Bloemenspeculatie in Nederland*, pp. 107–10.

21 As reported by the Italian historian Guicciardini. Coudemberghe's garden was started in 1548; twenty years later it had accumulated 600 exotic plants; on both points see van Indevelde, *Botany in the Low Countries*, p. 23.

22 Garber, 'Tulipmania'.

23 Segal, *Tulips by Anthony Claesz*.

24 Despite propagation via outgrowths, bulbs as such – the better sorts – were scarce, for the demand for new varieties was always pressing against the available supply.

25 van Indevelde, *Botany in the Low Countries*, p. 33.

26 S. Alpers, *The Art of Describing. Dutch Art in the Seventeenth Century* (Chicago, 1983), pp. 72ff. 'Attentive' and 'curious' were interchangeable as terms descriptive of Dutch paintings. 'Curiosity' had similar connotations also in seventeenth-century English.

27 As reconstructed by Bol, *The Bosschaert Dynasty*. The first known dated flower pieces of each of the aforementioned painters are between 1601 and 1608, though the same artists had already painted floral pieces before those dates: P. Taylor, *Dutch Flower Painting 1600–1720* (New Haven, 1995); Bol, *The Bosschaert Dynasty*. In a letter to Cardinal Borromeo dated 1606, Jan Breugel the elder, for example, writes that he is working on a new painting which includes more than a hundred different flowers, many of them 'trop in e'stimi per aver in casa' (too precious to have at home), and 'fatti tutti del naturel' (all done from nature): see G. Crivelli, *Giovanni Breughel pittor fiammingo* (Milan, 1868), quoted in Taylor, *Dutch Flower Painting 1600–1720* pp. 119 and 214.

28 Bol, *The Bosschaert Dynasty*, p. 25.

29 Bosschaert's last painting (1620), a very large piece with an apotheosis of flowers, was sold for 1,000 guilders to Prince Maurits, the Stadtholder. This was, however, an exceptionally high price. Bosschaert, who also traded in paintings, had sold a Veronese, *Europa*, for 100 guilders, and in 1613 a fruit piece by Georg Flegel for 66 guilders: Bol, *The Bosschaert Dynasty*, p. 26.

30 *Ibid.*, p. 30, plate no. 30.

31 See M. Bianchi, 'Collecting as a Paradigm of Consumption. Unifying and Discriminating Strategies in Consumer Choice', *Journal of Cultural Economics*, 21 (1997), pp. 275–89.

32 See D.E. Berlyne, *Aesthetics and Psychobiology* (New York, 1971).

33 Krelage, *Bloemenspeculatie in Nederland*, ch. 5.

34 Alpers, *The Art of Describing*, p. 85. See also N. Bryson, *Looking at the Overlooked. Four Essays on Still Life Painting* (Cambridge, MA, 1990).

35   In the course of time this element has faded in favour of a purely axiomatic theory of choice. This approach allows some of the problems of the theory, mainly those connected with the measurability of utility and of the inter-personal comparison of utilities, to be avoided. In this way, however, the motivation of action – the object of one's maximisings – is left unaddressed.

36   In economic theory novelty is subversive, since the main scope of the theory is to analyse the forces which converge to an equilibrium, not those which, like novelty, disrupt it.

37   T. Scitovsky, *The Joyless Economy. The Psychology of Human Satisfaction* (Oxford, 1992).

38   Garber, 'Tulipmania'; and 'Who put the Mania in the Tulipmania?'.

39   A desire for novelty can easily generate intransitivities and inconsistencies in the preference set: see M. Bianchi, 'Taste for Novelty and Novel Tastes. The Role of Human Agency in Consumption', in idem, ed., *The Active Consumer. Novelty and Surprise in Consumer Choice* (London and New York, 1998), pp. 64–86.

Colours and colour making in the eighteenth century

Colour is a subject at once familiar and remote. Everyone uses colour, and everyone has opinions about it, but those opinions are largely unexplored. Colour is an integral part of things, but it also has an existence separate from objects. The position of colour, as a part of personal experience, as a component of objects, as a focus for ideas, creates interesting challenges for its interpretation.

The fluid qualities of colour are unconsciously expressed in our description of its role in life and art. We understand that some kinds of colours rise and fall in popularity. We see that colours currently in fashion can give a 'new' look to even the most common object. Thus, the use of colour establishes links between people, commodities and contemporary social culture, because it contributes to definitions of new and old, desirable and not.

The study of colour has another place within the sciences. Colours and colour changes serve a practical function in experiment. Explanations of light incorporate colour theories. Theories of coloration – explanations of how colour is formed on an object – provide further points for enquiry.

The technology of colour making also plays its part in the definition of colour. We can imagine any number of colours, but until they can be placed in or on objects they have only a limited value. The techniques that allow their employ have requirements that define a standard to evaluate change. These form part of the strategy for the presentation of novel colours.

All these functions for colour exist now, but all were manifest in the eighteenth century as well. Then, as today, colour had an established place in contemporary sciences, and a ubiquitous presence in daily life. In addition, in an era when intellectual and practical pursuits were not always considered in isolation, colour was a potent site for their combination. Practical descriptions of colour were summoned to explain theories. The searches to find new colours and improve or imitate existing fashionable ones used theoretical ideas to enhance practice.

My interest here is to create a definition of colour as something simultaneously technical, scientific and experiential, and to use this to understand what colour can tell us about eighteenth-century culture. My discussion has two parts: one about colour and the ideas of fashion and novelty, where it figures prominently in consumption and social life; the second about colour, novelty and improvement as a way to consume fashionable ideas. In both, I ask more questions than I can answer; colour is a multifaceted topic, and it is under-studied.

For that latter reason, and to aid my later explanations, I will first present 'little histories' of four eighteenth-century colours.[1]

Turkey red

The word 'Turkey' in Turkey red refers to the place and not the fowl; it was also called Indian red or, in French, *rouge d'Andrinople*. The model was a vivid red found on cotton and linen textiles imported from India and the Levant. Today, we might describe this as 'basic', 'true' or 'common' red, the ancestor of that colour found on the ubiquitous red bandanna.

Although there are examples of a similar colour in all media, and testaments to its consistent and universal appeal, 'Turkey red' refers only to a colour used for dyed or printed textiles. Those textiles were principally export items, shipped to colonists and traders in the Americas, Africa and (ironically) the Middle East.

Turkey red took its colour from madder root, a traditional source for red dyes throughout Europe. The difference between common madder reds and this new colour was the result of the Turkey red process. To create the colour, the fibre received successive steepings in lye, olive oil, alum and dung; this was in addition to the dye bath and a final process called 'brightening'. The procedure was labour intensive and expensive, requiring days or weeks to complete.

Most historians of textiles consider the successful creation of Turkey red by European colour houses an achievement of the nineteenth century cotton printing industry.[2] However, attempts to imitate Turkey red at home began in the 1740s, and success made the reputation and fortune of several dyers, chemists and manufacturers in the decades before the development of synthetic dyes.

The efforts to reproduce Turkey red in Europe took several forms. Spies were sent to the Levant to learn the technique. Workers were imported to set up and operate dye houses specialising in Turkey red. There were investigations independent of the original, where the goal was to reproduce the colour without relying on the established process.

Over the decades, trained colour makers, scientific investigators and others with varying practical or theoretical skills developed techniques to make Turkey red. In France and Britain, patents, publication and other forms of public acclaim for one recipe did not preclude announcement of others. The Society of Arts received more than eighteen submissions concerning Turkey red in the years before 1785.[3] John Wilson, a dyer in Manchester, twice won a premium from the Society: once in 1761 for producing the best Turkey red and two years later for making the colour brighter.[4] In France, the first *privilège* to produce Turkey red was granted about 1747.[5] The *Imprimerie Royale* printed a version in 1765. A dozen others later applied for permission to manufacture their Turkey red process, and *brevets d'invention* were granted in 1783 and 1791.[6]

Emanuel Osmont, one of those grantees, won an award for adapting his process to produce a shade he called rose of Smyrna.[7] This discovery excited the interest of L.-A. Dambourney, author of a well-respected publication on dyeing[8] and himself the owner of a dye house specialising in Turkey red. In general, however, altering the process to make different colours was unusual; there were no corresponding 'Turkey' blues or browns. Although the concept of a final brightening stage was added to other dyeing routines, continued investigations of Turkey red attempted to reduce production time, cost or the materials involved rather than generalise the technique. Turkey red is an example of an important colour in eighteenth-century Europe, one where the colour and the technique to produce it were closely connected.

Nankeen

Nankeen was – and is – the name of both a colour and a fabric.[9] The original cloth was made from a natural yellow-brown coloured cotton found in China and later grown in India. Although it now means other fabrics, the modern material closest to the eighteenth-century nankeen cloth (and so the eighteenth-century colour) is probably what we call khaki drill.

When eighteenth- and early nineteenth-century sources refer to nankeen colour, they mean a brownish-yellow resembling the original cotton. Or rather, they mean a range that extends from a very pale yellow to one approaching good English mustard, often with a greenish undertone. Nankeen was not among the 112 colours mentioned in Colbert's industrial reforms of the late seventeenth century, so in France, as in Britain, there was no prescribed way to produce nankeen on textiles, even wool. Dambourney's manual lists three main, and twenty-two variant, recipes for nankeen; within these twenty-five recipes he clearly distinguishes at least ten different shades.[10]

Like Turkey red, nankeen is now a colour closely associated with early nineteenth-century printed cottons, but it is included in colour house records and in descriptions of objects several decades earlier.[11] Unlike the red, nankeen was not a colour name limited to textiles. Both the Derby and Sèvres works produced porcelain service which featured a colour called nankeen, and earlier in the century the shade (but not the name) was a speciality of faience makers in Rouen.[12] There is no contemporary pigment called nankeen, but the colours were easily made using ochres (iron oxides found in the earth) or the same buckthorn berries and weld that could create nankeen on textiles.[13]

Not all native colouring materials for yellow gave the brownish-green nuances of nankeen, but there was no effort to import and adapt traditional production methods of another region, as with Turkey red. There was, however, interest in better sources and production methods for the colour. More than one inventor promised a nankeen dye that would imitate the original and darken on use. Turmeric was suggested for nankeen on textiles and in watercolour painting in the latter part of the century, with mixed results. Again, new methods to make this colour were investigated by gentlewomen, retired army personnel, apothecaries and sentry guards, in addition to those with technical expertise.

Nankeen was never a single shade, and this makes it important to understand what was new about the result of any proclaimed 'new' recipe. It was not always the colour itself. Mineral and plant sources for yellow colours are abundant in Europe, from ochres or from liquids expressed from plant leaves, roots and seeds. The colours which came to be called nankeen were common in Europe before they were linked to the name. Once affiliation with this imported novelty was established, changes focused on improvements that would increase its similarities.

Nankeen colours were popular in a wide range of objects and familiar to a broad group of consumers. Creation of 'new' nankeen colours was not stemmed by publication of instructions or any other announcement.

Pompadour

In 1758, Cuthbert Gordon received a British patent for a substance he called 'cudbear', the result of a new processing method for the traditional dyestuff orchil. His technique improved the longevity of the popular but fragile violets and purples this lichen produced.[14] Gordon, a merchant, and his brother, a coppersmith, formed a partnership to sell cudbear, supplying printers and dyers throughout Britain. In 1765 they offered a colour sample card which included seventy-eight 'cudbear colours', ranging through all the red-purples to the violet-blues that you might expect from a substance well known to scientists as an acid/alkali colour indicator.[15] So it is fitting (and perhaps not coincidental) that cudbear could be used to produce a colour called pompadour, a fashionable colour which first appeared in Britain in the mid-1750s.[16]

As the name for a pink colour, pompadour disappears from and reappears on colour lists until the early twentieth century with no remarkable regularity. Like nankeen, it was clearly not one colour, but several. Colour charts such as Gordon's and other descriptions suggest pompadour could range from a deep purplish-brick colour to a silvery pink, and it was used for textiles, paints and porcelain.[17]

The origins of the name pompadour are as difficult to pin down as the colour. Allegations that it was a favourite of Mme de Pompadour have been shown to be untrue; nor was it a colour name used in France at that time. Pompadour may be the colour of the drapery in Drouais's portrait of the Marquise now at the National Gallery or it may be the pinks in her skirt, or neither. George Edwards's *Natural History of Birds* (1759) includes a South American bird with purple-red plumage called the Pompadour, but its origins are equally obscure.

Pompadour hints at a different kind of exotic origin from Turkey red and nankeen, and a false one at that. Like cudbear, it is unusual because the names can be traced in both the colour house and the draper's shop. Together, they establish an association between a colour name and a contemporary process, though in neither case was the connection exclusive.

Prussian blue

Of all the colours invented in the eighteenth century, the story of
Prussian blue was probably best known in its time. The scientific ideas
it incorporated were nearly as important as the colours that resulted
from the process. Prussian blue was the accidental laboratory invention
of a German colour maker and an alchemist.[18] Quick to see a value for
their 'mistake', they offered their discovery as a pigment that was less
expensive than natural ultramarine and more stable than the common
blues: indigo, azurite and verdigris.

It is difficult to say whether scientists or artists were more interested in Prussian blue. Both the colour and the process were rapidly
and widely disseminated, with instructions published in a variety of
books and journals including the *Philosophical Transactions* (1724), Shaw's
Chemical Lectures (1734), Dossie's *Handmaid to the Arts* (1758) and the
Dictionnaire de la chemie (1766). None of the recipes in the many sources
are identical; some publications suggest several. The overwhelming
impression from reading the descriptions is of considerable interest in
the chemical foundations of Prussian blue: how it was created and
how to use that information to make the colour less expensive, more
predictable, less likely to turn green with time, easier to work.

Prussian blue was an immediate success, and supplying the pigment to colour makers became a sub-speciality of the colour trades. Other
'Prussian' colours appeared, some using related production processes,
others merely relying on this designation to encourage a connection to
a successful scientific novelty.

Interest in Prussian blue extended beyond its possibilities as a
painter's pigment. By 1749, a French academician established a way to
use it as a colour for wool and silk.[19] Few written documents exist to
prove the extent of early use of Prussian blue on textiles, but anecdotal
evidence from objects suggests it was neither rare nor the standard for
silk, and used somewhat less for wool, cotton and linen. Prussian blue is
often the blue colouring material of eighteenth-century *indiennes*, as
indigo was difficult to manipulate under the conditions textile painting
and printing required.[20]

Prussian blue is an excellent example of a successful manufactured colour, and of the successful adaptation of a colouring material to
different uses. For consumers of ideas and objects in the eighteenth
century, it clearly confirmed the way science could improve practice.

A motif of these examples, like the concern of this chapter, is the
juncture of novelty and improvement in making colours. Each history

describes a different combination of those elements; each has similar features within different descriptions. Turkey red, though not a colour of fashion in the eighteenth-century West, was important to trade. Investigations into its production methods and its continued improvement were carried indirectly to other dye techniques and changed perceptions of the production process. Nankeen, a foreign name for a common colour, caught the attention of colour makers and the general public at different times over decades. Existing sources for yellow could be manipulated to give these colours, but different methods to make nankeen were connected to fashion cycles and changes in the production house. The painter's colour, Prussian blue, illustrates the perception that the challenges of eighteenth-century colour making were both intellectual and practical. Discovery and development of this blue pigment solved some long-standing problems for painters. Metamorphosis into a textile colour was a challenge itself, with a resolution that solved other problems. As a source to make pompadour colours, Cuthbert Gordon's cudbear demonstrates the close links that could exist between fashion and production innovations.

These anecdotes also reinforce ideas well established through the investigation of eighteenth-century objects and related contemporary writing. We accept that colour was an important determinant, increasing or devaluing the desirability of objects. In alliance with notions of consumption and fashion that are not limited to the circumstances of the eighteenth century, we expect that the value of specific colours would rise and fall. Here, we see that a colour could be fashionable in several media simultaneously, and the fashion for colours could change quickly. We can conclude from this information, too, that owning and using fashionably coloured objects was a visual acknowledgement of participation in the social culture of the period.

These stories about new colours raise other questions too, but those answers are hindered by the paucity of related studies. As the episodes of pompadour and nankeen show, we do not know the ways these colours of fashion varied and how variations were presented or used. Why was Turkey red unimportant to European textiles made for European markets for more than sixty years? Were all nankeen colours always called by that name after its introduction? If the colour ranges of Prussian blue and indigo are nearly the same, how certain was the eighteenth-century consumer that one colour was used and not the other?

There are also more general questions about colour which define some restrictions for this work. What do we mean when we talk about new colours? Is it a new shade or merely a new name? Which groups name colours and how do they choose? Do names depend on location and time? Was only part of a colour range available in any year or from any one supplier? Or are we isolating shifts in hue or tone that would have been unrecognisable in their time?

Examination of contemporary language is not helpful here. Until recently, colour was described only by comparison or in simile, leaving much leeway in the interpretation. Crimson is a red colour, less yellow than scarlet, but more so than purple. Nankeen is the colour of a natural brown cotton, *merde d'oie* that of goose droppings.

Some information suggests that names could mean several different colours. Other sources hint that the meaning of names changes over time. Neither statement can be accepted exclusively, and eighteenth-century documentation cannot be embraced uncritically. Jean Hellot, a French academician responsible for dye operations at the Gobelins tapestry works, noted in his treatise on wool dyeing that the current taste for scarlet sought a brighter, more orange colour than was once in fashion.[21] Hellot may have based this statement on a strong visual memory of the earlier scarlet colour, or he may have compared an old sample with a new one. Can we trust his memory? Was the old sample unaltered?

If we are to continue to investigate colours as part of the display of fashion, we must combine information from many sources, including eighteenth-century artefacts and contemporary writing about them. We must consider connections between the creation of colour and its use. We must learn about the transactions between colour makers and the merchants who imported or sold colouring materials; between colour makers and the painters, printers and dyers who created colour in or on objects; and about contacts and the influence of the public who bought fashionably coloured goods. Each group had an overlapping but unique role in the presentation and transmission of fashions for colour. The details of these exchanges have yet to be explored.

How, then, do we take advantage of what we know to place colour within eighteenth-century consumer culture? If we set aside fashion as the principal focus for the time being, and turn to ideas of novelty and innovation expressed through the creation of colour, we can look at the place of those endeavours in public life. Colour making, as all four stories noted, was a pursuit of many people in the eighteenth century. Developing new techniques to make colour was one way to join in some common public preoccupations.

First, though, this discussion of processes and novelty must acknowledge a key feature of that relationship. What do you want from a colour? The simple answer is 'a good colour', and the quest for novelty and improvement is founded on that idea. In the eighteenth century, the definition of good colour had two components: permanence and aesthetic appeal.[22]

Any good colour was beautiful, of course, and there is an aspect to this which suggests 'beautiful' might be 'fashionable' as well. Aesthetic goodness may be a difficult standard to articulate, but apparently eighteenth-century manufacturers and consumers recognised a beautiful colour on sight. Comparative judgements were also used to establish beauty, especially when the effort was directed to imitation of a known colour, such as Turkey red. Is this colour as beautiful as existing colours similar to it? All presentations of a new colour, whether in advertisement, scientific publication or popular discussion, note its beauty, confirming its value in fashion.[23]

However beautiful it might be, a good colour was also 'solid'. It did not fade or darken, peel or rub off in time. Good colour was unaltered by light, water, airborne acids and other sources of destruction. It did not ruin the medium it coloured or, as could happen with lead- and arsenic-based colours, the health of the consumer. These qualities were always considered when a novel colour or method was advanced. Improved performance was another feature of claims for colours directed to a wide public.

The model of beautiful and permanent dominated colour production and created ideals to judge suitability of new colours. In reality, few colouring materials passed all tests, and the resulting problems were familiar to both consumers and producers. Beautiful colours often faded quickly; permanent colours were dull. A goal in the investigation of colours was to overcome the deficiencies of existing shades. For this reason, colour making techniques were subject to constant improvement, even when an adequate method existed.

Thus, the description of a colour as 'new' was often linked to new production processes which aspired to make good colour better. Cuthbert Gordon's claim for his cudbear colours was one response to anecdotes about women walking out in the morning wearing a violet-coloured dress, and returning in one of pale lavender that afternoon. A virtue of Prussian blue was that it did not darken when mixed with or placed next to mineral colours. The collaboration of Josiah Wedgwood and George Stubbs over painting with enamels, like Alexandre Brongniart's experiments at Sèvres some years later, was an effort to make painting more permanent.[24]

Factors such as reduced cost were also considered improvements. An application technique that required less finely ground materials or lower temperatures in the production process would be less expensive to produce. Again, the visual effect of the resulting colour might be the same as before; frequently that was also a goal.

The difficulties of creating and maintaining good colour were part of common experience with objects. Directly and indirectly, the search for good colour was encouraged by public presentation of theoretical and scientific ideas in combination with practical ones. They inspired the search for new sources for attractive colours and new ways to fix colours more firmly. Direct associations between these realms were lodged firmly in contemporary notions of 'polite' culture. The associations were revealed in the lecture courses and in publications which attempted to explain science to the general public. Although modern discussions of these connections emphasise the use of astronomy or electricity to interpret the presentation of scientific practices to a consuming society,[25] colour and colour making were also components of this exchange. There were several reasons why this alliance was particularly attractive.

The idea that some limited number of colours might produce all others was already well known in the eighteenth century. Many colour systems in place before that time described a set of 'primary' or 'principal' colours; those which could combine to form all others.[26] Published instructions for making colour for all media included, and so reinforced, the concept. In this respect, the capabilities of red, yellow and blue were easily demonstrated in the dye house, the paint box and the enamelling kiln. Although they were not the only series proposed, by the early eighteenth century these three (plus black and white) dominated trichromatic explanations. Another value of trichromacy was its suggestion that colour and colour making functioned within some universal order. This notion lodged those topics squarely within Enlightenment ideas about the organisation of the world.

The assumption that certain colours might have a special practical significance seemed to be a logical extension of this experience. Find a 'good' red and you have half of a good orange and a good purple. Find a 'good' blue and yellow, and you might be able to make all colours easily. The concept of universal basic colours was important to the formation of the quest for new colours, but production realities tempered the ideal. Some secondary colours made from one colouring material were visually different from any combination of two primaries. Diluted solutions of dyes did not always yield a lighter colour the way the addition of white could for most pigments. Formulas for ceramic colours could achieve very different results merely by changing the grinding time or proportions of materials. Despite these inconsistencies, however, the search for improved colours was never completely rid of the search for principal or basic colours. The concept was simply too attractive to abandon.

The relationship of colour and light was also an important part of the presentation of science to the eighteenth-century public. Newton's theories figured prominently in discussions about the nature of light and his use of artist's colours as examples further strengthened the connection. Artist's colours were also described in philosophical terms by other scientists, for example Robert Boyle, and there is a tradition of published explanations and further experiment based on those works.[27]

Discussions about the use of theories about light in colour production today often describe its restricted benefit.[28] Historians note that efforts to exploit connections between colour philosophies and practical outcomes were limited until differences between additive and subtractive mixing were resolved in the nineteenth century. But explanations of colour offered by natural philosophers to the public and to their peers depended on both techniques and theories.[29] Colour and colour making were consistent examples of a topic that involved both scientific precepts and commonplace objects. For this reason, colour could be used to explain complicated principles.

Other features of colour carried this value further, reinforcing the idea that creating colour was a viable public demonstration of one's consumption of scientific ideas. Colour was familiar and accessible; it brought philosophical ideas close to everyday experience. Books and lectures directed to a popular audience strove to make connections between theories and methods, emphasising the familiarity and practicality of colour making alongside the scientific significance of colour.

Techniques and materials connected to the theories and practices of colour, including many used to demonstrate it publicly, were commonplace. Anyone could contemplate Newton's experiments with spectral colours. Even without a glass prism, one could find the refraction of light in the rainbow or in drops of oil on water. Materials to make colour were equally ordinary. Many, such as turmeric used to make nankeen or the olive oil of Turkey red, also served as spices. Others, like ochres, were found in the earth.

Using philosophical ideas of colour in the search for good colour supported the concept of useful knowledge and allowed the consumer to participate in the public culture of the age at the same time. One could exploit fashionable ideas to improve fashion itself. This connection is evident in the four examples above.

The imprimatur this extended to the public further reinforced the notion that any individual could use scientific ideas to find new colours, or new ways to make 'old' ones better. The use of pigments, glazes and dyestuffs to explain physical notions of colours was a powerful impetus to scientific amateurs and improvers to explore similar connections. Because it could join theory and practice within a familiar setting, interest in the improvement of colour was widespread. And although creating colour in an object was never as simple as directing a prism towards a beam of light, the requirements of a successful colour offered many opportunities to improve or simplify existing materials and methods. These attempts were consistent with philosophical ideas about the natural world, and its relationship to the manufactured one.

Experiment with colouring methods and the discovery of techniques to improve the goodness of colours was an important point from which to affirm individual beliefs about the place of science in improvement of life and manufactures, and their own position within that system. If the result was good enough, the affirmation might be publicly declared and offer some financial gain.

As all four anecdotes note, improvements to colour making appealed to people from a broad range of society. The requirements of a good colour offered many opportunities to improve materials and methods, and these opportunities were seized upon by many people. The acknowledged limits of the relationship between theory and practices in colour making did not curtail efforts to combine the two. Instead, it served to open the topic further. If special training in physics or chemistry was of limited value, anyone might function as well as the *savant*. It was only necessary to act on *beliefs* about the use of science to improve manufactures, and the improvement of manufacture for public benefit (and often a personal one, too).

The combined search for novelty and improvement had many facets. Participants aspired to demonstrate their understanding of public culture, to show that they were familiar with its ideals of improvement and its demonstration of this through science. They hoped to prove their place in an intellectual fashion by making or improving objects used in fashion. Personal experience was combined with available information. General understanding of practices made improvement to colour available, and even obvious as a way to depict these personal connections. To simplify processes, as with Turkey red; improve fastness, as with cudbear; or stability, as with Prussian blue and nankeen; to find new ways to make the colours of fashion and commerce were goals consistent with philosophical ideas about the natural world and social ideas about useful information. Inventing a new colour, or improving an old one, was a way to show that one was a consumer of science. As part of the goal of improvement, information about colouring materials was collected and published, and institutions in Britain, France and elsewhere offered rewards for improved methods and new sources. New recipes appeared as pamphlets, in journals and abstracts about science and art, in patent applications and in petitions for rewards. These, in turn, fuelled further study. Universally, eighteenth-century investigations into colour never ceased.

Notes

I am grateful to Maxine Berg and Helen Clifford for encouraging this contribution, and for standing by through several drafts. Elizabeth Garber and Miriam Milgram also offered solid advice at critical points. Archival research was funded in part by a National Science Foundation Doctoral Dissertation Improvement Grant (SBER 95–20395).

1 Much of the information to follow refers to colours used for textiles. The size and importance of the textile industry in the eighteenth century means a large body of information about investigations into dyeing and printing remains. It is important to remember that interest in, and ideas about, colour were not limited to those for textiles. When possible, I will show that the same concerns (and frequently the same end results) were desirable in any enterprise where colour was important, whether the medium was fabric, clay, glass, paper, plaster or painter's canvas.

2 T. Chateau, *L'Historie de la fabrication du rouge turc ou d'Andrinople et la théorie de cette teinture* (Paris, 1876); A. Dubuc, 'L'Enigme Rouennaise du rouge des indes', in *Le Textile en Normandie: etudes diverse* (Rouen, 1995), pp. 167–72; J. Jacqué, *Andrinople le rouge magnifique* (Mulhouse, 1992); A.P. Wadsworth and J. de L. Mann, *Cotton Trade and Industrial Lancashire 1600–1780* (Manchester, 1931).

3 [Royal] Society of Arts (hereafter [R]SA), Guard Book, vol. 5 (5), Letter of W. Thompson, 14 May 1760; [R]SA, Minutes of the Chemistry Committee 1759–60, regarding Turkey red, November 1760; [R]SA, Minutes of the Chemistry Committee 1760–61, Farmer to the Chemistry Committee regarding Turkey red, 26 March 1761; [R]SA, Minutes of the Chemistry Committee 1760–61, regarding a premium for J. Wilson, 21 May 1761; [R]SA, Guard Book, vol. 6 (135), Letter of Lescullier to Fitzgerald, 16 March 1762; [R]SA, Minutes of the Chemistry Committee 1762–63, regarding a second premium for J. Wilson, 1763; [R]SA, Minutes of the Chemistry Committee 1767–68, regarding submission of M. Abrahams, 4 June 1768; [R]SA, Minutes of the Chemistry Committee 1767–68, Letter of F. Rheinswald to the Committee, 14 January 1768; [R]SA, Minutes of the Chemistry Committee 1772–73, Letter of Le Grand to Lord Nuncham, read to the Committee, 18 February 1773; [R]SA, Minutes of the Chemistry Committee 1772–73, Letter of Knowck read to the Committee, 18 February 1773; [R]SA, Minutes of the Chemistry Committee 1777–78, Examination of Mikovini by the Committee, 21 March 1778; [R]SA,

A11/41, Letter of C. Taylor to S. More regarding nankeen and Turkey red samples, 7 November 1784; [R]SA, A11/40, Letter of Schede, 21 December 1784; [R]SA, A12/65, Letter of Schlögel and Hazard to Green, 18 February 1785; [R]SA, Minutes of the Chemistry Committee 1785–86, Letters from Taylor and Cooper, 3 December 1785; [R]SA, Minutes of the Chemistry Committee 1787–88, Letter from Black and Madvil, 15 January 1788.

4   [R]SA, Minutes of the Chemistry Committee 1760–61, regarding a premium for J. Wilson, 21 May 1761; [R]SA, Minutes of the Chemistry Committee 1762–63, regarding a second premium for J. Wilson, 1763.

5   Archives Nationales de France (hereafter AN), F[12] 2424, Notice of *Arrêt du Conseil* granting a *privilège* to Daristoy of Rouen for his secret to dye *rouge d'Andrinople*, 26 August 1747.

6   Archives Departmentales de la Seine-Maritime (hereafter ADSM), C151, Dossier concerning Alteriac, 20 January 1759; AN, F[12] 1329, Dossier concerning Chaubert, 28 January 1791; AN, F[12] 2259, Dossier concerning Goudar, 1765; AN, F[12] 2259, Dossier concerning Myot, 1765; AN, F[12] 1330, Dossier concerning Flachat, 12 February 1770; ADSM, C151, Dossier concerning Deschamps and Regimbard, 7 March 1770; AN, F[12] 1329, Dossier concerning de Lange, 30 May 1766, 10 September 1766, 22 February 1772; AN, F[12] 2259, Dossier concerning Eymard, 1776; AN, F[12] 2259, Dossier concerning Pinal, 1779; AN, F[12] 1330, Mémoire on dyeing by le Page, student of manufactures, 17 March 1779; AN, F[12] 2259, Dossier concerning Gallay, 10 April 1780; AN, F[12] 1334, Dossier concerning the secret of *rouge des Indes* by Pluard, 27 November 1781; AN, F[12] 1331, Dossier concerning de Lorme, July 1787.

7   AN, F[12] 994, Notice of a *pension* of 600 *livres* awarded to Osmont *maître toilier* of Darnetal, 13 May 1783; AN, F[12] 1334B, Dossier concerning Osmont's *rose de Smyrne*, 1783.

8   L.-A. Dambourney, *Recueil de procédés et d'experiences sur les teintures que nos végétaux indigènes communiquent aux laines & aux lainages* (Paris, 1786).

9   I. Wingate, ed., *Fairchild's Dictionary of Fabrics*, 6th edn (New York, 1979), p. 407.

10 Dambourney, *Receuil des procédés*.

11 [R]SA, Guard Book, vol. B (86), Letter of E. Bancroft to S. More regarding dyeing, 20 May 1771; Colour Museum, Bradford, Yorks., BRFCM 1991.42.28, Order book of Joseph and Mary Ware (1773–78), n.p.; British Library, Additional Ms. 54486, Commonplace book of Charles Clark, (*c.* 1790), n.p.; [R]SA, Minutes of the Chemistry Committee, 1783–84, regarding nankeen dyeing, 8 November 1783; [R]SA, A11/41, Letter of C. Taylor to S. More regarding nankeen and Turkey red samples, 7 November 1784.

12 S. de Plas, *Les Faiences de Rouen, du nord de la France et de la région parisienne* (Paris, 1977), pp. 24–5.

13 R.D. Harley, *Artists' Pigments c.1600–1835: A Study in English Documentary Sources*, 2nd edn (London, 1982), pp. 107–16.

14 British patent No. 727. To George Gordon and Cuthbert Gordon for 'A dye . . . called cudbear', 12 August 1758; C. Gordon, Memorial of M. Cuthbert Gordon, relative to the discovery and use of cudbear and other dyeing wares (n.l., n.d., *c.* 1785).

15 [R]SA, Guard Book vol. 8 (20), Letter (with sample card) of C. Gordon to the Chemistry Committee, 26 May 1761.

16 The Oxford English Dictionary lists 1756 as the earliest use as a colour name.

17 For a discussion of the vagaries of the colour 'pompadour' on ceramics, see H. Coutts, 'A Chelsea Derby Vase and its Sources', *Derby Porcelain International Society Newsletter*, 18 (May 1990), pp. 22–30.

18 L.J.M. Coleby, 'A History of Prussian Blue', *Annals of Science*, 4 (1939), pp. 206–11.

19 Archives de l' Académie Royale des Sciences, *pli cachete* No. 23, Deposited by P.J. Macquer, 23 April 1749.

20 J.S. Martin, 'Unraveling the Material History of Painted Silk Textiles Through Micro-Analysis', in C. Paulocik and S. Flaherty, eds, *The Conservation of 18th-Century Painted Silk Dress* (New York, 1995), pp. 46–50.

21 J. Hellot, *L'Art de la teinture des laines* (Paris, 1750), p. 277. Hellot first made this statement publicly when he read his *mémoire* to the Académie des Sciences six years earlier.

22 S. Lowengard, 'Standards before Standardization: Testing Color in Eighteenth-Century France', Society for the History of Technology Annual Meeting, 18 October 1997.

23 'Couleurs pour la peinture nouvellement inventées. Extrait d'une letter écrit à Londres 15 April 1730', *Mercure de France* (May 1730), p. 968; British Museum, Department of Prints & Drawings, Heal Collection, 89.45, Trade card of De La Cour, London (n.d., mid 1700s); J.-M. Haussmann, 'Observations de M. Haussmann sur Rouge d'Andrinople', *Annales de Chemie et de Physique*, 12 (March 1792), pp. 196–219.

24 Wedgwood Ms., E 18856-25, Letter of J. Wedgwood to T. Bentley, 17 October 1778; A. Lajoix, 'Alexandre Brongniart et la Quête des Moyens de Reproduction en Couleurs', *Sèvres*, 1–2 (1992–93), pp. 64–73, 52–8.

25 T. Hankins, *Science in the Enlightenment* (New York, 1985); A. Walters, 'Conversation Pieces: Science and Politeness in Eighteenth-Century England', *History of Science*, 35 (1997), pp. 121–54.

26 R. Kuehni, 'What the Educated Person Knew about Color A.D. 1700', *Color Research and Application*, 6:4 (1981), pp. 228–32; H. Lang, 'Trichromatic Theories before Young', *Color Research and Application*, 8:4 (1983), pp. 221–31.

27 R. Boyle, *Experiments and Considerations Touching Colours* (New York, 1964; reprint of 1664 edn); E.H. Delaval, *Experimental Inquiry into the Cause of Changes of Colors* (London, 1777); W. Eamon, 'New Light on Robert Boyle and the Discovery of Colour Indicators', *Ambix*, 27 (1990), pp. 198–202; J. Hoofnail, *The Painter's Companion* (London, 1762); A.E. Shapiro, 'Artist's Colors and Newton's Colors', *Isis*, 85 (December 1994), pp. 600–30.

28 J. Gage, *Color and Culture* (Boston, 1993); J. Golinski, *Science in Public Culture: Chemistry and Enlightenment in Britain 1760–1820* (Cambridge, 1992); M. Kemp, *The Science of Art: Optical Themes in Western Art from Brunelleschi to Seurat* (New Haven, 1990); L. Stewart, *The Rise of Public Science: Rhetoric, Technology and Natural Philosophy in Newtonian Britain, 1660–1750* (Cambridge, 1993).

29 J. Hadley, *Plan of a Course of Chemical Lectures* (Cambridge, 1758); T.S., *Arts Improvement* (London, 1703); P. Shaw, *Chemical Lectures* (Scarborough, 1734); R. Watson, *Chemical Essays*, 3rd edn (Dublin, 1783). For a published argument about the place of colour theories in colour making, see Mauclerc, *Traité des couleurs et vernis* (Paris, 1773); F. Watin, *L'Art du peintre, doreur vernisseur, Supplément à l'art du peintre doreur et vernisseur en réponse à la réfutation du Sieur Mauclerc* (Paris, 1753–73).

PART THREE

Public and private

Jewellery in eighteenth-century England[1]

To write the history of gold, claims one authority, is to write the history of humankind.[2] Within this unsubstantiated declaration, we might recognise a truth: that gold, the most valued and one of the rarest of minerals, exists culturally at the nexus of competing discourses of the economic, the aesthetic and the legal. A similar claim might be made for diamonds which, as one eighteenth-century authority expresses it, 'deserve the chief regard of all Jewels' because not only will they 'lie in the smallest space of any, and are therefore the most portable' repository of wealth, but also 'their superlative Hardness secures them from all injury by wear'.[3] Following the removal of Jewish merchants to London in the second half of the seventeenth century and the abolition of the duties on diamonds in 1732, London became the commercial centre of the diamond trade, working in tandem with Amsterdam where stones were generally cut and polished.[4] Diamonds were high points of interest for Londoners, and not only as worn in jewellery: when the Pitt diamond, consigned for sale on behalf of Thomas Pitt in 1702, was cut in London by Joseph Cope, a model was made, which in a glass case was an object of interest to Dorothy Richardson when she visited London in 1775[5] and was still a talking point when Sophie von la Roche arrived in 1786. Visiting what she calls 'the royal museum' but what was in fact Montagu House (subsequently the British Museum), she remarks that: 'amongst the precious stones models of the largest-known diamonds may be seen: Pitt in France, one from Tuscany, and another in Russia being the most perfect of all' (Figs. 10 and 4, Plate 5).[6]

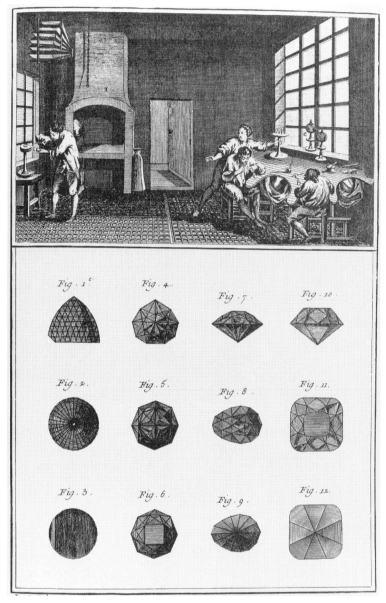

5 *Recueil de Planches, sur Les Sciences, Les Arts Libéraux, et Les Arts Mécaniques, Orfèverie Joallierie* (from Diderot's *Encyclopédie*, Paris, 1751–72)

Jewellery in eighteenth-century England comprised gold, silver and many gemstones, both authentic and fake. But above all it is diamonds that were both the actual preferred form of jewellery for anyone who could afford them, and the yardstick for luxurious consumption within speculative and imaginative discourse. Thus Rouquet, writing in 1755, identifies not only the prevalence of diamonds, stating that 'the use of diamonds is more received in England than that of other jewels; they are richer, less variegated, and less liable to imitation', but also have transcendent value and a capacity to signal symbolic worth:

> The pleasure of dress outstrips by far all the other passions; it is the first in childhood, and the last in old age. We would fain attract the attention of others, as we do our own; we use all sorts of means to compass this end: we cover ourselves with little thin plates of gold and silver, the lustre and richness of which metals naturally draw attention and respect: in short we try every thing that is capable of procuring a little homage to our dear individual, even if it be extorted. The brilliancy and value of jewels is one of the surest means of adding something to the importance of our being; they proclaim us from afar; they extend, as it were, the limits of our existence. It is not therefore at all surprising, that all nations should adopt them as ornament.[7]

If we consider the prominence of diamonds, imports of which increased throughout the century, and especially from 1770,[8] and the material characteristics of jewellery, which is designed to emphasise key points of erotic interest and draw the attention of the viewer (girandole earrings which, worn on either side of the face as a high fashion item, move with every turn of the head, diamond pins and brooches worn at the waist or on the bosom, hair ornaments, buckles on shoes that draw attention to the ankles of men and of women), we may propose that diamond jewellery was one of the conspicuous gauges of luxurious consumption in eighteenth-century England.[9] The phrase 'covered in diamonds'[10] is at one level a mere cliché of society conversation – it is, of course, not only improbable but also impossible that anyone could literally be covered in gemstones – but, like all clichés, it is founded upon consensual identification of a site of collective fantasy. This fantasy thus permits diamonds to function as a conceptual measure of acquisition, and of its concomitant element, loss. So a popular poem of 1778 has its protagonist, a 'woman of fashion', declare:

> My Diamonds are most of them gone, here and there;
> A few with false Stones now assist in the Glare.
> Thus what with my Gaming, my Tradesmen and Bets,
> Twenty thousand, I think, would not clear off my Debts.[11]

In this chapter I shall address some of the ways in which the problems raised by particular material characteristics of jewellery products highlight features of consumption as a defining characteristic of the modern city. Jewellery is, as I have implied above, a problematic category for historians and museum curators; apart from its exclusivity and its associations with wealth, vanity and exploitation,[12] it operates at transitional points where economic and aesthetic dynamics merge, it is designed for show but often hidden, it depends upon imported minerals which require superlative human skill for their transformation into a socially meaningful artefact. Jewellery is an extension to the body and is without apparent use value. At the same time the very preciousness of the materials with which it is constructed constantly threatens it with destruction: gemstones can be re-set, and gold can be melted down and used again. Within sociological literature on consumption, jewellery has, for these reasons, been recognised as a major element in theories of social need as articulated by writers like Simmel and Veblen. For Simmel, for example, sociological exchange as a relationship between people and things, 'finds its appropriate representation in the material of jewellery, the significance of which for its owner is only indirect, namely as relation to other people'.[13] I do not believe, as will become apparent, that this view adequately recognises the specific social characteristics of jewellery as material artefact. My concern here is not, therefore, to elaborate instances in which jewellery is a site of emulation or symbolic exchange, or of a bourgeois appropriation of aristocratic privilege (though much could be said on these counts). Rather, I shall focus upon ambiguities thrown up by jewellery's positioning along these conceptual boundaries. I shall engage with these ambiguities in an endeavour to re-establish the material significance of jewellery as artefact – a significance largely ignored in the sociology and psychology of consumption – while examining its uses within individual social practices that are themselves productive of, and participatory within, wider social meanings. Thus, while my conclusions will necessarily be tentative, questions of regulation and of governance will be germane to my argument.[14]

In 1738/39 a statute was passed in England which had an important effect upon the work of goldsmiths; this highly regarded community of craftspeople was ordered to destroy their marks and register new ones at Goldsmiths' Hall, consisting of initials rather than, as had been common, the first two letters of their surnames.[15] Controlling the production and distribution of gold and silver wares has always been closely tied to issues of national security since maintenance of the standard ensures a nation's economic independence and its ability to mobilise its defences. But precious metals, especially when wrought into artefacts that also carry aesthetic and philosophical values, are objects of desire,

and as such challenge the kinds of mechanisms of control and surveillance that had become, by 1738/39, so highly developed within the
powerful Livery Companies.[16] It is, therefore, interesting to observe
that the statute cited above appears specifically to exclude jewellery
from its provisions, stating: 'The Act then provides, that nothing therein
contained shall extend to any Jeweller's Works, that is to say, any Gold
or Silver wherein any Jewels or other Stones are or shall be set, other
than mourning rings, nor any jointed Night Ear-Rings of Gold, or Gold
Springs of Lockets.'[17] In the course of a long discussion with Customs
and Excise in the 1960s, Goldsmiths' Hall wardens concluded that the
exemption of jewellery (except mourning rings) from the Act was not
the consequence of muddled drafting but was due to the fact that the
only standard permitted for gold at that time was 22 carats which
would have been quite unsuitable for the parts of objects that needed
to be hard and springy (such as claws and the settings that hold stones
in rings) and that this is why 'gold springs of lockets' are particularly
mentioned.[18]

It has been argued that the period 1550–1750 saw 'an almost
complete retreat from efforts to control product innovation, the organisation of production and the content of training' among goldsmiths.[19]
Certainly, the diversification of goldsmiths' products by the mid-
eighteenth century is well established: the Assay Office Price List for
1767 itemises over thirty-one objects from snuffboxes and locks to
orange strainers and bottle tickets.[20] The evidence of wills confirms not
only the variety, but also the sentimental value placed upon such small-
scale objects made in precious metals. Thus, typically, when Dame
Anna Maria Shaw made her will in 1753, she left instructions for the
disposal of all her plate; her repeating watch, gold chain and cornelian
seal set in gold; her single stone brilliant diamond ring and the hoop
diamond ring 'which I usually wear'; her diamond buckle; her pearl
necklace and pearl earrings with the diamond bow; her diamond stay
buckles; her 'new ring set with diamonds which I made in remem-
brance of my late dear daughter'; her 'silver saucepan engraved with my
widow's arms'; and various gifts of money, clothing and furniture.[21]

Objects are here identified by their material make-up but articulated – and thereby projected into a narrative for the future – by the
sentiments of ownership. The plate, watch and the silver saucepan
should all have been hallmarked but diversification and emotional
investment of the kind manifest in wills written by women of substance
in eighteenth-century England, and resulting from what has become
known as a boom in consumer goods, created problems of governance.

It is therefore not surprising that the statute I have quoted suggests a degree of anxiety about boundaries, about what should or could be included; the necessity of maintaining the standard of gold and silver was seen as problematic in relation to the category of jewellery, even though jewellery invariably involved the use of precious metals. On the other hand, control is not necessarily confined to that which is defined in legal statutes. Nor is the law coterminous with practice or, indeed, with perception.

Although sumptuary laws were repealed by the parliament of 1604 under James I,[22] the rules for court events remained extremely strict and were vigorously policed by the heralds.[23] As late as 1788, the *Ladies' Complete Pocket Memorandum Book*[24] included, at the back, a lecture on luxury incorporating a reprint of Queen Elizabeth I's sumptuary laws, quoted from Stowe. Jewellery, and above all diamond jewellery, was a site of particular concern: Jeffries the jeweller, for example, in 1750 felt it necessary both to argue for jewels as investment purchases and to defend them as appropriate adornment for persons of birth and wealth:

> Persons of rank and fortune, that need not regard any reasonable loss, or the interests of money, are the proper purchasers of jewels; and the money laid out by such persons can no more be deemed luxury in them, than that which is expended in equipping and furnishing sideboards and cabinets, and on all other costly personal equipments in gold and silver. But it may be said that the latter is more useful and necessary than the former. To which it may be answered, that its uses may be supplied at a much cheaper rate, so the appearance and credit must be the remaining motive for laying out money in that way; which is the same in respect to jewels: And if the losses attending the purchasing these be an objection, it will be found to lie as strong against the other, in respect to fashionable elegant things, the workmanship of which, upon average, comes to at least $\frac{1}{4}$, if not $\frac{1}{3}$, of the purchase money.[25]

It would be disingenuous to suggest that the regulation of production and usage of everyday objects and items of apparel was solely – or even primarily – dependent upon legislation. As Alan Hunt points out, the relationship between regulatory legislation and enforcement is by no means self-apparent.[26] Sumptuary regulation in the early modern period involved 'the manipulation of social space, time and appearance'.[27] The Goldsmiths' Hall statute is protectionary: it is presumably primarily intended to protect the authority of the Assay Office by excluding categories of objects that challenge or undermine the clarity and efficiency of its procedures. It also serves to protect the interest of the consumer, even after death, since the hallmark on mourning rings is designed to assure purchasers of the quality of the metal they are buying. The question of enforcement is, as always, difficult to measure, but it is not apparent from surviving collections of mourning rings that the clause respecting these items was observed.[28] Equally, however, the statute can be seen as a defensive response to the mayhem created by a fascination with jewellery that gripped wealthy consumers in London from the early 1730s and which, I shall argue, was marked by its own forms of internal, popular governance, operating at the discursive level through social networks, clubbish exchanges, female letter-writing, acts of friendship, and many varied social mechanisms and forms of representation such as the writing of inventories. Not only did the numbers of jewellers' shops in London and in large centres like Newcastle increase dramatically during the eighteenth century,[29] but there is also evidence of an intense preoccupation with jewellery as owned and/or worn by observers of the social scene. Mrs Lybbe Powys records, for example, in 1771 while entertaining Sir Walter and Lady Blount to dinner: 'I was bid to take notice of a present his cousin the Duchess of Norfolk made him at their wedding, viz., an exceedingly fine pair of diamond buckles, very handsome indeed they are.'[30] Horace Walpole possessed a connoisseurial interest in antique gems but he is by no means unusual in his readiness to measure both individuals and events by the quantity and value of jewels on display. Writing to Horace Mann he describes the Princess of Saxe Gotha at a masquerade in 1742 as 'vastly bejewelled' through the services of Frankz who 'had lent her £40,000 worth, and refused to be paid for the hire, only desiring, that she would tell whose they were . . .' and when, in 1785, he wishes to assure the Duc de Nivernais that there is no need to ask his pardon, he reaches for the most complimentary metaphor current and tells his correspondent:

> What is it possible I should resent, but your conferring an obligation, which I can never return? A jeweller can give lustre to rude stones by cutting them into brilliants; but brilliants can receive no further splendour, and can owe nothing to any setting.[31]

The wording of the Goldsmiths' Hall statute of 1738/39 exempting jewellers' works from the hallmarking regulation, confirms that definitions and usage of jewellery were fraught with complexity and highly nuanced in terms of social practice. However, while mourning rings are recognisably jewellery to a twentieth-century eye, they are not

6 Gold mourning ring inscribed in reverse on black enamel
'EDW^D. LORD HAWKE OB: 17 OCT: 1781.Æ:76', 1781

exempt. This cannot be because they were not set with 'jewels or other stones'. Large numbers of surviving mourning rings are set with precious stones and, while simple gold bands with inscriptions were common, so too were elaborate concoctions involving crystal, diamonds and pearls, hair, imagery and inscriptions (Plate 6).[32] And we know that the practice of leaving money for the purchase of mourning rings was widespread.[33] Moreover, if the practice was to be all inclusive, it would have extended the production process since the gold band would have to be hallmarked prior to the application of enamel or the introduction of stones.

One of the most complete pieces of documentation concerning mourning rings, albeit prior to the 1738/39 statute, is to be found in the diary of Samuel Pepys, who died in 1703, in a 'List of all the Persons to whom Rings and Mourning were presented upon the occasion of Mr. Pepys's Death and Funeral'. All the persons are named, including those unable to attend because they were at sea or in the country, and are classified as relations, godchildren, domestics at his death,[34] former servants and dependants, general retainers, Royal Society, Admiralty, Oxford, Cambridge, Clergy, Laity and so on. 'Mourning', meaning cloth from which mourning clothes would be made, is given to relations, dependants and servants. The rings fell into one of three categories: those that cost twenty shillings, those that cost fifteen, and those that cost ten.[35] Some mourners received two sorts of rings. Such a large number of rings must have been available 'off the shelf' in the retail trade; they cannot have been fitted individually and this is another reason why they may never have been worn. The etiquette surrounding mourning rings was extremely complex and a bequest of money for a ring, or of a ring itself, required careful interpretation. There can be few clearer illustrations both of the extent of ring-bequests (to which the statute may be presumed to be a response) and of the principle of reciprocity and obligation attached to present-giving.[36] Walpole, for one, took great interest in this question: he records a friend receiving a present of a diamond mourning ring from a cousin and naming it 'l'anello del piscatore' in reference not only to the papal ring but also to the donor fishing for his estate. He also tells Henrietta Seymour Conway in 1764 that Lord Strafford, who has received a legacy of only £200 from the Duke of Devonshire, has written to consult Lady Suffolk as to whether he should go into mourning. 'She told him, for such a sum, which implies only a ring, it was sometimes not done; but yet advised him to mourn.'[37] Walpole's dismissive remark: 'Mourning rings are so much out of fashion amongst people of rank as plum porridge', made following the death of Lady Orford in 1781 should, in the light of the large numbers of surviving mourning rings from well into the nineteenth century, be treated with considerable caution, and as the reaction of a self-conscious sophisticate.[38]

Mourning rings appear, then, as a readily accessible and fairly historically unproblematic artefact. Large numbers survive, there is extensive quasi-legal documentation in wills, and funerary rituals are well researched.[39] On the other hand, it may be argued that mourning rings raise a paradigmatic question for the study of consumption. For who, in this instance, is to be regarded as the consumer? Is it the deceased who left instructions and provided funds? Is it the executors of the will who order and pay for their manufacture? Is it the mourners who wear them or, more likely, take them home and throw them into a drawer? The case illustrates graphically how consumption is a kind of diaspora and, as de Certeau has argued, a form of production.[40] What is produced are individual and conflicting narratives that criss-cross the field of production, perpetually colouring its meanings and changing its outcomes. In short, consumption is tied to ritual with all its transcendent associations, and is simultaneously, and contradictorily, individual and collective, historical and actual.

A further question arises as to what a 'mourning ring' comprises. The range of jewellery commonly described, and organised accordingly

7 Mourning ring: gold, enamelled in blue and white, the willow in hair, 1783–84
8 Mourning ring: gold and seed pearls; monogram SWH and willow leaves partly in hair over plaited hair, 1786

in museum displays, as 'mourning' consists of rings that are either a more or less simple gold band inscribed with the names and dates of the deceased (see Plate 6), or a ring surmounted by a crystal or glass-covered image depicting a funerary motif (urns, weeping willows, mourning female figures etc.) (Plates 7 and 8). The latter are distinguishable from rings celebrating friendship only by their content or iconography: friendship rings are characterised by inscriptions ('Amitiés' is common) and by motifs such as doves. Lockets and brooches serve the same function but are less widespread than rings. Relatively few plain gold bands from the eighteenth century survive and of those that do the later variants have scrolls and curves. The rings with imagery, though now more commonplace, were unlikely to have been cheaper than plain gold bands since execution of the often elaborate designs in sepia and hair would have been labour intensive.[41] So, given this situation, what was it that was intended to be encompassed by the term 'mourning ring' as specified in the 1738/39 statute, and why was this particular item singled out?

A clue may be found by close reading of textual evidence that reveals emphases and interpretative glosses suggestive of usage. Full and

9 Anon after Sir Godfrey Kneller, *Sarah Churchill, Duchess of Marlborough*, 1700

extensive documentation exists relating to the Duchess of Marlborough's jewellery. While Sir Godfrey Kneller's *c.* 1700 portrait of the Duchess of Marlborough as Mistress of the Robes and Keeper of the Privy Purse to Queen Anne suggests that she confined personal adornment to a diamond buckle at her waist (Plate 9),[42] documentary evidence indicates a long-standing and significant interest in jewellery; many lists and inventories survive, some of which indicate Sarah Churchill's interest in recording the origins and destinations of particular items which she accepted as gifts, or herself gave away or lent, as part of an extraordinary management and manipulation of public affairs and events.[43] An inventory prepared *c.* 1744 establishes an important distinction between 'mourning rings', some, though not all, of which are listed by weight, and other jewellery. Those distinguished by weight and therefore possibly by this date hallmarked appear to be relatively plain, while others are described as set with jewels and hair (as with 'Two mourning Rings with Chrystals at £3.10.0 per oz 2p.w. 10 gr' as opposed to other jewellery, such as 'a Ring with the Dss of Bedford's Hair & 8 Brilliants' and 'a mourning Ring set with 3 little Diamonds').[44]

In the light of this it seems likely that even the most costly category of Pepys's three types of mourning ring (those that cost 20s) were still of the type of simple gold band that ended up being viewed merely as gold for recycling in the inventories of members of the nobility and aristocracy. The Goldsmiths' Hall statute refers simply to 'mourning rings', but then goes on to deal with other kinds of jewellery set with gemstones. Thus a clear distinction is implied and 'mourning rings' must therefore, I suggest, here mean exclusively the kinds of simple gold bands that rapidly became redundant or recyclable in the eyes of recipients and which would, therefore, have been of particular interest to the Assay Office. We may, therefore, tentatively conclude that mourning rings without imagery were understood to be in some way institutional, collective and disposable while mourning rings featuring symbolic motifs and human hair were understood as individual and private.[45] This distinction seems to be reflected in the wording of trade cards (Plate 10). The inference must also, however, be drawn that jewellers' works, with their mixed media, were socially and economically, as well as technically, ungovernable. It is, we might conclude, not merely a matter of whether or not technically it is possible to assay the metal on a ring, but whether artefacts of this kind are not already socially beyond the control of institutions of governance such as the Worshipful Company of Goldsmiths.

I want to reiterate here that attaining an historical understanding of consumption requires us to interrogate forms of evidence for their nuances and their contradictions. For consumption, as Bermingham has stated, is tied up with concepts of subjectivity.[46] It is an 'exercise in identity'[47] and, therefore, by extension never something that is completed and done with; the individual consumer is caught in a sequential process of desire and fulfilment, of seeking and acquiring, of obtaining and disposing in which each stage contains within it the promise of another stage, as well as the recollection of what has preceded. Mourning rings may have a function on a particular occasion – a funeral – and may be essential to the pursuance of a required ritual. The conventional language of the will in which money is left for the purchase of rings (a matter often left to executors as, for example, in the case of Dame Barbara Ward who states, 'I give nephew Buxton and his brother Lenard Buxton each a ring and to nephew Warsham a ring. You may

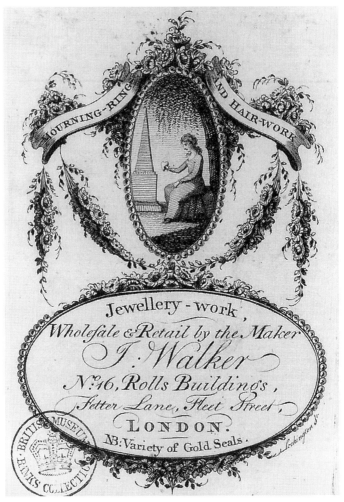

10 J. Walker, jeweller, trade card, 1704

do as you think proper to give more rings to my own neices (sic) or not'[48]) is merely one way in which social control is inscribed in law. After the functional dimension is fulfilled and the funeral processes completed, rings may transform into potential – gold capable of being melted down to be retained against a rainy day or a further necessity. Finally they may indeed be melted down and become another, different, piece of jewellery to be desired, purchased, worn and, again, disposed of. At no stage does the economic value preclude the ritual or sentimental worth of the object. Each complements the other. If jewellery is subject to sumptuary practices, it is subject also, and most

importantly, to individual and collective fantasies which work to produce dominant ideas of the social body. It may, therefore, be expected
that simple gold bands issued at funerals would be discarded as part of
the individual's and the social group's investment in the future.

The 1738/39 statute not only offers us information about the
technical distinctions formulated in the interests of policing the gold
standard, but also, however elliptically, suggests ways in which the
classification of objects was dealt with at this period. Why, we may ask,
are 'Night Ear-Rings of Gold' and the 'Gold Springs of Lockets' mentioned? What about the clasps of bracelets or the settings of girandole
earrings with their characteristic pendants? Most eighteenth-century
earrings have pendants – and girandoles (with a hanger from which
three pendants are suspended) were by far the most popular. The fact
that springy but nonetheless hard gold was required for the effective
production of these items scarcely explains their selection. It would also
seem, however, that legislation is responsive to social practice and to
the market in ways that may be instructive for an account of consumption. Mourning rings were not exempt from the requirements of
the hallmarking statute because, we may infer, at one level they were
understood to be functional in the sense that they were produced for a
particular event, a funeral, and lost a great deal of their significance
after that event. This meant they could be seen as disposable and,
therefore, could be drawn into the legislation designed to deal with
the manufacture and circulation of objects in precious metals. Those
drafting the statute thought of borderline cases: mourning rings were
included but two other categories deemed also to be functional were
excluded. In the case of the gold springs, we can accept the practical
reason: that a particular quality of alloy was required and so they could
not be included in the legislation. At the same time we should also
recognise the citation of lockets as evidence of the widespread popularity of this form of jewellery, a popularity confirmed by the incidence
of such items, containing portraits of friends and relatives, that appear
in wills from this period. Jewels containing portraits brought together
two forms of high status consumer object and made it possible to cus-
tomise jewelled artefacts, as well as to construct ambulant portraits.[49]

The third item of jewellery mentioned in the statute quoted
earlier and, like mourning rings, excluded from the hallmark require-
ment is 'jointed Night Earrings of gold'. So what exactly were these?
Diana Scarisbrick has pointed out that during the Georgian period
earrings, 'not withstanding the ordeal of piercing which had to be
endured', were 'essential to the appearance of the well-dressed woman'.[50]

Wearing earrings with a raised coiffure was one of the markers of the transition from childhood to adult status. Wilkie's painting *The First Earring*, exhibited in 1835, is a fictitious and historicised piece of nostalgia but it depicts a recognised rite of passage.[51] As Grace Boyle told her friend Ann Strafford on 18 September 1735:

> Many things have happened since I came here [i.e. to London] viz: the borring of my Ears, Papa's giving me a pair of £100 Earrings, a pink Diamond ring, & a pair of gold buckles the same of his own with 4 Guineas for my pocket. Mama's giving me a pair of star Earrings, a set of stay buckles, & an Ermine muf. So I think I came to town to some purpose.[52]

Ear piercing was, we may presume, accomplished with a needle and cat gut by hairdressers, as it was even as late as the 1950s. Once pierced, ears required what we now know as 'sleepers' to keep the aperture open if the owner was not wearing earrings. But night earrings were evidently not designed to be worn in bed.[53] Eighteenth-century references to night earrings suggest elaborate and costly jewellery far removed from a basic sleeper. The Duchess of Marlborough's *c.* 1744 inventory includes 'a pair of Diamond Ear-rings for night cloathes 2 brilliants in each'.[54] As these were valued at £60 there could be no question of their being paste, though, as Evans points out, many jewels worn in London and Paris were false by 1720.[55] Moreover, Scarisbrick cites a 1735 lottery advertisement in which '1 Pair of Rose Diamond Night Earrings' is one of the prizes and 'a pair of night earrings with pearl drops set with diamonds' in the sale of the Dowager Princess of Wales in 1773.[56] It is hard to imagine in what way these might have differed from earrings worn during the day. However, we find Lady Ann Strafford, who was a keen shopper and could certainly have afforded night earrings set with jewels such as those described above, sending her friend Jane Cockburn on a number of errands in London some time in the early to mid-1730s. Jane reports back as follows:

> I went according to Dear Lady Anne's commands to day to Mrs. Shanays & got the Buckle which if Papa comes out to morrow or monday shall be sent I could not meet with a necklace such as Lady Betty desired ready strung, but bespoke one which will be done by tuesday & come to about seven shillings: the night earrings I enquired after at seven shops but can meet with no such thing for they make none but with drops: but [tear] you may have tops without the drops that sort set in gold for fifteen & the garnett sort in gold for twelve or thirteen shillings I would not buy any of these but I have informed your Lady[sp] and

received further orders: Mrs Shanay had one pair of garnet, quite red almost: night earrings which I'm sure Dear Lady Anne would not wear, and she asked a guinea for them. I have at last got some bobs which I hope will do . . .[57]

Jane's letter is, of course, a delightful testimony to the pleasures and challenges of shopping in London as well as to the importance of jewellery as a category in young women's patterns of desire and acquisition. It shows that access to London in person was not a requisite to enjoying the advantages of the capital's retail trade, that it was customary to shop around, and that consumers had very precise ideas about what they wanted. It is also clear that Lady Ann Strafford and Jane Cockburn expected to be able to purchase simple (a ring without a pendant) and unadorned night earrings but that it was impossible to find them even having searched (if Jane is to be believed) seven shops. The commission and the extensive search must have been founded on some prior knowledge and some reasonable expectation of success but either there was a market shortage or, more likely, the standard night earring was becoming a more complex and bejewelled fashion item. Thus the choice is either to convert a pair of earrings by taking off the drops (which would have been relatively easy since many earrings were designed to enable removal of their pendant parts)[58] or to settle for some garnet earrings which sound to have been unattractive to the purchaser who is sure 'Dear Lady Anne' would not wear them. She is, in the end, obliged to buy some ear drops ('bobs') which she hopes will do as night earrings for her friend.

The major museum collections of eighteenth-century jewellery possess few examples of earrings without pendants from this period, and where they do exist they are much more elaborate than those for which Jane Cockburn was scouring London jewellers. On the other hand, relatively little eighteenth-century jewellery survives simply because it was dismantled by later generations, the gold melted and the gemstones re-set to newly fashionable designs. So, is there another tack we might try? The term 'night earring' must at some point – even if the connection had become obsolete – have linked the jewellery to the time of day. Night is, in one sense, merely to be understood as that period in the twenty-four hours when the sun is not visible but, as with all natural phenomena, there is in the act of naming a cultural process of interpretation at work. 'Night' stands in opposition to 'Day' as dark is in opposition to light. However, as Hogarth's series of four paintings of 1736 (engraved 1738, Plate 11) demonstrates, Night is also a term for a socially organised and historically specific mechanism for structuring

11 William Hogarth, *The Four Times of Day: Night*, 1738

time in ways that permit the interpretation and hence the governance of human behaviour and social interaction. Thus *Night* is the culmination of a sequence that commences with *Morning* and moves through *Noon* and *Evening*. For Hogarth this provides an opportunity for an increasingly pessimistic view of human depravity and social organisation.[59] Night, for Hogarth, is certainly not a time for sleeping.

We must clearly recognise that Hogarth's project is not to hold up a mirror to life but, rather, to construct a critical commentary upon a series of familiar quotidien events. Nonetheless, Night is indisputably here an action-packed time in the city. 'Night' as an adjective attached to apparel in the same period, similarly, does not signify things to wear when going to bed. Indeed, quite the opposite, as is evident when Clarissa Harlowe, who after her rape by Lovelace refuses to take off her clothes at all, descends to address her tormentor 'dressed in a white damask night-gown, with less negligence than for some days past'.[60] Ainsworth's *Thesaurus* of 1746 translates 'nightgown' as 'toga domestica' which demonstrates exactly the nature of Clarissa's clothing: she was wearing a dress designed for domestic (i.e. private) rather than public use. Dinner, the main meal of the day, was served later and later as the years went by so that, by one estimate, it moved from around noon in the 1740s to 4.00 p.m. by the 1770s.[61] Residents in the eighteenth-century city lived, as one historian has remarked, in different temporal worlds.[62] For the likes of Jane Cockburn, breakfast was around 10.00 a.m. and dinner between 5.00 and 7.00 p.m. Supper was taken from 10.00 until the early hours of the morning, depending upon one's social programme. Public life took place before dinner and 'Night' therefore, even for the gentry and nobility who were wearers of jewellery and who tried to avoid the filthy turmoil of the street depicted in *Night*, was a particular time in the diurnal round, a time that signalled, if not the theatre or the assembly rooms, then domestic privacy rather than public duty.

It would seem, therefore, that night earrings were, like mourning rings, linked to a shifting and transforming set of social expectations, that they were part of the intense privatisation of life in the early modern period which, as Brewer has pointed out, permitted people unprecedented access to cultural resources in their own homes,[63] and which brought with it 'an ever more sharply defined separation be-tween public sumptuousness and private luxury'.[64] Night earrings may, of course, have been worn in company, around the tea-table or over the performance of music, but the indications are clear: they were worn with 'night cloathes', that is they were worn essentially in private and domestic milieux. This specificity was, however, probably in the pro-cess of being superseded as the boundaries between apparel appropriate for public and for private events was blurred. Had night earrings continued to be plain gold rings, which is what Jane Cockburn seems to have been after, Goldsmiths' Hall would, presumably, have included them in the statute along with mourning rings.

Consumption, as I have suggested, cannot be understood simply as the counterpart to production. Consumers are, we have noted, also producers. The willingness of Jane Cockburn and Lady Ann Strafford to

adapt and extemporise indicates a vigorous and entrepreneurial engagement with consumer products. It would be easy, given the emphasis on
display in a society where shops and individuals' appearances are constantly scrutinised, recorded and transmitted to others through letters
and conversation, to ignore the question of private luxury. Shopping
for the discerning eighteenth-century commentator was a combination
of dazzling spectacle and dangerous threat to social order: Rouquet's
remarks on the way in which London shops make 'a most brilliant
and most agreeable shew, which infinitely contributes to the decoration of this great city' are well known.[65] Less widely recognised is the
scepticism represented by Hester Thrale Piozzi, who compares Parisian
shopkeepers with those in London:

> a Frenchman who should make his Fortune tomorrow by Trade, would
> be no nearer advancement in Society or Situation – why then should
> he solicit by Arts he is too lazy to delight in the practice of, that
> Opulence which wd afford so slight an Improvement of his Comforts?
> ... Was he to recommend his Goods like the London Shopkeepers
> with studied Eloquence and attentive Flattery ... he could not hope
> like them that his Flattery might one Day be listened to by a Lady of
> more Birth than Riches when employed on a different Subject, he
> could not hope like them that the Eloquence he now bestows on the
> Decorations of a Hat, or the varnish of an Equipage may one day serve
> to torment a Minister, or obtain a charge of honour for his son.[66]

Theories of consumption, following Veblen and Bourdieu, as
well as much recent historical research on particular examples of the
conduct of consumers, lay emphasis on the importance of visibility,
ostentation and display.[67] This makes good sense if we consider consumption in its economic aspects, as the opposite of production and
as 'the use of goods in the satisfaction of human wants' in outcomes
that result from 'consciously motivated behaviour'.[68] Moreover, as we
have identified, contemporary sources indicate that diamonds were one
of the publicly recognised criteria for gauging social success and social
propriety.[69] What, then, of expenditure – not merely of money but also
of time and effort in the process of acquisition – on jewellery that was
intended to be seen only by the subject's most intimate associates?
Does the ultimate in luxurious consumption consist in expenditure of
large sums of money on items for private or domestic use?

Private jewellery seems a contradiction in terms since jewellery
is, of its essence, a matter of display, of enhancing and extending the
appearance of the body. Nonetheless, if we move beyond the nuanced
and ever mobile distinctions between day and night to focus upon the

female body as a site of cultural formation, we find this very ambiguity in play as, perhaps, the most apt illustration of the notion of luxury as operating in the symbolic rather than the material order. Among the jewellery that Grace Boyle acquired from her parents on her arrival in London was a set of stay buckles. The significance of private consumption in mid-eighteenth-century England is, I propose, encapsulated in the linguistically ambiguous issue of concealment/ostentation with regard to this category of jewellery.[70] References to buckles and other kinds of jewellery connected with stays appear in a number of sources concerned with women's apparel in the eighteenth century. In 1730 the Rt. Hon. Ann Baroness Dowager Trevor wrote her will; she left a variety of jewellery to her children, including a diamond girdle, a pearl necklace, a gold tweezer case, a locket set with diamonds and diamond earrings. She also left to her daughter, Mary Bernard, 'my diamond buckles for my stays'.[71] The Duchess of Marlborough's jewellery inventories contain references to 'four Brilliant Buckles for Stays containing four and twenty Diamonds in each',[72] 'a Set of Turkey Buckles set in Gold for Stays' and two 'Loop(s) for the Stayes'. These are elaborate arrangements with a rose cluster, knots and 'endes' all composed of diamonds (Plate 12).[73] When the Rt. Hon. Lady Charlotte Scott wrote her will in 1747 she specifically bequeathed to Lady Caroline Scott, eldest daughter of her nephew the Earl of Dalkeith, along with a handsome dowry of £10,000, her small pearl necklace with twelve rows of pearls, pink coloured diamond ring set with small white diamonds on the shank, and 'my white diamond in the shape of an heart which I use as a hook for my stays'.[74] In 1753, as we have seen, Dame Anna Maria Shaw included 'diamond stay buckles' in the jewellery she bequeathed and Mrs Delany reported seeing Lady Spencer at court after her wedding in 1756 in white and silver which, as Buck points out, 'was only a background for a magnificent display of jewels':

> The diamonds were worth twelve thousand pounds, her earrings, three drops, all diamonds, no paltry scrolls of silver. Her necklace most perfect brilliants, the middle stone worth a thousand pounds and set at the edge with small brilliants ... Her cap all brilliants (made in the fashion of a small butterfly skeleton) had a very good effect with a pompon and behind where you may suppose the bottom of a caul, a knot of diamonds, with two little puffs of diamonds where the lappets are fastened and two shaking sprigs of brilliants for her hair; six roses all brilliants for her stays.[75]

Mrs Delany's testimony indicates that the diamonds for Lady Spencer's stays were fully visible. Moreover, the complexity of the

No. 1. A Pair of Pendants, the Tops Single Stones, Fossetts very much painted & thick the first Water and quite perfect. Six Brilliant Drops, two of them very large the other four much less. The Bar which these Drops hang upon has six little Brilliants and one a little bigger in the middle.

2. A Loop for the Stays, 1st The Rose in the middle contains one large Fosset. Eight less Fosetts and eight little ones round it. In the two Knots, two large middle Stones and twenty lesser Diamonds. The two Ends of this Loop have in them two longish Fosetts and sixteen lesser and thirty small ones.

3. The second Loop. The Rose in the middle contains one large Foset, eight less and Eight small ones. In the two Knots, two Diamonds and twenty lesser. In the Ends, two longish Diamonds, and sixteen less and the smaller.

4. The third Loop. The same Number of Diamonds and set in the same Manner.

5. The fourth Loop. The same Number of Diamonds and set in the same Manner.

6. The fifth Loop. The same Number of Diamonds and set in the same Manner.

7. The Diamond Loop for the Tip of the Stays, one and twenty Diamonds.

8. Four Loops for the Sleeves & Buttons. Four large Foset Stones in the Buttons set round with fifteen small Brilliants in each. In the Knot and Bottom part belonging to each Button fifteen Brilliants. In all Sixty. And all the small ones are Brilliants.

9. Four Buttons and Loops for the Neck set in the same Manner. All these are set with Fosetts containing in each three and twenty Diamonds.

10. Two other Buttons and Loops set in the same Fashion to Button up the Gown, all small Diamonds containing in both fifty Eight.

11. Four Brilliant Buckles for Stays, containing four and twenty Diamonds in each.

12. Eleven small Brilliants in a Pearl Bracelet.

13. Dog Earings. Two Foset Stones with two other little Diamonds.

14. Two little Emerald Drops and two Ruby Drops unpolish'd, with little Brilliant Sparks upon the Tops.   Drop Ears

* The little Pearl set round with Foset Diamonds for a Necklace, the Shoe Buckles and the Buckles for a Neck to ride in of Foset Diamonds are not numberd because part of these Things were made out of Lady Russell's Stay-Buckles.

16. A Set of Turkey Buckles set in Gold for Stays.

12 From a page of the Duchess of Marlborough's jewel inventory

Duchess of Marlborough's loops also suggests something which was visible and on display. Yet stays are unequivocally undergarments. As Buck herself mentions, stays are what give the dress its shape: they are its underpinning.[76] In terms of the construction of the female body as socially mediated artefact, stays – corsets made of whalebone and laced behind – are of pivotal cultural significance; they are the private and the concealed structure that works to translate flesh into a culturally normative artefact. It is from this very condition that derives the emotional and sexual charge of the scene in *Pamela* where Mr B. tries to persuade his imprisoned female servant to release to him the pages of her diary which he (correctly) suspects she has concealed about her body:

'Tell me, are they in your pocket?' 'No, sir,' said I, my heart up at my mouth. 'I know you won't tell a downright *fib* for the world,' said he; 'but for *equivocation*! no jesuit ever went beyond you. Answer me then, are they in neither of your pockets?' 'No, sir,' said I. 'Are they not,' said he, 'about your stays?' 'No, sir,' replied I; 'but pray no more questions; for, excuse me, sir, but ask me ever so often, I will not tell you.' . . . 'Artful girl,' said he; 'what's this to my question? Are they not *about* you?' 'If,' said I, 'I must pluck them from behind the tapestry, won't you see in which apartment?' 'Still more and more artful!' said he. 'Is this an answer to my question? I have searched every place above, and in your closet, for them, and I can't find them; I *will* therefore know where they are. Now,' said he, 'it is my opinion they are about you; and I never undressed a girl in my life; but I will now begin to strip my pretty Pamela, and I hope I shall not go far before I find them.' And he began to unpin my handkerchief.[77]

In fact, Pamela has sewn her papers into her clothes, but what this passage demonstrates is that the term stays is understood precisely to mean an undergarment that cannot be seen. How, then, can jewellery for stays be explained?[78] One possibility is that women did, indeed, wear items of jewellery that were not normally visible, that their stays were adorned with diamond buckles, rather as though a woman today might wear a bra with a diamond fastening or suspenders made of gold. The other possibility is that this is a case of usage creating new meanings: that women themselves had elided the notion of the undergarment with the gown that went over it. If this is the case, then 'buckles for my stays' merely means buckles that would be worn (decoratively – since stays did not need buckles) on the bodice. The Victoria and Albert Museum possesses a number of diamond buckles that would have been too small for shoes and which may have served this purpose. The fact that some of the items named above, especially the Duchess of Marlborough's loops and Lady Charlotte Scott's heart-shaped diamond, must have been distinctive and spectacular objects supports this thesis. Both possibilities appear to be true. As Aileen Ribeiro explains, the word 'stays' came to mean not only the undergarment ('so crucial a part of women's existence') but also the bodice of the gown. 'Stay buckles' are small jewels, often roses or bows, that adorned the bodice in the area of the stays. At the same time, some items were actually attached to the stays directly, such as stay hooks (often of precious material) which were hooked to the front of the stays and then used to suspend items such as watches or perfume flasks.[79] Lady Charlotte Scott's diamond stay hook described above was clearly of this type.

I want to conclude by suggesting that the semantic slippage between stays and bodice points to the eighteenth-century female body and its adornment as a site of ambiguity around questions of revelation and concealment, questions that are crucial to an analysis of consumption that moves beyond an empirical mapping of artefacts. It is in usage that consumers make meanings that connect artefacts with the politics and poetics of the public sphere. And jewellery, with its connotations both of the individual body and of universal exchange value, occupies a distinctive place in these processes of negotiation. Jewellery, designed to attract the eye and one of the period's most financially and imaginatively invested consumer products, is ineluctably here identified with the shifting status of the body as accessible to sight and, simultaneously, bounded by prohibition. I conclude, therefore, with a conundrum. For, if consumption is to be understood as implicated in a culture of visibility, one essential facet of that element of the seen, of spectacle, must be the dimension of the fantasised invisible. The semantic elision around the naming of items of female dress, or the practice of appending precious jewels to female underclothes, stages with great vividness the interdependent relationship of the seen and the imagined upon which all consumption is ultimately predicated.

Notes

1   I would like to thank Maxine Berg and Helen Clifford for their patience and encouragement. I also wish to thank the following for the advice they have generously given during the course of researching this topic: David Beasley, Anthea Jarvis, Victoria Lane, Claire Phillips and Diana Scarisbrick.
2   New York Natural History Museum, educational film.
3   D. Jeffries, Jeweller, *A Treatise on Diamonds and Pearls in which Their Importance is considered: and Plain Rules are exhibited for ascertaining the value of both: and the True Method of manufacturing DIAMONDS*, second edn, *with large Improvements* (London, for the author, 1751), p. 98.
4   See G. Yogev, *Diamonds and Coral: Anglo-Dutch Jews and Eighteenth-Century Trade* (Leicester, 1978), p. 140 *passim*.
5   'In Glass cases under the windows great variety of Gems &c – Models of the Emperor of Germany's, the King of France's, & Pitt's Diamonds'. Ms. Ryl Eng Ms. 1124, f. 227–8. Dorothy Richardson was the granddaughter of the antiquarian Richard Richardson: see M. Pointon, *Strategies for Showing: Women, Possession and Representation in English Visual Culture 1665–1800* (Oxford, 1997), ch. 3.
6   *Sophie in London: Being the Diary of Sophie von la Roche*, trans. C. Williams (London, 1933), p. 157.
7   M. Rouquet, *The Present State of the Arts in England* (London, 1755), pp. 89–90.
8   Yogev, *Diamonds and Coral*, p. 141. A crucial factor, and one which resulted in considerable speculation, was the discovery of diamond mines in Brazil; until that time India had been the only source.

9   There is also evidence from other periods and locations that the meanings of jewellery are often overdetermined. See, for example, Diane Owen Hughes's magisterial article, 'Distinguishing Signs: Ear-rings, Jews and Franciscan Rhetoric in the Italian Renaissance City', *Past and Present*, 112 (1986).

10   As, for example, with the comment of a young woman at the Queen's Drawing Room in 1787 who observed that Queen Charlotte was 'dazzlingly fine in diamonds, she was covered in them' (*The Harcourt Papers*, ed. E.W. Harcourt, Oxford, 1880–1905, vol. VI) and Mrs Powys, who described seeing someone fat, plain and unfashionable, though 'covered in jewels', *Passages from the Diaries of Mrs Philip Lybbe Powys of Hardwick House, Oxon,* ed. E.J. Climenson (London, 1899), p. 152. Queen Charlotte's fondness for diamonds was much satirised: see M. Pointon, 'Intrigue, Jewellery and Economics: Court Culture and Display in England and France in the 1780s', forthcoming in M. North, ed., *Markets for Art* (Aldershot and Vermont, 1999).

11   *The Woman of Fashion. A Poem. In a Letter from Lady Maria Modish to Lady Belinda Artless* (London, 1778), p. 23.

12   Not surprisingly, jewellery features little in histories of class, labour and everyday life which have focused upon other issues. The recent excellent work on consumption, in so far as it addresses jewellery, does so as a category within a range of consumables (see, for example, C. Fairchilds, 'The Production and Marketing of Populuxe Goods in Eighteenth-Century Paris', in J. Brewer and R. Porter, eds, *Consumption and the World of Goods* (London, 1993). There remains a split between the work of jewellery historians, who are concerned with objects, and that of economic and social historians who focus upon production and circulation. This chapter is an attempt to bridge these approaches and is part of a larger, long-term project on the display culture of jewels and jewellery.

13   G. Simmel, *The Philosophy of Money* (1st pub. 1900; ed. D. Frisby, trans. T. Bottomore and D. Frisby, 1978; 2nd edn enlarged, London, 1990), p. 177. See also T. Veblen, *The Theory of the Leisure Class: An Economic Study of Institutions* (London, 1925) and, tangentially, P. Bourdieu, *Distinction. A Social Critique of the Judgement of Taste* (1st pub. 1979), trans. R. Nice (London, 1986).

14   I adopt the term 'governance' as used in A. Hunt, *Governance of the Consuming Passions: A History of Sumptuary Law* (Houndmills, 1996), where it is explained (p. 3) as 'the results of concerted and persistent action of social agents through "projects" conceived as the practices (and their associated discourses) directed towards the control of other social agents and institutions'.

15   12 Geo II, known as the 'Plate Offences Act'. All statutes relating to goldsmiths are contained in a single volume in Goldsmith's Hall Library, 736 Q 1. A summary of all the statutes affecting goldsmithing is to be found in *Touching Gold and Silver: 500 Years of Hallmarks*, exhibition catalogue, Goldsmiths' Hall, 7–30 November 1978.

16   On goldsmithing as a business in this period see D. Mitchell, ed., *Goldsmiths, Silversmiths and Bankers: Innovation and the Transfer of Skill, 1550–1750* (Stroud, 1995).

17   12 Geo II, 21.

18   Goldsmiths' Hall takes the line, in this correspondence, that jewellery in accordance with modern usage should no longer be exempt: Goldsmiths' Hall Library, Ms. G II 9 (1226). Wedding rings were incorporated into the assay requirements in 1866. The 1973 Act (enforced in 1975) finally brought the mountings of rings set with jewels within the legislation for hallmarking. I am grateful to David Beasley for information concerning this history.

19 J. Styles, 'The Goldsmiths and the London Luxury Trades, 1550–1750', in Mitchell, ed., *Goldsmiths, Silversmiths and Bankers*, p. 113.

20 Goldsmiths' Hall Library, G II 1 (3). The list for 1829 (G II 1 (6)) offers a great increase in the range of items. It should, however, be borne in mind that this may merely represent the increased effectiveness of the hallmarking legislation rather than an increase in the range of objects.

21 Dame Anna Maria Shaw, PROB 11, 819, quire 328, fos 335–6. For transcripts of a selection of wills written by women in this period and frequently listing such items see Pointon, *Strategies for Showing*, appendix.

22 *Blackstone's Commentaries*, Book iv, vol. ii, p. 129.

23 See, for example, the publication in 1760 of *An Account of the Ceremonies Observed in the Coronations of the Kings and Queens of England; viz. King James II and His Royal Consort; King William III and Queen Mary; Queen Anne; King George I; and King George II and Queen Caroline* (London, 1760). Part II, published later, is an account of the coronation of George III. For an authoritative general account, see F.E. Baldwin, *Sumptuary Legislation and Personal Regulation in England* (Baltimore, 1923).

24 This was a commercially produced diary.

25 Jeffries, *A Treatise on Diamonds and Pearls*, pp. 143–4.

26 Hunt, *Governance of the Consuming Passions*, p. 195.

27 *Ibid.*, p. 185.

28 Claire Phillips of the Victoria and Albert Museum is in the process of inspecting the rings in that collection, but believes they are not all hallmarked.

29 Hard quantitative evidence is lacking but, in addition to extensive (if not manifestly reliable) eyewitness accounts that establish how people perceived jewellery to be an increasing retail area, the petition from 'Goldsmiths, Silversmiths, and Plate-workers remote from London' in 1700 which led to setting up Assay Offices in York, Exeter, Bristol, Chester and Norwich and, the following year, in Newcastle upon Tyne, suggests thriving trade in goldsmithing which would also have affected jewellers (1700 Stat 12 Will. III Cap. 4 and 1701 Stat Anne Stat 1. Cap. 9, sect. 3, in Goldsmiths' Hall GII I (4)). See also M.A.V. Gill, *A Directory of Newcastle Goldsmiths*, PhD thesis, privately printed, Goldsmiths' Hall, 1980.

30 *Passages from the Diaries of Mrs. Philip Lybbe Powys*, p. 132.

31 Horace Walpole to Horace Mann, 26 February 1742, and Horace Walpole to the Duc de Nivernais, 6 January 1785, in *The Yale Edition of Horace Walpole's Correspondence*, ed. W.S. Lewis (London and New Haven, 1937–80), vol. XVII (1955), p. 342 and vol. XLII (1980), p. 130. Frankz, the editors suggest, is probably a moneylender.

32 As might be expected, the more elaborate examples proliferate in the 1780s, but there are also lots of dated examples from the earliest years of the century onwards. See C.C. Oman, *Victoria and Albert Museum Catalogue of Rings 1930* (Ipswich, 1993), pp. 120–9.

33 See Pointon, *Strategies for Showing*, appendix.

34 It was common to specify a bequest to a servant provided he or she was living with the testator or testatrix at the time of the death: a device to ensure the necessary care of the individual in old age.

35 *The Diary of Samuel Pepys* (London, 1904–5), vol. I, pp. liv–lix.

36 There is an important anthropological literature dealing with the nature of the gift, but see, especially, the *locus classicus*, M. Mauss, *The Gift: The Form and Reason for Exchange in Archaic Societies* (1950), trans. W.D. Halls (London, 1990).

37   Horace Walpole to Horace Mann, 30 January 1757, and Horace Walpole to Henrietta Seymour Conway, 29 October 1764, in *Horace Walpole's Correspondence*, vol. XXI (1960), p. 52 and vol. 38 (1974), p. 453.

38   Horace Walpole to Horace Mann, 11 February 1781, *Horace Walpole's Correspondence*, vol. XXV (1971), p. 124.

39   For two useful general surveys, see N. Llewellyn, *The Art of Death* (London, 1991) and J. Litten, *The English Way of Death* (London, 1991).

40   M. de Certeau, *The Practice of Everyday Life*, trans. S. Rendall (Berkeley and Los Angeles, 1988; 1st pub. 1984).

41   I am grateful to Claire Phillips for a discussion on this subject.

42   A contemporary copy of this portrait is in the National Portrait Gallery, London.

43   For an excellent biography of her life, see F. Harris, *A Passion for Government. The Life of Sarah Churchill, Duchess of Marlborough* (Oxford, 1991).

44   Valued by Mr Eyemaker, British Museum Add. Ms. Althorpe Papers D15.

45   On mourning jewellery with hair, see M. Pointon, 'Wearing Memory: Mourning, Jewellery and the Body', in G. Ecker, ed., *Trauer Tragen* (Munich, forthcoming 1999).

46   A. Bermingham, *The Consumption of Culture 1600–1800: Image, Object, Text* (London, 1995), p. 13.

47   *Ibid.*, p. 15.

48   Dame Barbara Ward, PROB 11/822, quire 126, fos 196–7, quoted in Pointon, *Strategies for Showing*, p. 372.

49   The phenomenon of portraits in jewellery and a gift economy in eighteenth-century England is a topic of my work in progress.

50   D. Scarisbrick, *Jewellery in Britain 1066–1837* (Norwich, 1994), p. 277, though it should be noted that there were spells in the eighteenth century when it was fashionable to wear no earrings: see J. Evans, *A History of Jewellery 1100–1870* (New York, 1970; 1st pub. 1953), p. 158, quoting the *Lady's Magazine* for 1774.

51   Part of the Vernon Collection, given to the Tate Gallery, London, in 1847.

52   Strafford Papers, British Library Add. Ms. 22, 256 (36). I am grateful to Dr Karen Stanworth for drawing to my attention the Strafford Papers.

53   It is necessary here to correct the inference I drew in Pointon, *Strategies for Showing*, p. 53, n. 80.

54   Valued by Mr Eyemaker, British Museum Add. Ms. Althorpe Papers D15.

55   Evans, *A History of Jewellery*, ch. 7.

56   Scarisbrick, *Jewellery in Britain*, pp. 248, 230.

57   Jane Cockburn to Lady Ann Strafford, n.d., *c.* 1735, British Library, Add. Ms. 22, 256 (33). There is no goldsmith or jeweller named Shanay in A. Heal, *The London Goldsmiths 1200–1800: A Record of the Names and Addresses of the Craftsmen, their Shop-Signs and Trade Cards* (Cambridge, 1935).

58   I am grateful to Diana Scarisbrick for this information.

59   For a detailed analysis of the traditions of representing times of the day, of which Hogarth's series forms a part, see S. Shesgreen, *Hogarth and the Times-of-the-Day Tradition* (Ithaca and London, 1983).

60   S. Richardson, *Clarissa or the History of a Young Lady*, ed. A. Ross (Harmondsworth, 1985; 1st pub. 1747–48), p. 899, Letter 263.

61   P.J. Grosley, *Londres* (Lausanne, n.d., authorship and date attributed in London Library copy, 1770), vol. I, p. 191. Foreign visitors provide information about basic routines that native inhabitants take for granted, but this particular testimony seems to be based on observations of the merchant class.

62   R.B. Schwartz, *Daily Life in Johnson's London* (Madison, 1983), p. 89.

63   See J. Brewer, *The Pleasures of the Imagination* (London, 1997), especially ch. 4.

64   See Hunt, *Governance of the Consuming Passions*, p. 193. See also A. Ribeiro's identification of the growing distinction between formal or full dress and informal or undress that developed through the eighteenth century in England: A. Ribeiro, 'Eighteenth-Century Jewellery in England', *Connoisseur*, 199 (October 1978), p. 75.

65   Rouquet, *The Present State of the Arts in England*, p. 119. See also Grosley, *Londres*, p. 62: 'Les boutiques du Strand & des rues qui le continuent, sont ce que, dans le détail, Londres offre de plus frappant aux yeux d'un étranger. Toutes fermées de grandes glaces, toutes ornées en dehors d'architecture antique, d'autant plus déplacés qu'ils sont plus rigoureusement traités, toutes brillantes & par les choses qui s'y vendent, & par leur élégante disposition, elles forment un coup d'oeil auquel Paris n'offre rien de comparable'.

66   Hester Thrale Piozzi's Italian Journal, 14–16 September 1784, Ms. Ryl. Eng. 618/1, John Rylands Library, University of Manchester.

67   Veblen, *The Theory of the Leisure Class*, and Bourdieu, *Distinction*; see also C. Walsh, 'The Design of London Goldsmiths' Shops in the Early Eighteenth Century', in Mitchell, ed., *Goldsmiths, Silversmiths and Bankers*, and the collection of essays in Brewer and Porter, eds, *Consumption and the World of Goods*.

68   C. Campbell, *The Romantic Ethic and the Spirit of Modern Consumption* (Oxford, 1990; 1st pub. 1987), p. 38.

69   On the improper acquisition and wearing of diamonds by older women, see M. Pointon, 'Intriguing Jewellery: Royal Bodies and Luxurious Consumption', *Textual Practice*, 11, 3 (1997).

70   Due to its financial value, jewellery is frequently hidden in jewel caskets and cabinets. I am concerned here, however, with jewellery worn on the body but invisible in public.

71   The Rt. Hon. Ann Baroness Dowager Trevor, PROB 11/751, quire 367, fo. 318, signed 3 August 1730, proved 29 December 1746, transcribed in Pointon, *Strategies for Showing*, p. 313.

72   By 1751 Jeffries was complaining about the present fashion for the 'extraordinary use of small Diamonds in the decorations now fashionable in jewelling': Jeffries, *A Treatise on Diamonds and Pearls*, p. 5.

73   Ms. British Museum Add. Ms. Althorp Papers D15 (Jewellery 1723?–1744?), 'A List of the Jewels which my Lady Russell has of the Duchess of Marlborough'.

74   The Rt. Hon. Lady Charlotte Scott, PROB 11/757, quire 264, fos 58–9, proved 2 October 1747, transcribed in Pointon, *Strategies for Showing*, p. 355.

75   *The Autobiography and Correspondence of Mary Granville, Mrs. Delany*, ed. Lady Llanover (1861–62), vol. II, p. 297, quoted in A. Buck, *Dress in Eighteenth-Century England* (London, 1979), p. 15.

76   *Ibid.*, p. 15.

77   S. Richardson, *Pamela; or Virtue Rewarded* (Harmondsworth, 1980; 1st pub. 1740), pp. 270–1.

78   I am grateful to Anthea Jarvis, Curator of Costume, Platt Hall, Manchester, who has confirmed that stays are undergarments and that a stiffened outer garment was universally referred to as a 'body'.

79   Ribeiro, 'Eighteenth-Century Jewellery in England', p. 80. I am also extremely grateful to Dr Ribeiro for a personal communication on this matter, 15 September 1997.

7 ⊘◉ HELEN CLIFFORD[1]

A commerce with things: the value of precious metalwork in early modern England

In a short story by George Sand, the author, claiming historical authenticity, describes how a provincial baron, who had been leading an untamed feudal existence, is persuaded to engage with contemporary society at the time of the French Revolution.[2] It is not the baron's desire for money, but his 'commerce with things' and people which jolts him into the present. In English, the word 'commerce' implied from the sixteenth century the concept of trade and 'the exchange between men of the products of nature and art'. By the seventeenth century its meaning had come to embrace all kinds of 'dealings', meetings and interactions, including a commerce of ideas.[3] This chapter explores aspects of the communication between people and things in terms of ideas of value and exchange, during a period which witnessed an unprecedented increase in the number of goods available. We are only just beginning to investigate what these goods meant to those who wanted and acquired them, and to look at consumption beyond the point of purchase.[4] People value objects in different ways. There is a shifting relationship between priorities of intrinsic value, respect for workmanship and personal association.

Objects made in precious metal provide a particularly appropriate focus for an exploration of ideas about value. As the material from which they are made ties it to the coinage, its processing, manufacture, sale and possession are usually documented in detail. Moreover this documentation often provides separate costings for materials and workmanship. There is a constant theme that runs through the written evidence connected with precious metalwork, the balance between materials and their manufacture. Samuel Pepys's complaint, that he paid as much for the workmanship as for the metal, on settling his bill for two cups is a commonplace. William Fitzhugh, ordering silver from his London agent in 1688, stipulated that it 'be strong and plain, as being less subject to bruise, more serviceable and less out for the fashion'.[5] Retailers frequently had to explain to, and negotiate with, their customers about the balance between these two elements. Benjamin Vulliamy, a London clockmaker, who also supplied wrought silver, explained to one of his clients in 1814, that 'Cup No.2 would probably be really larger than the drawing & would weigh more than No.1, for there is less work & considerably more silver in it for the same Money'.[6] Vulliamy also took the precaution of requesting that the order be 'a Ready Money transaction (a thing of consequence in silver work) calculated on putting the greatest possible quantity both of silver and work for the sum stated'.

By looking at ideas surrounding sterling worth, recycling, fashioning and refinement in connection with precious metalwork, I hope to throw light upon their complex interrelationship. The period 1650 to 1750 saw a growth in consumer preference for fashion over intrinsic value. In the second half of the eighteenth century innovations in manufacture and the invention of substitute materials, like Sheffield plate, heralded the triumph of novelty and variety over quality of materials.

Sterling worth

The intrinsic value of precious metal places objects made of the material at the top of the hierarchy of goods, not only in terms of sterling worth, but also in terms of design and workmanship. The desire for the products of the goldsmiths' craft is deeply engrained within Western culture, and has often been used to illustrate the temptation of earthly vanities against the achievement of heavenly virtues (Plate 13). Silver 'things', like centrepieces, and cups and covers, were once the prime indicators of power and status, both in terms of wealth, and in their form and workmanship of taste. They were integral to the construction of both personal and national identities. It was not for nothing that Charles I followed his predecessor's example in attempting to maintain the exclusivity of Cheapside to the goldsmiths.[7] It was the main thoroughfare of the City of London and part of the processional route for diplomats and royalty. The glitter of the goldsmiths' shop windows convinced many visiting commentators that London was the wealthiest capital in Europe (Plate 14). It is only 'in looking at the prodigious quantity of plate piled high and exposed there', noted the German

13 German woodcut, fourteenth century

traveller, von Archenholz, in 1785, that one can 'form a proper idea of the riches of a nation'.[8]

We know that the English were long pre-occupied with the standard of precious metal. The method of testing its purity by means of assaying is first clearly described in an English text of *c.* 1181.[9] England developed one of the earliest and most sophisticated controls over the quality of silver and gold, introducing in 1300 the first documented example of consumer protection, in the form of a mark to guarantee the sterling (coinage) standard of silver.[10] This control of

14 S.H. Grimm, *Coronation procession of Edward IV passing through Cheapside in 1547* (detail)

the quality of the metal seems to have been maintained at the expense of concern for the standards of workmanship.[11] In 1607 the Court minutes of the Goldsmiths' Company record a complaint by its membership that the 'true practise of the art & mystery of Goldsmithrie is not onely grown into great decaye but also dispersed into many partes, so as now very few workmen are able to finish and perfect a piece of plate singularly with all the garnishings and partes thereof withoute the help of many & several hands'. This was explained by the observation that

many of the idler sort betake themselves to the sole practise and exercise of some slight and easy part . . . some to be onely hammermen and
for the most parte doe also faile in the general manage and use thereof
and make it their whole practise to worke nothing else but bell saltes
or onely belles, or only casting bottles or some such onely thing and
nothing else other some planish some to grave and chase; some others
to be spoonmakers and some to be badge makers. And by suche theire
owne unskillfullness and wilfull ignorance is also of late required and
crept in the use and helpe of sundry inferior handy craftes as pewterers
founders and turners for the perfecting of divers workes to the great
scandall and disgrace of this misterie.[12]

This implies that specialisation had developed to such an extent that
individual goldsmiths were incapable of making a single piece from
design to finished product. On the Continent, in contrast, the tradition
of submitting a masterpiece to complete an appenticeship was still very
much alive in the seventeenth century, and there were no comparable
controls over the standard of the metal. Although the French introduced 'the Touch of Paris', the English refined and rigorously upheld
the system of identifying place of assay, date and person responsible for
the quality of the silver. The 1607 memorandum sought to reinstate the
presentation of the masterpiece 'to be begunne and finished' by the
apprentice 'withoute the helpe or instruction of any other'. Subsequent
cases brought before the Court of the Company show, however, that
this was ineffective.[13]

Until the development of deposit banking in the late seventeenth century the traditional way of investing wealth had been to
purchase wrought silver.[14] Its intrinsic value and convertibility into cash
has meant that of all commodities those of precious metal are among
the best documented. Compared with bags of coin, wrought plate gave
added value to the consumer, in that it could be displayed. As Elizabeth Smythe advised her son in the 1630s, 'money spent on strong
substantial plate will doe you more service and credit than in your
purse'.[15] For Pepys a bag of gold was 'no honourable present' compared
with a gift of wrought silver.[16] Payment in wrought plate, circumvented,
in some cases, the opprobrium of being paid in money. For example,
Daniel Defoe's Roxana is rewarded for intimate services as a courtesan
with a dinner service and a set of dressing plate, which at the end of
the novel she presents, not without irony, to her faithful Quaker friend.[17]

Yet having precious metal converted into plate involved a charge
for workmanship and until the advent of an 'antique' market for plate
in the late eighteenth century, the conversion of wrought silver into

cash involved the loss of the value of that workmanship in the transaction. When plate was traded in to pay debts, fund other expenses or to be refashioned, the owner received back only the value of the silver. The cost of constructing and decorating a piece could not be recouped. This is why Stafford Briscoe, a goldsmith on Cheapside who specialised in dealing 'in all Sorts of Second Hand plate', could advertise in *The General Evening Post* in 1751 'An entire fresh Sortment of several thousand Ounces of old Plate, to be sold for a Trifle more than the Weight'.[18] Buyers of the wares would have been those who were not prepared to pay the cost of new silver, its working and the duty payable on the articles.

Recycling

The recyclability of silver was thus at the heart of its attraction. Newly wrought silver was often paid for in battered, broken and old-fashioned plate. The new was created from the old. For example, at Corpus Christi College, Oxford, in 1783, the fellows happily sent a sixteenth-century chalice and covered cup which had belonged to their founder to be melted and 'exchanged for some useful articles, viz – a Tea urn, Tea Pot and three hand candlesticks with extinguishers'.[19] The objects which survive in collections today represent only a small percentage of a far greater quantity of plate that was regularly melted down according to the demands of debt and of changing fashion. James Boswell had no hesitation in turning the silver lace on his old hat into 'a small supply'. He reports in his *Journal*, 'No sooner thought than done. Off it went with my sharp penknife and I carried it to a jewellers in Piccadilly and sold it for 6s 6d which was a great cause of joy to me'.[20]

The practice of recycling silver is only the most clearly documented example of a more general pattern of behaviour. 'Few goods were lightly abandoned', writes Woodward, 'fewer still were left to rot by the roadside. Nearly all items discarded by one person could be used by another in an unaltered form, in repaired or partially reconstructed state, or in a totally new guise via the process of re-cycling'.[21]

While economic historians have been able to reconstruct aggregate figures of the costs and quantities for the production of some commodities, it is usually impossible to quantify how much these new products incorporated old materials, or how important the role of repair was to individual businesses, as compared with the manufacture and sale of entirely new goods. We are only just beginning to appreciate, for example, the importance of the second-hand clothes trade and the way that people recycled their own clothes. Samuel Pepys was proud to note in his diary that he was wearing a 'gray cloth suit and faced white coat, made of one of' his 'wife's pettycoats'; while his 'new silk Camelott suit' had been made from an old cloak'.[22] The London merchant Alexander Cook in 1741 advised his agent Mr Nemes, a brazier in Cheapside, to buy new watches, 'except aney should fall yr way that are pretty good & look well & can be had for forty or 50 shillings, it may be Mr Trimer the Pawnbroker has some'. In the same letter Cook asked for 'a second hand silver hilted sword chased ye gripe of it solid for a middle sized man, the price not to exceed forty five shillings, except you meet with a very handsome one that will answer well ye maygive a crown more . . . it will doe as well as new, I am told ye sord cutlers sells old as well as new'.[23]

The purchase and sale of second-hand goods, and the offering of repair and alteration services by shops, played a crucial role in maintaining the relationship between retailers and their clients. Not only did these sales provide much needed ready money when capital was locked up in materials, they also provided reasons for regular contact with customers. As the silversmith Joseph Brasbridge stated, 'only get people to come to your shop, and when there, you can easily convince them that they cannot go to a better'.[24]

Dependence on the trading of old for new goods, whether involving recycling or sale 'second hand', meant that networks of communication crossed specific trade or guild barriers. For example, there was a close tie between basketmakers, china dealers and silversmiths. The accounts of the basketmaking firm of Scotts, surviving from 1698, show that amongst their regular customers were silversmiths who came to them for 'laping', or wickering, that is the binding of handles and finials in wicker to insulate them from heat conduction.[25] China men and potters were charged 3d a handle, silversmiths usually 6d, and private customers 8 to 9d a handle.

Another example of the ties which existed across the trades is illustrated through the relationship of milliners, and more particularly lace sellers, with goldsmiths. From the evidence of the writings of Pepys and others, it is clear that in the seventeenth century men looked upon lace as a necessary article to embellish their wives and advertise their own status.[26] Joseph Addison observed that when china mania first appeared in England, 'women exchanged their Flanders point lace for punch bowls and mandarins, thus picking their husbands' pockets', for the man who fancies that he is buying a fine head for his wife is really funding the purchase of a china vase. During the seventeenth and eighteenth centuries it was a popular fashion to ornament clothes with gold and silver lace. Household bills of the seventeenth and eighteenth centuries show that it had long been customary for gold and silver lacemen to take back lace.

Just as women converted goods bought for them into objects which they desired more, they also turned one aspect of recycling into a fashion which generated its own array of novel objects. Parfilage, or drizzling as it was called in England, was a pursuit that first came into vogue at Versailles during the reign of Louis XVI. It consisted of picking out or unravelling the gold and silver threads of laces, braids, tassels and embroideries from outworn coats, dresses, uniforms and furnishings for the purpose of reselling them to the goldsmith, who melted them down and recovered the weight of the precious metal. Drizzling soon became a socially accepted pastime. The 'parfileuses' carried with them small embroidered pouches containing the necessary tools for cutting the stitches. These tools were taken to parties and social functions, and even to the theatre. As the fashion grew, sets of implements specially made for use in parfilage became obtainable, contained in richly decorated cases. According to one eighteenth-century writer, 'a bold and beautiful parfileuse might make over 100 Louis-d'or a year by this industry'.[27] In her novel *Adèle et Theodore*, published in 1782, Madame de Genlis included an incident which actually befell the Duc de Chartres. 'One day before the promenade', she writes, 'we were all assembled in the salon, when Madam de R—— remarks that the trimmings of gold of my coat would be excellent for unravelling. At that very instant a movement of gaiety compelled her to cut one of my fringes; immediately I was surrounded by ten women who, with a grace and a charming vivacity, undressed me, snatching away my coat and putting all my trimmings in their bags'.[28] For these voracious ladies, the intrinsic value of the lace was more desirable than its workmanship.

Fashioning

Just as the fashion for parfilage was a foreign import, so too was skilled goldsmiths' work. While sixteenth- and seventeenth-century consumers looked to France, Germany and the Netherlands for fashionable highly wrought plate, native goldsmiths sought to block competition from 'aliens and stranger workmanshipp', which was 'in better reputation and request than that of our owne nation'.[29] One of the first documented examples of this increasing appreciation of 'fashioning' appears in 1644: when Parliament proposed that the contents of the Jewel House should be sold, pawned or melted down, the House of Lords demurred, on the grounds of the veneration in which this plate was held. 'The fastion of it and the badges upon it', made it, in their eyes, 'more Worth than the Plate itself'.[30] The associations, coupled with the workmanship, made it too valuable merely to melt down. These expressions are some of the first recorded examples of a growing antiquarianism, an appreciation of the age, 'curious workmanship', and historical and personal connections of plate. During the seventeenth century it is possible to track the development of a language of discrimination in the arts, or at least an attempt to establish criteria of judgement that could be employed by antiquaries, collectors and connoisseurs.[31] Claire Pace has described the evolution of the language of antiquarianism in which craftsmanship was increasingly valued.[32] Desirable objects were those which were made 'with care or art, skillfully, elaborately wrought'. Gombrich refers to the growing need in the seventeenth century for an eye which could 'distinguish the genuine from the false and the hall marks of devoted craftsmanship from shoddy short cut methods'.[33]

Coinciding with this refinement of the language of collecting and appreciation is the appearance in England of elaborately worked plate, often made by foreign goldsmiths who were masters of embossing and chasing. Embossing, the beating out of silver from behind, required thinner sheet metal than English goldsmiths had previously been accustomed to using. As a consequence the cost of the workmanship often accounted for more than the price of the silver.

If customers could not buy fashionable plate in England they attempted to import it. In a letter written to Lord Montague in 1769, Horace Walpole refers to the attraction of foreign-made plate, which when imported into England was defaced at the hands of the customs officials, who being concerned only with the metallic quality destroyed the workmanship for which it was desired.

> Plate, of all earthly vanities is the most impossible. It is counterband in its metallic capacity, but totally so in its personal: and the officers of the Custom House not being philosophers enough to separate the substance from the superficies, brutally hammer both to pieces and return you only the intrinsic.[34]

Walpole's remarks reveal much about superior standards of workmanship on the Continent, and the shifting balance in favour of skill versus intrinsic value. By the first decades of the eighteenth century the impact of the deposit banking system and the foundation of the Bank of England in 1694 had made themselves felt. At the same time one of the most ambitiously decorative styles was emerging in France, to be christened later in the century as 'Rococo', and first appearing in the silverware of the French designer Juste Aurèle Meissonnier.[35] Unlike almost every previous style it arose not via exterior architecture, but from the arts of the interior. It was individualistic, without rules, orders or authority, allowing plenty of scope for imaginative interpretation and creative craftsmanship. It was a style that demanded an appreciation of workmanship. The 'curious' element in Rococo silver was its elaborate ornament and complex shape, which relied heavily on the modellers' skill, and casting for its reproduction. Robert Campbell, writing in 1747, begins by describing the goldsmith as foremost a 'former' of 'sensible figures, either by casting in moulds or forming them with the Hammer' and that 'they may be reckoned of some Kindred to Sculpture and Statuary'.[36] The skills of the goldsmith were crucial to the popularity of the Rococo and its dissemination. Expert modellers who had begun their careers in metal went on to experiment in ceramic: the Elers brothers in Staffordshire, Nicholas Sprimont at Chelsea, Andrew Planché at Derby and Samuel Bradley at Worcester. Jean Voyez, who came to London as a silversmith, worked as a modeller for Robert and James Adam as a woodcarver, and went on to work at Chelsea and Bow, before being employed by Josiah Wedgwood. Wedgwood put such a value on his skill that he paid his full salary of 36s per week to keep him from working elsewhere.

Such skills did not come cheap. The cost of commissioning a suite of silver, including a ewer and basin, four cups and covers, six large candlesticks, two cruet frames, a tea waiter, six hand waiters and an ink stand, show just how expensive workmanship could be in relationship to material. The plate was commissioned by the Goldsmiths' Company from Paul de Lamerie in 1741, to replace silver sold in 1677 and 1711. The ewer and basin (Plate 15) was agreed by the Goldsmiths' Court to be fashioned 'in a very curious and beautiful manner' and is one of the most highly worked examples of English Rococo silver to survive. The silver was charged at 5s 8d per troy ounce, the making at 5s per ounce and gilding at 4s per ounce. The total order amounted to 2,357oz 10dwt of silver, which is £667 19s 2d. The fashioning cost £465 0s 2d, and the gilding £193 13s 10d. The chasing of the ewer and basin and four cups came to an additional £44 2s and the engraving £29 14s.[37] Compare this bravura performance with Lord Fitzwalter's bill from the same silversmith in 1736. For two salvers weighing 30oz 5dwt he paid 6s 2d for the weight, amounting to £9 6s 6d, and only 12d an ounce for fashion at £1 10s, indicating that they must have been rather plain.[38]

15 Ewer and basin, silver gilt, Paul de Lamerie, London, 1741

These figures, which relate to grander pieces of aristocratic plate, given in isolation seem rather meaningless. By using accounts from Oxford colleges which survive in great detail and over a long period of time, it is possible to give a more general picture of the consumption of humbler items of plate. In Table 1 comparative costs of silver bought by three Oxford colleges in the eighteenth century are given, showing the relationship of weight to fashion. Table 2 provides a comparison with other services offered by Oxford goldsmiths to the colleges and their cost to the consumer. By returning to the published household accounts of Benjamin Mildmay, Earl Fitzwalter it is possible to provide an even wider context for the consumption of silver.[39] In Tables 3 and 4 a range of commodities are listed of a similar price range, and bought within one to four years of each other.

Mildmay was a 'progressive' consumer in the sense that he bought newly invented commodities, like his 'ring with 4 branches, 4 buttons, 4 round saucers & a large basin', bought in 1728, and only later to be named as an epergne. He also paid for silver in 'the newest taste' in the emerging 'Rococo' style, and yet another example of a desirable French

Table 1   Comparative costs of wrought silver bought by three Oxford colleges between 1710 and 1800, divided between cost of metal and cost of workmanship

Date	Object	Weight in troy ozs	Cost of silver	Cost of fashion
1710	4 spoons[a]	7oz 18dwt	£2 3s 6d	13s
1730	punch ladle[b]	2oz 8dwt 12gr	14s 12d	7s 6d
1732	6 spoons[c]	14oz 15dwt	£4 8s 6d	12s
1749	48 silver hafts[d]	61oz 8dwt	£18 8s 5d	£6
1753	4 tumblers[e]	24oz 14dwt	£7 12s 4d	£1 16s
1760	pair candlesticks[f]	29oz 9dwt	£8 6s 8d	£7 15s
1778	argyle[g]	16oz	£4 18s 6d	£2 10s
1800	sugar and cream basin[h]	14oz 13dwt	£5 5s 2d	£5 5s

[a] New College Oxford Archives, 11373, invoice from John Wilkins to the College, 1711.
[b] BNC, Hurst, Tradesmen's Bills, 43, invoice from John Wilkins, Oxford goldsmith to the College, 11 December 1731.
[c] *Ibid.*, 45, 11 August 1732.
[d] *Ibid.*, 62, 31 May 1749.
[e] *Ibid.*, 63, 16 June 1753.
[f] *Ibid.*, 71, 13 December 1759.
[g] NCA, 11,393, invoice from George Tonge, Oxford goldsmith, to the College, 12 March 1778.
[h] BNC, Hurst, Tradesmen's Bills, 120, invoice from Lock & Son to the College, 21 July 1800.
Source: Vouchers in the archives of Brasenose College, Oxford, and New College, Oxford. (Information gathered from the Oxford colleges was made possible by a Leverhulme funded Research Fellowship, awarded 1993–95, for the study of Oxford college silver.)

import. Yet 'progressive' patrons of the Rococo style were not necessarily all at the wealthy end of the market. Thera Wijsenbeek-Othius's study of 458 inventories from the cities of Holland for the period 1670 to 1795 identifies, 'progressive' and 'traditional' patterns of consumption, over the same period and right across social categories. Lifestyle related to the ownership of silver was not only determined by wealth, as some people owned more luxury goods than they could actually afford, while others who were rich lived soberly.[40] These findings tally with the more specific study of the ownership and use of silver in Gloucestershire between 1660 and 1740 in which Tony Sale found that most collections were of small value, and value did not necessarily reflect the wealth and status of the owner.[41] The Rococo style not only

Table 2   Cost of goods and services supplied by Oxford tradesmen to two
Oxford colleges, 1755–66

Date	Service or type of goods	Cost
1755	cleaning 24 spoons[a]	2s
	2 salt glasses[b]	1s 9d
1758	cleaning silver at Christmas[c]	5s
1774	red leather case to a tureen[d]	15s
1780	2 pairs silver patent snuffers[e]	£5 5s
1766	2 dozen mahogany spoon cases[f]	£2 2s

[a] BNC, Hurst, Tradesmen's Bills, 69, invoice from John Wilkins to the College,
8 August 1757.
[b] *Ibid.*
[c] *Ibid.*, 790, invoice from Edward Smith, butler, to the College, 29 May 1759.
[d] *Ibid.*, 90, invoice from Edward Lock, Oxford goldsmith, to the College, 26 January
1774.
[e] *Ibid.*, 100, 17 December 1781.
[f] NCA, 3312, invoice from George Tonge to the College, 28 September 1767.
Source: See Table 1.

Table 3   Comparative cost of luxuries, 1731–32

Date	Object(s) bought	Cost of metal	Total cost
1731	4 large silver candlesticks	£27 10s	£29 3s 8d
1730	Kneller's portrait of the Duke of Schomberg		£31 10s
1730	frame to above		£20 10s
1730	year's land tax for London house		£32 12s 6d
1731	carved stone chimney piece		£23
1731	16 dozen bottles of Rhenish wine		£26 6s
1732	large mirror glass and 10 blue leather dining chairs		£33 6s 0d

Source: A.C. Edwards, *The Account Books of Benjamin Mildmay, Earl Fitzwalter*
(London, 1977).

flourished in the grand serpentine carved cornices of country houses
like Claydon, but in the hundreds of Bilston enamel snuffboxes, japanned
letter-racks and porcelain perfume bottles that flooded the market in
the mid-eighteenth century. Commentators like the crotchety Defoe
could only ineffectively complain of 'the barrenness of the people's
fancy, when they are so easily taken with shows and outsides of things'.[42]

Table 4   Comparative cost of 'necessaries' and semi-luxuries, 1731–33

Date	Object(s) bought	Cost of metal	Total cost		
1733	large kitchen spoon	£1 1s	£1	9s	12d
1734	seven barrels of oysters		£1	7s	1d
1732	dozen china soup plates		£1	1s	0d
1733	Miller's, *Gardener's Dictionary*		£1	10s	
1733	two 7 inch brass locks		£1	1s	
1731	leather fire screen			6s	0d
1732	pinchbeck metal snuffbox		£1	11s	6d

Source: A.C. Edwards, *The Account Books of Benjamin Mildmay, Earl Fitzwalter* (London, 1977).

Refined behaviour

Metals are refined to produce pure materials, in the same way that 'refined' behaviour indicated quality. As John Brewer has argued, for the eighteenth-century English 'Politeness and refinement had little value unless they were shared; they had to be put on display to be shown to others'.[43] People were increasingly aware of how objects could be used to communicate 'politeness'. Another crucial aspect of our 'commerce with things' is how we use objects, commodities as a form of communication, creating coded behaviour, only decipherable by the initiated. Far from being 'Toys of no use! high prized commodities Bought to no end! estates in oddities', these objects were crucial elements within a developing language.[44] Their 'fashioning' meant more than their intrinsic value. The young fop who sat behind Carl Philip Moritz at the Haymarket theatre in 1782 obviously failed to communicate his taste and/or refinement by 'continually putting his foot on the bench ... in order to show off the flashing stone buckles on his shoes', and treading on Moritz's coat-tails if he 'didn't make way for his precious buckles'.[45]

For David Hume, refinement also involved an appreciation of craftsmanship, apart from the inherent value of materials, as a valuable means of heightening the gratification of the senses.[46] Part of being refined meant appreciating the nuances of style, recognising novelties and using fashionable objects as part of a wider non-verbal language of display and use. It is evident that some consumers needed enlightenment about just what these new objects were (Plate 16). The London goldsmith James Coutts had to inform one of his provincial customers

16 Tea set, silver gilt, William Addy, London

that the smart 'kettle will not be sold without taking the stand & Lamp with it, probably your spouse mistakes what we call a stand for a tea kettle its not a flat plate like a salver but a frame of silver in which the Lamp is fix'd and the Kettle fits into that Frame, there's no such thing used here, as a silver Kettle without such a stand or Frame'.[47] No doubt Mrs Andrews would have made her new acquisition the centre of her tea-table, conveying to her guests that she too was now in the height of fashion, although the form had first appeared in the 1690s, and this object was purchased second hand.[48] Thomlinson recorded that in a clergyman's home near Durham, 'Aunt would have £50 to furnish her drawing room, i.e. £20 for silver tea kettle, lamp and table'.[49] The silver object seems to have made up the grandest single decorative contribution to the room. *The Female Spectator* of 1744 reported that a fashionable tea-table was more costly to maintain than two children and a nurse.[50]

The tea-table was one of the major growth areas of luxury production and consumption, and a key area for the understanding of the dynamics of household organisation and communication. As the Duc de Rochefoucauld observed on his visit to England in 1784, tea drinking provided 'the rich with an opportunity to display their magnificence in the matter of tea-pots, cups and so on'.[51] Tea pots, kettles, cups and canisters, cream boats, milk jugs, tea and mote spoons, sugar tongs

17 Robert Cruikshank, *The Tea Party – or English Manners and French Politeness*, 1835

and basins, and eventually complete boxed equipages were invented to furnish the tea-table.[52]

Proof of one's refinement was an understanding of the codes of behaviour which involved the use of objects (Plate 17). A French visitor to the home of Richard Morris recalled taking tea

> at the twelfth cup, I must put my spoon across it when I wished to finish . . . it is almost as ill-bred to refuse a cup of tea when it is offered to you, as it would [be] indiscreet of the mistress of the house to propose a fresh one when the ceremony of the spoon has notified her that we no longer wish to partake of it.[53]

The rules of refined behaviour changed constantly, as the Duchess of Northumberland, after a two-year absence on the Continent, observed. She noted in her diary a change in the service of seven o'clock tea at St James's Palace, when 'formerly the Queen made Tea herself at the Table and the King carried it about to the Ladies. Now, two Pages of the Backstairs enter'd each with a waiter carrying a single cup of Tea with a cream pot and Sugar'.[54]

Refinement often involved using an increasingly complex array of objects to distance oneself from bodily contact. 'The french are an indelicate people', Dr Johnson observed after his visit in 1775.

At Madame [du Boccage's], a literary lady of rank, the footman took the sugar in his fingers and threw it into my coffee. I was going to put it aside; but hearing it was made on purpose for me I e'en tasted Tom's fingers. The same lady must needs make tea à l'Anglaise. The spout of the teapot did not pour freely; she bade the footman blow into it. France is worse than Scotland in everything except climate.[55]

Dominated by women, the tea-table was an ideal focus for the critics of consumption, and an oft-used device for poets, authors and playwrights from which to develop intrigue and humour.

Conclusion

This chapter has attempted to map a subtle shift in our 'commerce with things', through an analysis of attitudes towards a specific category of luxury goods. Lorna Weatherill places silver 'frontstage'. Sale's analysis of silver ownership in Gloucestershire confirms that silver appeared in the highest status rooms of the house, in the best chamber, the closet and the parlour chamber.[56] It had been liberated from the older arenas of display, the buffet and plate cupboard, to take a more active role in social commerce. In Weatherill's analysis silverware is more often recorded in inventories of the gentry (61 per cent), professional people (55 per cent) and dealing tradesmen (43 per cent), and is concentrated in the three most advanced areas: London (44 per cent), Kent (41 per cent) and the north-east (34 per cent). There was, however, little change in the proportions of households owning it from 1675 to 1725. This should be compared with the ownership of other goods like pewter and looking glasses which more than doubled over the same period. Overall, however, Weatherill's findings conform to the general pattern of other analyses of inventories, the number of commodities increased, but their relative value fell.[57]

Although Weatherill suggests that these figures might represent a more 'traditional attitude of investing in things of known value', this does not fit the move from quantitative 'hoarding' to qualitative appreciation. David Mitchell's analysis of the annual weight of silver assayed at the Goldsmiths' Company between 1600 and 1700 presents a comparable picture of restricted growth.[58] He explains his findings by referring to alternative investment opportunities, growth in the second-hand market, competition from other materials, and the production of lighter weight silver goods. It is the latter reason which also accounts for an increase in volume that does not appear in the official figures. The new consumer goods in silver were made of thin rolled sheet, some so thin that they exempted themselves from the hallmarking regulations. Between 1758 and 1777 the London Assay Committee found various, 'new invented articles of small plate, not particularly named in the Act [for the Better Preventing Frauds and Abuses in Gold and Silver Wares, 1758], or named in the Assay Office list of prices'.[59]

By the 1760s fused plate, that is copper sheet sandwiched between silver, and thin gauge stamped silver competed with heavier cast and raised silver. At a third or even a fifth of the cost, consumers could purchase objects which in terms of form and decoration were identical to their sterling silver fellows. The refinements in steel for making dies, and the flattening of sheet metal by means of rollers from the 1720s, meant the same tools could be used for the manufacture of both silver and Sheffield plate. The cost of working Sheffield plate, thin sheet or heavier gauge silver was the same, only the cost of the materials differed. As Matthew Boulton explained to one of his customers who was purchasing a tea urn, 'the price you were pleased to fix for it was but £20 ... it was impossible to guess exactly at the weight of the silver it would take – The fashion is charg'd at 2s per oz, but as the tea Urn is light the fashion is naturally dearer per oz than it would have been had the kitchen been heavy since we must pay the same for the making of a light one as for a heavy one'.[60] As concern for fashionability increased, so these imitative wares, made of cheaper materials, must have gained in desirability relative to the very objects which they emulated.

What exercised the manufacturers in the precious metal trades was the speed with which these imitative commodities were made and how skilful the imitations were. The Sheffield silversmith Richard Morton explained to the 1773 Committee reporting on the conduct of the assay offices that:

> he had seen plated work of almost every pattern that was made in Silver, and so well imitated that he has been obliged to file the Coat of Silver off before he could distinguish the difference, and his customers have declared they could not discover the Difference between Plated and Silver Work if he has not mentioned it.[61]

When customers valued 'fashion' above intrinsic worth silver could not compete. The 'bright-cut' wares which appeared in the 1770s may have been a last-ditch attempt by silversmiths to compete with their imitative rivals (Plate 18). This innovative technique of engraving required deep cutting, creating individual 'v' shaped indentations which heightened the reflective quality of the material. It was difficult to

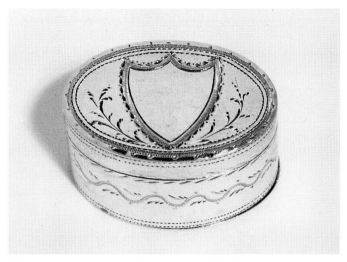

18 Nutmeg grater, silver, Birmingham, 1798–99

execute in Sheffield plate, which only had a thin coat of silver above the copper base.

For manufacturers and retailers higher profits could be made on fused plate than silverware. Customers for silver expected long periods of credit, typical of commissioning, while plated products were sold 'ready made' over the counter for 'ready money'. Businesses like those of Boulton and Fenton & Creswick in Sheffield came unstuck when customers expected credit, the capital locked up in the material impeding the flow of cash.[62] In a way the competition between silver and plate encapsulates wider changes in the market-place and associated meanings and messages, the triumph of wares 'ready made after the newest fashion' over 'bespoke' objects.

In a society where investment was no longer widely made in silver, and where novelty and variety as indicators of taste were competing with quality of materials, London silversmiths responded to demand by displaying fused plate and silver side by side in their shops. For example, the sale by auction of a London dealers' 'stock in trade' in 1786 included as much Sheffield plate as wrought silver:

> upwards of One Thousand Ounces of fashionable Plate, and . . . Two Hundred Pair of plated candlesticks, fifty plated Tea-urns . . . 50 elegant japanned Tea-Trays one Hundred dozen of knives and forks, One Hundred and Twenty Dozen of Buckles.[63]

Consumers had to face a new set of decisions: to continue in the 'traditional' mode of purchase, which placed retrievable and recyclable intrinsic value alongside design, or to preference design, variety and novelty above potential investment.

Notes

1   I would like to thank Maxine Berg and John Styles for their advice on this chapter.
2   G. Sand, in her short story *Mauprat*, quoted by N. Elias, *The Civilising Process* (Oxford, 1997), p. 320.
3   See, further, R. Williams, *Keywords: A Vocabulary of Culture and Society* (London, 1976), p. 70.
4   For example, A. Vickery's work on Elizabeth Shackleton, in J. Brewer and R. Porter, eds, *Consumption and the World of Goods* (London, 1993), p. 232.
5   P. Glanville, *Silver in England* (London, 1987), p. 165.
6   Public Record Office, Chancery Masters Exhibit, C.104.57, Letter book, Benjamin Vuliamy to Mr Turner, 20 September 1814.
7   W. Chaffers, *Gilda Aurifabrorum. A History of English Goldsmiths and Plateworkers and their Marks Stamped on Plate* (London, 1883), p. 8, for example Orders in Council passed 1629, 1631, 1634 and 1637. The 1634 Order observed that 'uniform show which was an ornament to those places and a lustre to the City is now greatly diminished'.
8   Brewer and Porter, *Consumption and the World of Goods*, p. 29.
9   M. Campbell, 'Gold, Silver and Precious Stones', in J. Blair and N. Ramsay, eds, *English Medieval Industries* (London, 1991), p. 111.
10 S. Hare, 'The History of the Goldsmiths' Company from their Records', *Proceedings of the Society of Silver Collectors*, II, 11–18 (Spring 1982), p. 174. Attempts at regulating the standard date back to 1238. In 1300 the mark of the leopard's head was introduced to signify 'work that was of a true alloy', that is 92.5 per cent sterling silver. In contrast the French were first to introduce town marks, first mentioned in 1275 and maker's marks at Montpellier in 1427.
11 This decline is paralleled in many other London trades where Corporate controls on worksmanship were weak.
12 Goldsmiths' Company Records, Court Minutes, Wednesday, 4 November 1607.
13 There were in 1607, for example, several complaints against the importation and sale of Nuremburg silver.
14 S. Quinn, 'Balances and Goldsmith-Bankers: The Co-ordination and Control of Inter-banker Debt Clearing in Seventeenth-Century London', in D. Mitchell, ed., *Goldsmiths, Silversmiths and Bankers. Innovation and the Transfer of Skill 1550–1750* (London, 1992), pp. 77–83.
15 P. Glanville, *Silver in Tudor and Early Stuart England* (London, 1990), p. 47.
16 R. Latham, ed., *Shorter Pepys* (London, 1993), p. 197, 24 May 1662, on the Queen's gift of £1,400 sterling to Lord Sandwich.
17 D. Defoe, *Roxana. The Fortunate Mistress* (Oxford, 1981; 1st pub. London, 1724), p. 182.
18 G. Wills, 'Stafford Briscoe, A London Silversmith', *Burlington Magazine* (1983), p. 52. Briscoe appears to have been the first silversmith to use the newspapers for advertising, and among the few to have done it at all during the eighteenth century. In 1751 he placed fifteen advertisements from 8 January up to and including 30 April, at around seven-day intervals.

19 Corpus Christi College Archives, H/4/1/2, note dated 17 November 1783 in an inventory of goods and plate 1694–1794.

20 *Boswell's London Journal 1762–1763* (London, 1952), p. 114 for 28 December 1762.

21 D. Woodward, 'Swords into Ploughshares': Recycling in Pre-Industrial England', *Economic History Review*, 2nd ser., 38 (1985), pp. 175–91.

22 Latham, *Pepys*, entries for 13 June 1661, p. 141, and 29 June 1667, p. 801.

23 Public Record Office, Chancery Master's Exhibit, C.104.141, papers relating to Alexander Cook, London merchant, Letter book, 1741, entry for 21 March 1741.

24 J. Brasbridge, *The Fruits of Experience* (London, 1824), p. 52.

25 J. Banister, 'A Link with Pauld De Lamerie', *Apollo* (March 1961), pp. 61–2 and 'A Basketmaker's Accounts with Some Eighteenth Century Silversmiths', *Proceedings of the Society of Silver Collectors*, I, 9, (1967), pp. 21–4.

26 Mrs B. Palliser, *History of Lace* (London, 1976), p. 349, quotation from *The Lover*, 10, 1714.

27 I would like to thank Claire Brown of the Textiles Department, Victoria and Albert Museum, for drawing my attention to S. Groves, *History of Needlework Tools* (London, 1966), which includes a chapter on 'The Practice of Parfilage'; see esp. p. 127.

28 *Ibid.* The German actress Caroline Bauer, who came to England in 1829 as a prospective bride of Prince Leopold, recalled how her suitor gained enough money by his drizzling to buy a handsome silver soup tureen which he presented to his young niece, Princess Victoria of Kent, on the occasion of her eleventh birthday.

29 Goldsmiths' Company Records, Court Minutes, Wednesday, 4 November 1607.

30 Glanville, *Silver in England*, p. 268.

31 S. Warneke, 'A Taste for Newfangleness: The Destructive Potential of Novelty in Early Modern England', *Sixteenth Century Journal*, 26:4 (1995), pp. 881–96.

32 C. Pace, 'Virtuoso to Connoisseur: Some Seventeenth-Century English Responses to the Visual Arts', *The Seventeenth Century* (London, 1993), vol. II, p. 174.

33 E.H. Gombrich, *The Sense of Order: A Study in the Psychology of Decorative Art* (Oxford, 1979), p. 17.

34 W.S. Lewis, ed., *Letters of Horace Walpole* (New Haven, 1982), vol. X, p. 289.

35 T. Murdoch, 'The Huguenots and English Rococo', in C. Hind, ed., *The Rococo in England* (London, 1986), p. 60.

36 R. Campbell, *The London Tradesman* (London, 1747), p. 141.

37 Goldsmiths' Company Archives, Court Minutes, no. 14, p. 379, 9 December 1741.

38 Essex Record Office, D/DM F13, 15 May 1736, part of a total bill for £971 3s 11d covering the period 14 February 1727 to 15 May 1736.

39 A.C. Edwards, *The Account Books of Benjamin Mildmay, Earl Fitzwalter* (London, 1977).

40 Thera Wijsenbeek-Olthius, 'A Matter of Taste. Lifestyle in Holland in the Seventeenth and Eighteenth Centuries', in *Material Culture: Consumption, Life-Style, Standard of Living, 1500–1900, Proceedings of the Eleventh International Economic History Congress*, (Milan, 1994), pp. 55–70.

41 Tony Sale, 'Ownership and Use of Silver in Gloucestershire, 1660–1740', *Transactions of the Bristol and Gloucestershire Archaeological Society*, 113 (1995), p. 127.

42 D. Defoe, *The Complete English Tradesman* (New York, 1970), in his chapter on 'fine shops and fine shows', p. 183.

43 J. Brewer, *Pleasures of the Imagination: English Culture in the Eighteenth Century* (London, 1997), p. 107.

44 W. Broome, 'The Widow and the Virgin Sisters, Being a Letter to the Widow in London', in D. Davison, ed., *The Penguin Book of Eighteenth-Century English Verse* (London, 1973), p. 29.

45 R. Nettel, trans and ed., *Carl Philip Moritz: Journeys of a German in England in 1782* (London, 1965), p. 61.

46 J. Lubbock, *The Tyranny of Taste, The Politics of Architecture and Design in Britain 1550–1960* (New Haven and London, 1995), p. 118.

47 Coutts Bank Archives, Letter from James Coutts to Mr Alexander Andrews, London, 4 January 1731.

48 G.B. Hughes, 'Tea-Kettle and Urn Stands', *Country Life*, 13 September 1956, p. 549.

49 L. Weatherill, 'The Meaning of Consumer Behaviour in Late Seventeenth- and Early Eighteenth-Century England', in Brewer and Porter, *Consumption and the World of Goods*, p. 216.

50 Hughes, 'Tea-Kettle', p. 549.

51 S. Houfe, 'Meer Cocksparrows', *Country Life*, 31 August 1995, p. 59.

52 B. Woodcroft, *Subject Matter Index of Patents of Invention, Patent Office* (London, 1857), C. 73.15, no. 1076, accompanied by a sketch illustrating a sectional view.

53 Quoted by I. Quimby, 'Silver', *American Art Journal*, 7 (1975), pp. 68–80, from E.W. Balch, trans., 'Narrative of the Prince de Broglie', in *Magazine of American History*, 1 (April 1877), p. 233.

54 G.B. Hughes, 'Old English Teapoys', *Country Life*, 8 September 1955, p. 504. For 26 December 1772.

55 Anon, 'Notes on Furniture: The Tea Equipage', *Apollo* (London, 1956), p. 124.

56 Sale, 'Ownership and Use of Silver in Gloucestershire', p. 12.

57 C. Schammas, 'Changes in English and Anglo-American Consumption from 1550 to 1800', in Brewer and Porter, *Consumption and the World of Goods*, p. 191.

58 Mitchell, *Goldsmiths, Silversmiths and Bankers*, p. 12.

59 W.S. Prideaux, *Memorials of the Goldsmiths' Company* (London, 1896–97), vol. II, pp. 265–7.

60 Birmingham Central Library, Boulton Letter Books, Letter book E, p. 626. Letter from Matthew Boulton to Lord Boston, Grosvenor Street, London, 1 November 1772.

61 T. Gilbert, *Report from the Committee Appointed to Enquire into the Manner of Conducting the Several Assay Offices*, London, 29 April 1773, p. 68.

62 Sheffield City Library, Bradbury Archives; Fenton Creswick & Company, 19 September 1795, responded to Schlesinger and Frankel in Hamburg that 'The profit is so small on silver Goods that we don't allow any Credit'.

63 *A Catalogue of the Neat and Genuine Stock in Trade of a Wholsale dealer, to be sold by Mr Warre*, 6 and 7 December 1786.

PART FOUR

Excess, taste and fashion

Making a science of taste: The Revolution, the learned life and the invention of 'gastronomie'

Introduction

In the first year of the nineteenth century, the former magistrate Louis Philipon de la Madelaine expressed in print the sense of liberation shared by many of the middling sort across France in the wake of the triumph of moderatism over Jacobinism. *L'Élève d'Epicure*, which celebrated the joys of wining and dining, was a political and social world apart from the work of 1783 for which Philipon's name is known today, a treatise upon public instruction which had insisted that 'Sobriety, a virtue for the rich man, is necessity for the poor ...'[1]. In seventeen years, the Revolution had completely transformed the social meaning of food in France for many. The gastronomic genre of the first quarter of the nineteenth century overturned a particular politics of food which had held sway in journals, cookery books and manuals of domestic economy since at least the 1760s, and had enrolled a particular self-image of sensibility, utility and economy which appealed to a growing audience in the late old regime, including literary figures, *salonnières* and *savants*. This chapter will explore some of the consequences of that transformation, which was not by any means unquestioned. It will consider the competing domains of practices and discourses – the scientific, the aesthetic, the gastronomic and the philanthropic – which were involved within gastronomic writings in attempting to stabilise the nature and significance of food, taste and consumption.

Early nineteenth-century writers drew upon the most unlikely combination of elements in renegotiating the meaning of food. The chapter will travel from cannibals to chemistry, from the dining club to the soup kitchen. But it will also show that gastronomic writings over the period were a major setting for debates about the place of learning in the new society. Uniquely, food writings were a setting at which many different commentators came together in an exchange of insults which enabled the political and social problems of new regime eating and erudition to be resolved. Ultimately, it was the generation of a scientific underpinning for gastronomy itself, the invention of a science of taste – indeed, the partial assimilation of what had previously seemed two conflicting perspectives – which heralded the success of the nineteenth-century French culinary tradition.

Gastronomy and Republicanism

It is appropriate to begin in 1800, with a poem, *La Gastronomie*, published by the former *justice de paix* Joseph Berchoux. This was to set the terms of the debate for the following decade, by launching an attack against both Republicanism and its Spartan moral precepts of self-denial and *vertù*. It achieved this aim through transforming the meaning of the classics: familiar Republican tropes were exploded or inverted. The Persians, far from being the soft and corrupt despots who so often formed the backdrop for admonitory accounts of the Spartans' vigour, were here the epitome of civilisation and the perfection of the culinary art. The robust heroes of Homeric tales ate a 'coarse food' and 'Would not have esteemed our crayfish *coulis*'. For Berchoux, the Republican model of government was not compatible with the advancement of taste, delicacy and the arts.

Moreover, his gastronomy was an explicit move away from the moderate consuming practices of the late eighteenth century. Instead, the indulgence of the passions was an escape from political turmoil. To fit this view of eating as anti-political enterprise, Berchoux reformed a classical account of the emperor Domitian halting the business of the Roman Senate:

> I do not come to tell you
> To watch over the security of the empire;
> To arouse your zeal, and take your advice
> On the fates of Rome and the conquered peoples;
> To debate peace and war with you:
> Futile projects on which you ought to keep quiet.
> What's at issue is a turbot; deign to deliberate
> On the sauce that should be prepared for it.[2]

Despite the facetious language in which much of this was couched, it also had a genuine political message: hunger created an honesty which prevailed over the contrived excesses of Republican heroes, ancient or modern; food unravelled the tightly controlled self-presentations of Sparta and exposed them as overly dramatic poses. The actualities of hunger had underlined the importance of food against the writings of those who sentimentalised the plain diet of the rustic labourer. Even the nature of the food to be consumed by the *gastronome* was determined by these personal encounters with hunger: gastronomic writers insisted upon the central importance of solid dishes rather than tempting dainties.

Food could thus be the focus of dissatisfaction with neoclassical Republicanism. Different foodstuffs were employed to recreate the social hierarchy that had been lost during the height of the Jacobin Republic. Thus, for Alexandre-Balthazar-Laurent Grimod de La Reynière, perhaps the best known of the gastronomic writers of the 1800s, sturgeon, fawn or carp were 'food fit for princes, or at least, for Republican suppliers'.[3] Food and wine were the consolations which replaced the monarchy within the individual, according to Berchoux's description of one memorable meal whilst a Revolutionary soldier:

> Abundance is united with delicacy:
> The truffle perfumes the plump chicken from Bresse . . .
> I drink to my friend, to hospitable manners . . .
> No longer a soldier, I rule, I'm a king,
> And already the terror has fled far away.[4]

The new Maecenas

Gastronomy was an enterprise which also responded to the new social conditions emerging after the Revolution.[5] The rapid changes in political fortunes, accompanied by the collapse of the paper money economy, had enabled a host of *parvenus* without high birth or social status to amass vast sums in a very short time in the immediate aftermath of the Revolution.

> Since a necessary result of the revolution was to produce a reversal of fortunes which placed them in new hands, and the spirit of most of these financial mushrooms was principally concerned with purely animal pleasures, we thought to render them a service by offering them a sure guide in the most solid part of their most cherished affections. The heart of most opulent Parisians has suddenly metamorphosed into a gizzard; their sentiments are no more than sensations, and their desires

no more than appetites; so to give them, in a few pages, the means of receiving the best value for their money and inclinations where good food is concerned, is to serve them appropriately.[6]

A new technology of sensibility had to be constructed to suit these new consumers, one which recognised that they were differently put together, lacking the refined tastes and delicacy of the old regime rich. Grimod's writings were both an effort to re-educate the nouveau riche, the 'Amphitryons, the true Maecenas of Gourmands' and an accommodation of the old regime eating to the new eaters.[7]

Gastronomic writings thus reflected the patronage crisis at the end of the old regime. Men of learning of the 1800s were being faced with agonising decisions about the social meaning of talent in a world in which many of the older genres of fine arts, literature and even the sciences no longer received automatic respect and patronage by those with the money. The right-wing *libraire* Charles-Jean-Auguste-Maximilien de Colnet de Ravel offered authors his own version of a Berchoux-esque gastronomic poem in 1810, aimed at training authors to become successful *parasites* – that is, uninvited guests at the tables of the rich. Once again, Colnet's work produced hunger and food as the common currency which undercut philosophical and political differences; in reality, at the heart of the literary successes of the old regime were not reason and enlightenment, philosophy and politics but the simple common denominator of hunger and thirst:

> Haven't we seen thinking poets,
> The ardent reformers of my sad fatherland, as *gourmand philosophes*
> Surrounding the tables of those great men
> Whom they found so futile, so despicable?
> They wanted to put a stop to abuses of power;
> 'The dignity of man' was their sole refrain.
> But at the first glimpse of the best kitchens,
> They knew how to soften their anti-social doctrines . . .[8]

Gastronomy privileged hunger and eating over learning and politics. It is thus not surprising to find that gastronomic writings such as those of Grimod de La Reynière demoted the concerns with regimen that had typified culinary writings from the 1760s.

Gastronomy against the sciences

Although perfectly familiar with the effects of different foods when cooked or raw, and the fine details of climate, season, age, sex and constitution which altered the effects of foods upon the individual body, according to the Hippocratic canon, Grimod briskly dismissed those who bowed to such regulations from the circle of true *gourmands*: 'The digestion is the stomach's business, and indigestion is that of physicians'. The extent to which gastronomy was to predominate over learning was evident in the frontispiece to Grimod's first gastronomic publication, the *Almanach des Gourmands* of 1803, displaying the 'Library of a Nineteenth-Century Gourmand', with items of food displayed on the shelves in place of books. In successive issues of the *Almanach*, the frontispieces intermittently continued the theme of gastronomy as the substitute for philosophy and the learned life, as for example in 'The meditations of a *Gourmand*', the frontispiece to the 1809 issue, which shows the *gourmand* in his cabinet engrossed in thought – about food. This was really to take the battle into the central territory of the *philosophes'* self-construction.

The perversion of scientific claims to alimentary expertise was perhaps most clearly evident in the satire which Berchoux wrote to capitalise upon the success of his poem. *Le Philosophe de Charenton*, published in 1803, was a sustained attack upon the modern scientific practitioner; it purported to describe the voyages of a profoundly un-scientific man and his suicidal cousin Fremer, who was learned in all the sciences. However, not one of these helped him to find pleasure in life, for he was wholly materialist:

> [The narrator, conversing with Fremer, whom he has just discovered attempting to kill himself:] I believed that ... [the sciences] would have taught you to love the company of men and to fulfil your [earthly] destination ... – Ah, my friend, it's precisely because I know every-thing, that nothing pleases me ... It's because I am a metaphysician that I know that my soul is no more than a diffuse substance, suited for movement; the which substance is so slight a thing, that it doesn't justify the trouble of being preserved for such a long time, organised as it is. It's because I am a geometer, that I have discovered that the world is just a machine, a sort of clock, in which I do not care to figure as a useless cog. It's because I am an anatomist, a naturalist, a physiologist, a chemist, botanist, mineralogist ... – For God's sake, cousin, can't you forget all the things filling up your head, and live like me in salutary ignorance, which so far has kept me in good health, happiness and contentment? ... – No, my dear fellow; it's as impossible for me to stop being learned, as it is for you to become so.[9]

The most sustained joke in Berchoux's armoury was that concern-ing eating. Citing Jean-Jacques Rousseau, the *philosophe* laid a moral injunction upon the eating of animals. When, at a certain point in their travels, the two ended up amongst the cruellest people upon earth, the cannibalistic Jaga tribe, Fremer was delighted with their barbarity and shared portions of his future wife's shoulder at their banquet. Evidently philosophical vegetarianism did not extend to cannibalism. However, the eating of human flesh was a metaphor for lack of sensibility, for on their return to France Fremer was co-opted by the Jacobins, in whom he recognised an even greater barbarity than in his Jaga dining companions. The message was clear: feelings founded upon philosophical reasoning – indeed, a life founded upon such reasoning – were not worth experiencing; they yielded no pleasures and produced no humanity. It was the pursuit of scientific knowledge which had deadened people to the horrors of the Jacobin regime; feelings, when exposed to philosophical analysis, became warped and distorted.

The final twist in Berchoux's tale returns us to cannibalism once more, and proves how far Berchoux must have been familiar with the most up-to-date alimentary science. From 1800 a group of philanthropic ex-nobles and *savants* were involved in state commissions set up to organise an extra-institutional system of charitable provision for the poor.[10] As part of the process of refining the contents of the soup served up in public soup kitchens, the pharmacist Antoine-Alexis Cadet de Vaux experimented upon the process of obtaining gelatine from boiled bones whose nutritional value would otherwise go to waste. His pamphlet on the topic was published by order of the Minister of the Interior in 1804. He concluded that bone soup, suitable for even the most delicate eaters, would supply the nutritional deficiencies of the poor, who were forced against nature to renounce the costly consumption of meat.

Private and public philanthropy appear here intimately linked to enterprises of urban reform in which a particular diet based on scientific principles was being enforced upon the lower classes. But such perspectives were not perceived as politically neutral by contemporaries. Berchoux ended his scientific satire with the last will and testament of the *philosophe* of Charenton, in what was a parody of a paragraph from Cadet de Vaux's (then unpublished) memoir. After requesting that his body be preserved for science, Fremer continued:

> When I have remained some years as a skeleton, I wish to be employed to make soup, which shall be distributed to *philosophes* of slender means. I am very attached to this philanthropic destination for my bones, and I would be annoyed if they should ever be employed to make knife handles, breeches buttons, whistles and the like.[11]

Berchoux's pre-emptive attacks demonstrated the extent to which the politics behind this philanthropy of food was open to question, hence also the alimentary chemistry which underpinned it; what was at stake here was the meaning of taste and the relations between politics, sciences and passions. To what extent was a science of physiology a necessary or sufficient explanation of the workings of the passions? The central focus of contemporary scientific accounts of taste was a particular account of the physiology of the organ of taste which persisted through several decades. A sensible membrane lined the mouth, tongue, throat and stomach, with different areas conveying sensations of different flavours to the brain.[12] The passions could thus be explained as the results of physical phenomena which were reducible to scientific analysis.

Conflicting accounts of sensibility were at issue in pro- and anti-gastronomical writings in the 1800s. For Berchoux, it was the *savants* who suffered from a lack of sensibility by virtue of the materialist explanatory models they adopted, and even their philanthropic claims could be critically viewed as evidence of this. For Grimod de La Reynière, an excess of sensibility was the mark of old regime weakness. The true *gourmand* possessed a robust appetite, yet was far from being insensible, for gastronomic expertise depended upon the possession of a developed and discriminating organ of taste. But gastronomy was far from being perceived as a neutral enterprise in its own right. Republican appeals for self-restraint as a mark of true patriotism, denoting economy, Spartan morality and sobriety were still current. If *gastronomes* could satirise philosophy, others could turn the tables on them. Jean-Baptiste Gouriet's *L'Antigastronomie, ou l'homme de ville sortant de table* of 1806 managed to satirise both cherished gastronomic precepts and the opposite end of the spectrum, the self-denial and stoicism of its opponents, through parodying Berchoux's poem. The stick used to beat the *gastronomes* here was medical: indigestion and obesity would punish those who over-indulged. Passing the scythe of neo-Galenism through successive courses, Gouriet's anti-*gastronome* denounced every foodstuff as unhealthy and invoked the pleasures of abstinence:

> Ah! fear those artificial sweetnesses;
> Fear those highly spiced dishes,
> And all those seasonings,
> Slow and pernicious poisons
> Whose evildoings I know;
> Fear every dish, whatever it may be,
> One is too hot, the other too cold,
> One is dry or melancholic,
> Another bilious or phlegmatic . . .[13]

The anti-*gastronome* claimed that poetry, the divine art, was not a suitable vehicle for the earthy manifestations of *gourmand* greed. *Gourmands*, he opined, would be haunted by nightmares; significantly, these were nightmares about the collapse of civilisation and the occurrence of terrible disasters.[14] Moreover, the poet reversed Berchoux's linking of reason with insensitivity, claiming that *gastronomy* diminished sensibility by hardening the heart towards the hunger of others. It was questionable for contemporaries, then, whether gastronomy was truly modern; whether it was evidence of the progress of reason through human society, or whether, in fact, it was simply another manifestation of the barbarous excesses of passion which were so vivid in everybody's mind.

At the centre of the criticisms of anti-*gastronomes* was the issue of how far taste could truly be discriminating when unaccompanied by learning; were not *gourmands* just (in the original sense of the word) indiscriminate gluttons? A contemporary caricature illustrated the dichotomy that contemporaries perceived between the two styles of eating; the scientific eater was slender, his table orderly and geometrical, and his food included items whose healthful properties were frequently attested by regimen authors and philanthropists. The *gourmand* was obese, his principal foods were roasts (judging by the debris beneath his feet), and he drank wine instead of water. The line between philanthropy and cannibalism, between gastronomy and gluttony, between rational order and passionate disorder was thus to be drawn by capturing the meaning of 'taste'.

Making a science of taste

Thus gastronomy was invented amidst an apparently irreconcilable split between the art of eating and the sciences, between diners and *philosophes*, between neoclassicism and *gourmandise*. By the middle years of the Napoleonic empire, there were attacks against both gastronomy and a purely science-based understanding of food; if gastronomic writers were being denounced for their non-intellectuality, Cadet de Vaux's bone soup was being abandoned: on grounds of taste.[15] At what point did these apparently distant poles of the scientific and tasteful come to be reconciled? We can turn to the allegedly posthumously published *Cours gastronomique* of 1809, by Charles-Louis Cadet de Gassicourt, for illumination of the rehabilitation of the sciences in the eyes of *gastronomes*.[16] Cadet de Gassicourt was a member of a gastronomic dining club and an *avocat*-turned-pharmacist who was in fact the nephew of Cadet de Vaux. Thus he was well placed to appreciate both sides of the science–gastronomy divide. The *Cours gastronomique* was an attempt to reconcile the two positions by making scientific knowledge an obligatory part of gastronomic expertise. Like his gastronomic predecessors, Cadet invoked a repertoire of familiar figures: the *parvenu* amphytrion, Manant-Ville, whose social *gaucherie* manifested itself in evident but ineffable ways and who feared that his son, Saint-Charles, lacked the proper manner and learning of a gentleman, and the parasitic Chevalier de Versac. Although at first glance another in a series of volumes devoted to the retraining of the *nouveau riche*, from table settings onwards, Cadet's contribution actually performed a far more intricate task. Uniquely, he reinvented these risible characters by introducing to the dinner-table a succession of *savants*, from a professor of 'phagotechny . . . the art of eating well, which leads to the art of living well; and the man who knows phagotechny knows as much history, physics, philosophy, literature as he needs to shine in the most illustrious circles . . .', to the naturalist Aristophilus (or 'wealth-lover') and the chemist Oxigénius.[17] There was also a straw man who represented the anti-gastronomic viewpoint, criticising the dinners because they were not occasions for 'expounding upon the arts and sciences'. He called upon the *convives* to teach Manant-Ville about the self-denying Spartans: 'Then your conversation will be in keeping with good taste and morality whilst still being gastronomic.' What the character sarcastically termed 'that scientific dinner of M. de Manant-Ville' was, in this view, none of the sort.[18] Here the alternative model of eating, dating from the late old regime, was being invoked: one could be erudite and continue to talk of food, but only by invoking historical examples of self-restraint and self-denial.

Against the anti-*gastronomes*, then, gastronomy had to be shown to require both the erudition of historians and *savants*, and the wit of authors. Unlike previous gastronomic writers, Cadet de Gassicourt used contemporary medical physiology of the organ of taste and up-to-date chemistry of the nutritive principles to define the terms '*goût*' and '*aliment*'. For chemical, medical and natural historical writers, reliance on taste was an instinctive guide to the best or most suitable foods for the individual, implanted in animals and man by nature. These *savants* depended upon their power to make claims about the physiology of taste in order to capture the content of diet. However, *savants* also sought to pin down the possible loose ends that might result from man's social state by claiming that they alone, with their expert and complex knowledge of the effects of each foodstuff, were in a position to compensate for the moments when nature was insufficient and taste failed, or when taste was duped by the addition of seasoning.[19]

Thus *savants* could appeal to a two-sided account of taste which drew its authority from the combined powers of nature and the sciences to defend their hegemony over food. Cadet de Gassicourt used these current medical and chemical accounts of the operations of taste to underpin his 'phagotechny'. The tongue was differentially sensitive to different flavours across its surface. A truly artistic cook was one who knew how to play upon the sequence of physiological effects produced by these flavours: effectively, a scientifically trained cook. But the skills of *gastronomes* were also necessary. A cook who could command such skills could not be judged by a simple *gourmand* or *polyphage* who would eat anything and everything, but only by someone with very highly developed senses.[20] Thus the *Cours gastronomique* asserted a scientific foundation for gastronomic theorising. As the chemist, Oxigénius, put it: 'There you are, sirs, gastronomy is already justified by physiology; it will be even more so when we apply the principles of chemistry to it . . .'[21] This scientific underpinning for gastronomy managed to separate the *gastronome* from the glutton in two ways: first, by proving that scientific, literary and historical erudition was at the heart of gastronomy; and second, by demonstrating that the two figures were distinct at the physiological level.

But the moral message of the book was at the end. After eating an omelette popular at the time of Louis XV, composed of cockscombs, capon's testicles, mushrooms and fillets of quail, Manant-Ville, the host, fell ill of an indigestion. The *savants* thronged to his bedside after dinner to give advice to the suffering amphytrion on how to avoid the problem in future. Wringing the hand of Oxigénius, Manant-Ville admitted: 'I would not be here, my dear doctor, if I had earlier studied the chemical effects of an over-long dinner with you; but, corrected by experience, I wish at last to know the nature of our daily food, and I pray you to give us an elementary notion of the relations between gastronomy and the sublime science of Hermes–Lavoisier in that regard.'[22] The last laugh, evidently, was to go to the *savants*. And Oxigénius's account of the chemical operations of food replaced gastronomic classificatory schemes with a medico-chemical model of the interplay of different foodstuffs, a scientific version of the complex interweaving of tastes that gastronomic literature advocated:

> I believe that, seated at a well-furnished table, the *philosophe* should choose with taste and discernment those dishes which can please him without risking his health; he will make use of the insights of chemistry so as not to associate within his stomach those substances which may excite too great a fermentation, or [which] amalgamate in a heavy and indigestible manner.[23]

It was by means of modern chemistry, the 'sublime science of Hermes–Lavoisier', that Cadet de Gassicourt hoped to bring about the resolution of the differences between gastronomy and dietetics. Chemistry was to allow the perpetuation of scientific knowledge as a *desiderata* at the tables of the wealthy whilst stripping learning of its previous political associations and its self-denying reputation.

Conclusion

In the quarter-century of gastronomic writing between *La Gastronomie* of 1800 and *La Physiologie du goût* of 1825, a science of taste was gradually fashioned which combined the old regime's fascination with the medical and physiological processes of digestion with the new era's obsession with antiquity and lavish displays of wealth. The scientific version of gastronomy evidently did not win out immediately; in 1813 came the last major attack against the *Almanach des Gourmands*, published in the official journal *Gazette de France* by 'F.X.', which described the *Almanach* as an 'apology for all vices and for the disordered passions of human nature'.[24] Moreover the fictional saving of Manant-Ville from the clutches of the dreaded indigestion can be contrasted with the sober reality of the death, in 1806, of a physician who was also one of Grimod de La Reynière's *convives*, Docteur Gastaldy, following his fourth helping of salmon.[25] But by the time the provincial judge Jean-Anthelme Brillat-Savarin published the first edition of his classic *Physiologie du Goût, ou Gastronomie transcendentale*, in 1825, it was no longer necessary to negotiate possible areas of conflict between learned sobriety and gastronomic self-indulgence.

This may partly reflect the fact that the fortunes of men of learning had meanwhile improved to the extent that those of a middling order had once again become part of the social elite, able to participate in the management and allocation of social status. Just as men of letters had promoted the patronage of amphitryons for authors, Cadet de Gassicourt portrayed parasitism as a possible solution to the hardships of *savant* life in an imperial society which seemed not to value learning for itself, nor to pursue the goals of public happiness with any particular zeal. The *Cours gastronomique* ended happily ever after when the naturalist Aristophilus acquired a paid post, thanks to the intervention of Manant-Ville. However, Brillat-Savarin described his experience of the pleasures of the table as shared with his social equals, including several physicians, rather than as the parasite of amphitryons. If *savants* such as Cadet de Gassicourt conceded political ground to the popularity of gastronomic writings, the social setting for gastronomy itself was rapidly altering in the early nineteenth century. As Aron has compellingly suggested, the amphitryon was replaced by the nineteenth-century bourgeois consumer, who fuelled the restaurant trade and created gastronomic spaces even in modest homes, and it was this shift, only partly adumbrated in the writings of Grimod de La Reynière, which ultimately marked the difference in consumption patterns between the old regime and the new.[26]

Notes

1 Louis Philipon de la Madelaine, *Vues patriotiques sur l'éducation du peuple, tant des villes que des campagnes* (Lyon, 1783); quoted in Dominique Julia, *Les Trois Couleurs du tableau noir. La Révolution* (Paris, 1981), pp. 100–1.

2 Joseph Berchoux, *La Gastronomie, ou l'Homme des Champs à table, pour servir de suite à l'Homme des Champs par J. Delille*, 2nd edn (Paris, 1803; orig. pub. 1800), pp. 39–40.

3 *Almanach des Gourmands, ou calendrier nutritif, servant de guide dans les moyens de faire excellente chere; Suivi de l'Itineraire d'un Gourmand dans divers quartiers de Paris, et de quelques Variétés morales, nutritives, Anecdotes gourmandes, etc. Par un vieux Amateur*, 2nd edn (Paris, an XI/1803), p. 87 (of carp, but similar references exist for other foods).

4 Berchoux, *La Gastronomie*, p. 83.

5 On the Thermidorean *parvenus*, see Michel Bruguière, *Gestionnaires et profiteurs de la Révolution: L'administration des finances françaises de Louis XVI à Bonaparte* (n.p., 1986), especially chs 3 and 4 concerning the problematic moral standing of the financier in the second half of the 1790s; also Denis Woronoff, *The Thermidorean Regime and the Directory 1794–1799*, trans. Julian Jackson (Cambridge and Paris, 1984), esp. pp. 115–17.

6 *Almanach des Gourmands*, pp. j–ij.

7 *Ibid.*, p. 158. On the seventeenth-century usage of the term 'amphitryon', see Philip Stewart, 'L'Ambigu ou la nourriture spectacle', in Roland Tobin, ed., *Littérature et gastronomie, huit études* (Paris and Seattle, 1985), pp. 85–111.

8 [C.-J. de Colnet de Ravel], *L'Art de dîner en ville, à l'usage des gens de lettres. Poëme en IV chants* (Paris, 1810), p. 70.

9 [Joseph Berchoux], *Le Philosophe de Charenton, par l'auteur de la Gastronomie* (Paris, an XI/1803), pp. 9–11.

10 On Cadet's philanthropic involvement, see Dora B. Weiner, *The Citizen-Patient in Revolutionary and Imperial Paris* (Baltimore and London, 1993), pp. 157–9; idem, 'The Role of the Doctor in Welfare Work: The Philanthropic Society of Paris, 1780–1815', in Jean-Pierre Goubert, ed., 'La médicalisation de la société française, 1770–1830', *Historical Reflections/Réflexions historiques*, 9, 1 and 2 (1982), pp. 279–304; Catherine Duprat, *Pour l'amour de l'humanité. Le temps des Philanthropes. La philanthropie parisienne des Lumières à la monarchie de Juillet* (Paris, 1993), vol. I, esp. pp. 433–42. The results of experimentation with poor soup ingredients were recorded in Antoine-Alexis Cadet de Vaux, Augustin Pyramus de Candolle, Benjamin Delessert and Antoine-Augustin Parmentier, *Recueil de rapports, de mémoires, et d'expériences sur les soupes*

économiques et les fourneaux à la Rumford, suivi de deux mémoires sur la substitu-tion de l'orge mondé et grué au riz (Paris, 1801).

11   [Joseph Berchoux], *Le Philosophe de Charenton*, p. 215.

12   See, for example, Polycarpe Poncelet, *Chimie du goût et de l'odorat, ou principes pour composer facilement, & à peu de frais, les Liqueurs à boire, & les Eaux de senteurs* (Paris, 1755), pp. viij–ix; Jean-Baptiste Lafon, *Dissertation sur la diges-tion, présentée et soutenue à l'École de Médecine de Paris, le 26 Fructidor an II* (Paris, an XI/1803), ch. 1; [Charles-Louis Cadet de Gassicourt] *Cours gastro-nomique, ou les diners de Manant-Ville, Ouvrage Anecdotique, Philosophique et Littéraire; Seconde Édition dédiée à la Société Epicurienne du Caveau moderne, séante au Rocher de Cancalle; Par feu M. C***, ancien avocat au Parlement de Paris* (Paris, 1809), pp. 66–7.

13   Jean-Baptiste Gouriet, *L'Antigastronomie, ou l'homme de la ville sortant de table, poeme en IV chants. Manuscrit trouvé dans un pâté, et augmenté de remarques importantes* (Paris, 1806), pp. 14–15.

14   *Ibid.*, pp. 97, 65 respectively. Note that nightmares were a classic symptom of the form of indigestion termed 'dyspepsie nidoreuse' by the medical student J.-B. Lebrun in a thesis, *Recherches sur la dyspepsie idiopathique, ou digestion laborieuse. Dissertation présentée et soutenue à l'École de Médecine de Paris; le 4 nivôse an XII* (Paris, an XII/1803), cf. pp. 13, 17.

15   Société philanthropique de Paris, *Comptes-rendus et rapports . . . 1814* (Paris, 1815), p. 16, according to Weiner, *The Citizen-Patient*, p. 159.

16   The general consensus seems to be that this work was written by Charles-Louis Cadet de Gassicourt. However, in 1809 he was far from dead, being engaged as military pharmacist on a Napoleonic campaign. The mystery will require further resolution.

17   Cadet de Gassicourt, *Cours gastronomique*, p. 18. 'Oxigénius' refers to the construction of a legend around the discoverer of oxygen, Antoine-Laurent, marquis de Lavoisier.

18   *Ibid.*, pp. 175–6.

19   See, e.g., Antoine Coulomb, *Essai sur les alimens considérés comme cause de maladies; présenté et soutenu à l'École spéciale de médecine de Montpellier* (Montpellier, [1806]) p. 23; Guillaume-Camille Faure, *Considérations sur la digestion, présentées et soutenues à l'École de Médecine de Paris, le 28 Nivôse an XIII* (Paris, an XIII/1805), p. 15; Cadet de Gassicourt, *Cours gastronomique*, p. 295.

20   *Ibid.*, pp. 66–7.

21   *Ibid.*, p. 185.

22   *Ibid.*, p. 286.

23   *Ibid.*, pp. 295–6.

24   Quoted in Giles MacDonogh, *A Palate in Revolution: Grimod de La Reynière and the Almanach des Gourmands* (London and New York, 1987), p. 99.

25   *Ibid.*, pp. 66–7.

26   Jean-Paul Aron, *Essai sur la sensibilité alimentaire à Paris au XIXe siècle* (Paris, 1967), pp. 10, 32, 40.

'Quality always distinguishes itself':[1] Louis Hippolyte LeRoy and the luxury clothing industry in early nineteenth-century Paris

The First Consul enlarged France, LeRoy re-established the throne of Fashion on its most solid base, luxury.[2]

Louis Hippolyte LeRoy was the most celebrated milliner (*marchand de modes*) working in Paris in the first quarter of the nineteenth century.[3] His reputation reached beyond France to the areas of Europe conquered by Napoleon, and ruled over by his relations, but also to those that were not – including Russia and Britain.[4] Many of his clients were drawn from these different European monarchies and aristocracies, confirming his reputation for the production of high quality fashionable clothing.

During the eighteenth century French culture was regarded as a model for the elite groups of other European countries. The court of Louis XVI and Queen Marie Antoinette at Versailles was known for the sumptuous decorations of the palace and the luxurious dress of their courtiers. After the Revolution of 1789 many of the nobles who had formed the elite, including the two brothers of Louis and his one surviving daughter, left France and established a court in exile in Britain. In 1792 the First Republic was declared and this was followed by the period known as the Terror from 1793 to 1794. For a time there was no court and luxurious display in dress was not only politically incorrect but also personally dangerous. The centre of power and public display moved to Paris, where there were opportunities to see and be seen around the shops and gardens of the Palais Royal, the Tuileries, at balls and the many theatres.

With the establishment of the more stable Directory government in 1795 there was a return to the use of luxurious ornament and
display in dress by the five Directors and their circle, which included
the hostesses Madame Tallien, Madame Recamier and Madame
Bonaparte. Under Napoleon's rule as First Consul in 1799 and Emperor
in 1804 this trend continued. He believed in the importance of the
luxury trades to the economy of France as well as the power of conspicuous display to strengthen the public's awareness, at home and abroad,
of the assurance and solidity of his new regime. The new elite was made
up of military men, army contractors, returned *émigrés* and their wives
and daughters. In 1802 Napoleon made formal dress (elaborate gowns
for women, breeches for men) mandatory for receptions at the Tuileries,
and the coronation in 1804 confirmed a new style of court dress that
included the elaborate use of embroidery. The restored Bourbon courts
of 1814 under Louis XVIII and Charles X in 1824 continued this use
of luxury and incorporated many of Napoleon's elite.[5] Against the
context of change and continuity in France this chapter will examine
the role of luxury in the garments and accessories that LeRoy supplied,
the implications of this for his client base, and how it contributed
to the way that LeRoy was able to market his business.

Historiography and sources

Recent work has seen a growth of interest in the activities of the
milliner, because of attempts to understand the growth that took place
in France in the eighteenth century in the production and consumption of fashionable clothing and accessories.[6] According to Daniel Roche,
the milliners of the eighteenth century promoted the move from the
consumption of necessities to the consumption of luxuries and were
central to the production and distribution of fashionable clothing. They
also helped to create habits that embraced the idea of obsolescence
which paved the way for changes that ocurred at the end of the nineteenth century.[7]

Investigation into the growth of mass production and consumption has concentrated on the end of the nineteenth century as the
most important period of change.[8] This has been linked to the development of the department store and innovations such as the factory
system of working, the introduction of the sewing machine and increases in communications, made possible by the telegraph and the
railway. This has then been linked to an increase in consumption
provided by an expanding middle class.[9] The court's consumption of

luxury items has been considered mainly as important in providing a model for emulation by this socially ambitious middle class.[10] It has also provided moral commentators ammunition to descry the terrible financial, medical, public and private consequences of expenditure on fine clothing.[11]

The pre-mechanised period of the first half of the nineteenth century has not received much interest even from dress historians who have considered the luxury market for clothing mainly as the history of uniquely gifted individuals who created works of art in the form of garments and accessories that can now be viewed as part of design history.[12] Traditionally, particularly in British accounts, Worth has been seen as the first of this stream of designers who even today continue to produce luxury clothing in Paris.[13] Therefore those that worked before the middle of the nineteenth century have been regarded as being of lesser status and the system of clothing production and distribution has been seen as inferior and parochial.

Research into patterns of consumption has focused on the spread of fashionable clothing and accessories from the elite to the middle and lower classes. This has led to the 'social emulation' theory that the lower classes copied the consumption practices of the elite class because there existed a universal desire for material things that was only held in check by a lack of spending power.[14] This position has been challenged by writers such as Lorna Weatherill, Dick Hebdidge and Amanda Vickery, who consider that a much more complicated model to account for consumer behaviour is required.[15] Emulation has a negative passive connotation but Hebdidge, considering twentieth-century street styles, prefers to consider the 'appropriation' of fashions and symbols which has a positive role in creating social solidarity amongst a particular group. This agrees with the views expressed by Douglas and Isherwood, who consider that the most important information that goods convey is not, as is often thought, about status but about personal identity.[16] Gender differences in patterns of consumption have been revealed in the research undertaken by Daniel Roche. His work on inventories, of the belongings of people from the lower classes, has demonstrated that by the end of the eighteenth century women's wardrobes showed more variety than men's and had a higher monetary value. Although men were concerned with presenting an appearance too, Roche argues that women were taking the lead in this new consideration for fashion and personal identity.[17]

For other historians such as Amanda Vickery, it has been important to defend the female consumer against the historical charges of frivolity and vanity as well as charges that women were solely motivated by a sense of competition with their own sex combined with a need to attract the male sex. This has led to a consideration of the role of fashion and taste in the manipulation of female consumption.[18] This in turn has been linked to the proliferation of fashion journals that appeared in the late eighteenth century and included coloured plates of fashionable clothing and a text that discussed fashions.[19]

Jennifer Jones has examined the relationship between the fashion press, the construction of the feminine and the role of the milliner. It has been widely accepted that during the eighteenth century new fashions were set by the court at Versailles, particularly by the collaboration between Queen Marie Antoinette and her milliner, Rose Bertin. By examining the fashion press for the years after the Revolution, when there was no court and no 'one' clear female fashion leader, Jones is able to demonstrate that a much more complicated system was being formulated. According to Jones, the fashion journals established the importance and mystery of the creation of fashion, particularly concentrating on French female identity, and centring around both 'erecting a cult to the creativity of the *marchande de modes*' and at the same time making the reader feel that good taste rather than luxurious dressing was what was required to launch new fashions. Thus being distinguished as fashionable was not connected to quality or any particular class, and was achievable by everyone. The political ideals of the early 1790s were therefore able to be synthesised into this new critique of fashion.[20] It is against this background of historical debate that I will examine LeRoy's business.

The sources used for this analysis will include surviving textiles and garments, fashion journals and paintings, as well as two of LeRoy's account books.[21] Written sources also include an obituary notice published in the new fashion journal *La Mode*, invoices sent to clients, letters, memoirs, notarial documents and records of business associations and disputes.[22]

Maison LeRoy

LeRoy began his career during the old regime as a *perruquier/coiffeur* supplying headgear to the women at the court of Queen Marie Antoinette.

During the Revolution many of those who had produced luxury clothing found themselves without work, but LeRoy survived to advise the Convention on fashion and during the 1790s expanded his business to produce a wider range of clothing. He achieved this partly by

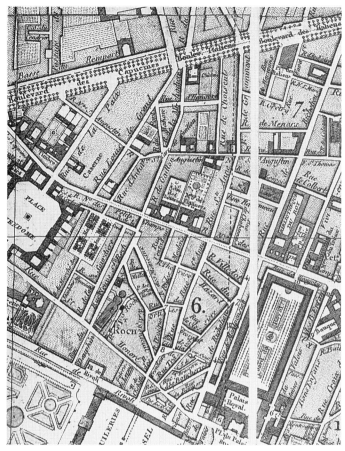

19 Map of Paris showing the location of Maison LeRoy. Plan Routier de la Ville de Paris, 1814

forming various partnerships, the first of which was in the form of a marriage on 29 prairial year 4 (May 1796) to a milliner from Orleans by the name of Françoise Renée Guyot.[23] By 1800 the business was based in the rue des Petits-Champs in the fashionable area west of Les Halles and LeRoy was listed as a milliner (*marchande de modes*) in the Paris directory. He was successful enough by 1802 to have moved to the more prestigious address of Maison Boutin, rue de la Loi (also known as rue de Richelieu) (Plate 19).[24] He had a new business partner by the name of Madame Raimbaud and they were working together at the time of the coronation (December 1804) of the Emperor Napoleon I and the Empress Josephine, when they produced her coronation robes. According to the wardrobe accounts of the Empress Josephine, the partnership ceased after 1805.[25]

For the next fourteen years LeRoy continued to work from the Hôtel Boutin, adapting his business to meet the needs of the changing regimes. In 1821 the lease for the Hôtel Boutin expired and this may have confirmed LeRoy in his decision to retire. He had laid plans for this time and had been training his niece, Esther, to succeed him, whilst not totally losing control of the business.[26] The new establishment was called 'LeRoy nièce et Compagnie' and was based at 36 rue de Rivoli. In 1824, possibly because of involvement in clothing for Charles X's coronation, LeRoy applied to have their arrangement dissolved.[27] Esther continued to place an entry in the trade directory as a dressmaker (*couturière*) until 1841 when she was still using LeRoy's name to adver-tise the business, testifying to the enduring quality of his reputation.

> Leroy nièce. seule succ. de la maison Leroy, robes et modes r.St Honore, 332.[28]

Esther was first entered in LeRoy's account book as an employee working in the shop (*au magasin*) in 1818.[29] Between the years 1811 and 1821 there were twenty-five employees listed, sometimes noting that they worked in different departments such as the shop (*magasin*), hats and accessories (*modes*), sewing – possibly repairs – (*couture*) and clothing workshop (*atelier de robes*). Others were listed as a salesman (*commis*) or merely 'in this house' (*ceans*).[30] A full range of garments and accessories were supplied to clients, including formal and informal clothing for indoor and outdoor wear. These also included corsets, hats, gloves, fans, bouquets, handkerchieves, stockings and shoes.

Fashion and marketing

> LeRoy, as a coiffeur and as a milliner,
> led fashion and did not follow it.[31]

The kind of clothes available in the early nineteenth century demon-strated progression both in terms of fit and the quality of construction.[32] A greater variety of fabrics were also in use, from heavy velvets and satins to fine woollen cashmeres, sheer cotton muslins and silk gauzes. LeRoy used the highest quality fabrics and trimmings to produce his garments, which he normally supplied himself to the customer.[33]

During the Convention and the Directory LeRoy continued to be known for his headgear such as *toques* (a brimless hat based on the Roman helmet), whilst also producing clothing (Plate 20). At the time of the Directory his major innovation was to reintroduce the use of gold embroidery on garments.[34] This demonstrated acute sensitivity, on

20 Sheet of caricatures by J.B. Isabey

LeRoy's part, to the changing attitude towards the use of luxury, as this kind of embroidery had been associated with the old regime, and therefore had been an anathema during the Revolution and the rule of the Convention.[35] For the clients of Napoleon's court LeRoy continued to use all kinds of materials for embroidery, including silver and gold plate, cut steel and precious stones (Plates 21 and 22). This made these outfits, necessary as court dress, extremely expensive and, according to the Duchesse d'Abrantès, Napoleon reintroduced a form of sumptuary law to save his courtiers from too much expense. This limited the amount of embroidery on the border of a gown to four inches for those under the rank of a princess.[36] When LeRoy supplied court dress it was an opportunity for him to control the complete *toilette* which apart from the gown and train would include the *coiffure*, *cherusque* (a fan-shaped standing collar), gloves, a fan and a bouquet. Napoleonic court dress had been established by the garments worn by Josephine and the other high-ranking women at the coronation of 1804. After instructions by Napoleon, this had been outlined by the artist Isabey and translated into clothing by LeRoy. For Louis XVIII's court LeRoy developed a different kind of embroidery, added lappets (*barbes*) to the

21 Gérard, *The Empress Marie Louise*
22 Sample of gold embroidery with the Napoleonic imperial emblem of the bee

coiffure and changed the design of the sleeve (*sabots*).[37] As these were not radical changes (not a return to the wide hoops of the old regime, still worn at the British court), it also provided a sense of continuity and stability during a time of change. Apart from court dress the use of very costly and ornate embroidery and lace was particularly evident on court commissions of full dress for masqued balls and weddings.

Several of the gowns supplied for the wedding gift (*corbeille de mariage*) of Catherine of Württemberg in 1807 were commended for their novelty. One was a gown of pink satin embroidered in steel and the other two were of crêpe with appliqued painted velvet flowers.[38] Other innovations concerned daywear, and Auger cites the occasion when LeRoy cut up an expensive cashmere shawl to create a cloak for the Empress Josephine. Portraits and fashion plates of the period show that many varieties of coats and gowns were eventually created from the cashmere shawl. LeRoy also invented the apron gown (*robe à tablier*) and examples are evident in the Empress Josephine's accounts. The names for garments, accessories and colours demonstrate the impact of new fashions, derived from sources such as other cultures, historical characters and dress, and military campaigns. Some examples are colours such as 'Marie Louise' blue, 'earth of Egypt' and 'Spanish tobacco' and gowns and trimmings 'à la Sevigné', 'Cossack', 'Arab', 'Gothic' and

'Queen Matilda'. Headgear included the 'Napoleon', 'Jockey', 'Cossack' and 'Polish'. Other new fashions that LeRoy invented show subtler nuances unrecognisable as 'fashions' today, such as straw hats trimmed with feathers of the same colour (*chapeaux de paille*) and reversible satin ribbons faced in a contrasting colour (*ruban double face*).[39] According to Auger, even in retirement LeRoy never stopped thinking about new fashions and even talked about bringing back the small side hoops (*demi-paniers*) that he had known in his youth.[40] Contemporary reports about LeRoy reveal a man who believed in his own pre-eminence in the profession of millinery, and this is demonstrated by the following quotation: 'being recognised as the manufacturer with the best taste in Europe there was no-one in a position to judge him'.[41] The same documents have recorded LeRoy's opinion about the qualities needed to create his products: they depended on taste, fashion and imagination. He saw his role as that of an artist and arbiter of taste but surviving documents also reveal a man with considerable business acumen.[42]

The financial rewards from his commercial enterprise were evident from the comfortable lifestyle that he and his family were able to lead. As well as having a home in central Paris, where his clients also lived and shopped, he kept a fleet of carriages and was described by contemporaries as an extremely well-dressed, elegant man with an arrogant air.[43] His appearance and his lifestyle emphasised his status as a supplier to the courts of France and Europe. His history of close contact with the French court, dating back to the time of the old regime, gave him a reputation for knowing court secrets and this served to further enhance his celebrity and attract new clients.[44] The vignette at the top of LeRoy's business stationery shows that he advertised himself as milliner to the Empress (*Marchand de Modes de sa Majesté l'Impératrice*) and that he supplied all kinds of the highest quality lace and embroideries as well as court dress and presentation dress (Plate 23).

LeRoy also advertised his business in the Paris trade directory. Two examples demonstrate how he adapted the entry to suit the changing regimes with reference to the Empress Marie-Louise in 1814 and the Duchesse d'Angoulême in 1817: both 'first ladies' of France during the years referred to.

1814
marchand de modes. de S. M. L' Impératice et Reine, rue Richelieu, 89.

1817
marchand de modes, et robes de la cour, de Madame et des cours étrangères, rue Richelieu, 69.

23 The heading of LeRoy's invoice, 1807

Guides to France were available in other countries. In England, in 1814, LeRoy's name was entered in *A New Picture of Paris* as supplier to the late Empress (Josephine), stressing his high status in relation to the other suppliers listed.[45] His business premises at Maison Boutin, rue de Richelieu, also helped to promote his reputation as a person of wealth and taste who could be relied upon to provide his clients with the kind of elegant surroundings in which they would feel comfortable. The clients were waited upon by servants in livery of light blue with collars and piped decoration of black velvet. LeRoy organised exhibitions of his garments, for which he issued invitation cards to selected people, whilst footmen stood guard at the front entrance of the Maison; emphasising the importance and exclusiveness of the occasion.[46] Once these garments had been sold they would be seen within a circle of other potential clients.

These clients were also recorded in paintings by artists such as Gérard and Isabey and possibly in fashion plates; although recent work on fashion journals has shown how difficult it is to credit particular fashion plates to particular makers at this period. The text accompanying the plates often simply made reference to '*modistes*' and did not name individual makers, thereby retaining the role of 'conveyor of fashion changes and arbiter of taste' to themselves.[47]

A high-ranking client such as an empress, whose actions and appearance were followed by the fashion press and general newspapers of France and abroad, was a way to advertise and promote LeRoy's reputation as the leading arbiter of fashion and taste.

Clients and modes of consumption

> I counted amongst my clientele two empresses and all the crowned
> heads of Europe ... The coronation started my fortune.[48]

LeRoy's assertion that his clients included all the crowned heads
of Europe may have been a slight exaggeration, but surviving records
do demonstrate some justification for his claim. The coronation of
Napoleon and Josephine as Emperor and Empress in December 1804
was an extremely high profile event that was reported in the world's
press.[49] It may have been this event and the new ornate form of court
dress that first brought his clothes to the attention of potential clients
from other countries.

Sources for an examination of LeRoy's clients include memoirs,
invoices and wardrobe accounts; however, his two surviving account
books offer the most comprehensive information over a ten-year period.
Between 1812 and 1821 there were approximately 603 different clients'
accounts and approximately half of those were for people who were
connected to the French or foreign courts.[50] There were 162 French
titles and 85 foreign titles. Of the foreign titles 33 were British, 19 were
Russian and 20 were German or Austrian.[51] The largest number of
clients were without titles and consisted of 294 French commoners
and 42 foreign commoners, making 336 in all. The British accounted
for the largest group of foreigners without titles: 23 were British, six
were Italian, six were German, four were Russian, one was Dutch, one
was Irish and one was possibly American.[52] Most of the clients were
female, but approximately 59 were male though mainly they made
purchases for female friends or family.[53] Many of the purchases that
clients made were over one year only, but some clients made purchases
over at least ten years, such as the Empress Josephine, the Empress
Marie Louise and Princess Pauline Borghese.[54]

During Napoleon's empire the highest ranking French clients
were the Emperor Napoleon himself, the Empress Josephine and the
Empress Marie Louise. The Emperor Napoleon manipulated the consumption of his courtiers so that they presented what he considered to
be the correct appearance. He discouraged what he saw as the indecent
display of women's fashions in the Directory period, whilst making
clear his approval of those women at court receptions whom he thought
dressed well. He also encouraged habits of rapid replacement of garments by reprimanding those who appeared too often in the same
outfit.[55]

LeRoy's most important client was Napoleon's wife, Josephine. According to Auger, at some time during 1796 LeRoy deliberately targeted Josephine and won her custom at the expense of other suppliers.[56] She looked upon LeRoy as her protégé and continued to purchase clothes from him as Empress and after the divorce from Napoleon in 1809, until her sudden death in 1814. Contemporaries have described Josephine as not physically beautiful but as a very attractive, graceful person who knew how to dress with taste.[57] As the wife of a man who rose from General-in-Chief of the French army to First Consul and then Emperor, she had a position to uphold when appearing in public at his side or representing him alone. In her own right she gained a reputation for good manners, diplomacy and charitable behaviour – often trying to mediate between the old aristocracy and Napoleon. Josephine's purchases from LeRoy included court dress, masquerade dress and all kinds of daywear, hats and accessories. Her personal preference was for simplicity, but her purchases from LeRoy often reflected the presentation of a 'public' appearance (Plate 24).

In her memoirs Madame Remusat said that Josephine was always aware of her background setting, such as the interior decoration of palace apartments, and that she selected her clothes accordingly.[58] The life of her garments demonstrates continual change. Many items were worn only briefly and then either remade as something different or given away to members of her family and the ladies of her household, who therefore indirectly became LeRoy's clients.[59]

Josephine's expenditure on clothes from LeRoy, after 1804, was between 7,000 and 10,000 francs per month, though this pattern could be distorted by extra purchases.[60] For example, in February 1807 her purchases came to 24,882 francs.[61] In 1809 Josephine's wardrobe expenses consisted of about twenty suppliers who ranged from jewellers to lace merchants and laundresses. LeRoy's supplies accounted for between 30 and 60 per cent of this monthly expenditure.[62] After the divorce from Napoleon in December 1809 Josephine continued to make purchases, but they reflected her reduced income and loss of public duties. She died in 1814 at a time when she was being fêted by the Allied leaders and her daughter's (Hortense, Queen of Holland) account shows purchases of suitable mourning clothes.[63] LeRoy's business was unaffected as he had already become supplier to Napoleon's second Empress in 1810.[64]

Marie Louise was the daughter of Francis I of Austria and the niece of Queen Marie Antoinette who at the age of 18 was married to the 42-year-old Emperor Napoleon. LeRoy supplied a large part of her trousseau, including the wedding dress, costing 12,000 francs, which

24 Gérard, *The Empress Josephine*, 1808

was of white satin embroidered with jewels and spangles.[65] It was worn with the same gold embroidered crimson velvet train lined in ermine that LeRoy had supplied for Josephine to wear at the coronation. Like Josephine, Marie Louise spent large sums of money every month on clothes both for herself and for her family in Austria, including her stepmother the Empress of Austria.[66] She continued to patronise LeRoy after the wedding and her name is entered in the account books until 1821, by which time she was living in her new position as the Duchess of Parma.

In terms of rank and the quantity of regular purchases from LeRoy, during and after Napoleon's empire, the female members of Napoleon's family were very important customers. At different times they ruled over parts of the Italian states such as Tuscany and Naples, Spain, the German states and Holland, but they were encouraged by Napoleon to preside over courts that owed their luxurious appearances to French suppliers.[67] Purchases and payments could be made by an intermediary such as a lady-in-waiting.[68]

Other high-ranking clients included the wives to seventeen out of Napoleon's twenty-six marshals as well as those who had been newly ennobled and given high political positions. One example was the Duchess de Bassano, the wife of the Emperor's most important minister, who was known as one of the most elegant hostesses at Napoleon's court. She appears in LeRoy's account books in 1812 already owing 11,806 francs for purchases in 1811.[69] She continued to make purchases until 1819 and these ranged from court dresses to riding habits. In 1813 she also purchased a striped gown for her daughter and even a white satin bonnet trimmed with white roses for her daughter's governess.[70] The pattern of other family members, and particularly a new generation, being introduced to LeRoy as clients is repeated throughout the account books. This included not only sisters and daughters but also the husband and father of the family. One example is the Rovigo family, who made purchases between 1812 and 1820. The Duc de Rovigo, whom Napoleon appointed Minister of Police between 1810 and 1814, made purchases between 1812 and 1813. The Duchesse de Rovigo made regular purchases between 1812 and 1820 for herself and for her four daughters, one of whom eventually, between 1818 and 1819, had her own account.[71] Despite their identification with Napoleon's regime, like many others they were eventually accepted at the court of Louis XVIII.

There exists an intriguing suggestion by the Irish poet Thomas Moore, in his satirical poem *The Fudge Family in Paris*, that after the restoration of the Bourbon monarchy, in 1814 and 1815, LeRoy became unfashionable due to his identification with Napoleon's court.[72] This requires further investigation, but Louis XVIII did give orders in 1814 that LeRoy was to remain supplier to the imperial court. LeRoy's account books show that the highest ranking women at the Restoration court were his clients. They were the Duchesse d'Angoulême (only surviving child of Queen Marie Antoinette), the Duchesse de Berry, who became the leading hostess of the younger faction, and the Duchesse d'Orléans (later to be Queen of the French).

LeRoy's account for the Duchesse d'Angoulême began in May 1814 when preparations were being made for the ceremonial entry into Paris.[73] She purchased everything required from a taffeta corset, at the modest price of 40 francs, to a gown of tulle with embroidered silver spots (priced at 1,166 francs), headgear, gloves and a bouquet of roses and lilies.[74] There is a predominance of white in these purchases which was traditionally the colour associated with the Bourbons, as was the lily. The court dress included in the same order lists a pair of lappets that formed part of the new official head-dress. Her purchases continued until the limit of the account book in 1821 amounting to between 15,000 francs and 20,000 francs per month.[75] She had little personal interest in clothes but acknowledged that she was obliged to present an appearance that was appropriate to her rank.[76] The Duc de Berry (younger son of the Comte d'Artois and nephew to Louis XVIII), was concerned that his wife Marie-Caroline was being overshadowed by the duchess's fine appearance and he was instrumental in persuading his wife to patronise LeRoy for her clothes.[77]

Apart from court functions, Captain Gronow has said in his memoirs that there were sixteen main families that held receptions during the Restoration period. Ten of these families had members who were LeRoy's clients: the Beauffremonts, the Chabots, the Choiseuls, the Crillons, the Gonthauts, the Grammonts, the Mailliés, the Montmorencies, the Talleyrands and the La Tour du Pins.[78] Some of the old nobility such as the Comtesse Choisi and the Duchesse de Clermont-Tonnerre certainly made purchases only after the Restoration.[79] There were other high-ranking foreign clients who were not linked to the French regimes and these demonstrate the extent of LeRoy's reputation.

Although Britain became the centre of anti-Napoleonic activity in Europe, this had not prevented a continuing interest in French fashions. In 1814 the British were able to visit France once more. The highest ranking clients who made purchases from LeRoy, included the Duchess of Bedford, the Duchess of Devonshire, the Duchess of Wellington and the Marchioness of Lansdowne.[80] The Duchess of Wellington made only modest purchases between 1814 and 1815, but these nevertheless included the required court dress which was of tulle embroidered in silver.[81] Other celebrated society hostesses included Lady Stuart and Lady Jersay, who in 1817 purchased a range of items including a lace trimmed corset, several gowns, headgear and a fichu amounting to 775.77 francs.[82] After the British clients the largest group consisted of Russians.

The Russian clients included the Empress and the Tsar's sister Catherine, the Grand Duchess, who made purchases in 1816 when she was going to be married for the second time. The most expensive item, at 7,500 francs, was a court dress of gold and silver with a mosaic design. These purchases were sent to her in two cartons, by courier as far as Strasbourg, at a cost of 86 francs, including customs duty.[83] Other high-ranking clients included the Princess Grassalkovich, Countess Kotchoubey, wife of a Russian minister, the Countess Tolstoy and Countess Bocholz.[84]

The Polish aristocrat and mistress of Napoleon, Countess Marie Walewska, made regular purchases between 1812 and 1816.[85] According-ing to her biographer, the Countess had arrived in Paris as a young unsophisticated woman and she had then learned from LeRoy how to dress and even apply make-up.[86] Her individual purchases were not very expensive but demonstrate complete outfits. For example, in July 1815 she purchased two white robes, one of crêpe, trimmed with satin, crêpe and blonde lace, and one of taffeta edged in satin. The accessories were a white straw hat trimmed with white, periwinkle blue and camellia satin ribbon and three white roses, together with matching boots of periwinkle blue.[87]

Other European aristocrats included the Prince of Monaco, Prin-cess Metternich, the Princess of Lichtenstein and Princess Esterhazy, who spent some years in London as the Austrian ambassadress.[88] Apart from the aristocracy of Europe there were those who were connected to the aristocracy and the court, such as ladies-in-waiting like Madame Remusat and Madame de Montmorency. Madame Campan, who edu-cated the female children of the elite, was also a client.[89] Then there were the wealthy middle-class clients, many of whom at the moment remain obscure. They do, however, include Madame Gros Davillier, (*negotiante*), the banker Mr Douaud, Mr Delaroche (*médecin*), Dr Hyde at the hotel de Paris and Mr Colin, notary living at the place Vendôme.[90] The theatrical profession provided clients, such as the acclaimed Italian singer Madame Grassini, Monsieur Derivise of the Opéra and the actresses Mademoiselle Mars of the Théâtre Français, who pur-chased daywear.[91] Madame Clothilde of the Théâtre Imperial at the Opéra purchased day clothes including cotton percale dresses, a red velvet *toque*, for which she supplied an aigrette, and in 1815 a Neapolitan costume of red, black and green trimmed with gold.[92] Examples show that clients made purchases that ranged from a few hats to the com-plete *toilette*.

Conclusion

Apart from a brief period after the Revolution, there was always a court with an elite that was encouraged by the monarch to purchase elaborate dress. Although court dress did not make up the majority of garments purchased from LeRoy, it was important to his business in two ways. These items were very expensive to the customer and profitable to LeRoy, and they were high profile garments that could be powerful marketing tools.[93] They helped to promote LeRoy's reputation as a fashion leader and arbiter of taste and this may have stimulated those of lesser rank and financial means to make some kind of purchase from him, however small. Accessories and daywear did not carry the same restrictions of rank and pocket. As about half of LeRoy's clients were untitled, a future study of their purchases would help in an understanding of consumer habits in the first quarter of the nineteenth century.[94]

Notes

Many thanks to Richmond Parish Lands Charity, the Pasold Research Fund, Winchester School of Art and the University of Southampton for financial assistance towards this research, and for the advice and support of Professor Colin Jones, Professor Lou Taylor and my supervisor, Dr Lesley Ellis Miller.

1 Sir John Vanburgh, *The Confederacy*, Act II, Scene I (London, 1705).
2 H. Auger, 'Notice Sur L.H. LeRoy', *La Mode* (1829), p. 311.
3 The workers' statistics for 1807 provided by the prefect of police, record 2,500 milliners and 12,000 dressmakers at a time when the population of Paris was 580,600: D. Roche, *La Culture des apparences* (Paris, 1989; English translation, *The Culture of Clothing: Dress and Fashion in the Ancient Regime* (Cambridge, 1994), pp. 285–6). *The Almanach du Commerce*, which required an entry to be paid for, in 1809 lists 113 milliners (*marchands de modes*) and 10 dressmakers (*couturières*). The category of workers known as milliners developed from the corporation of mercers in 1776. At this time they sold many kinds of headgear and trimmings as well as decorating the gowns that the dressmakers stitched. During the late eighteenth century the milliner became the higher status occupation and eventually stitched and decorated the gowns and other items of clothing. During the first half of the nineteenth century the terminology for the clothing trades imperfectly described the occupation.
4 There is also some evidence that LeRoy's clothing was known in America. Jerome Bonaparte, Napoleon's brother, was married twice and his first wife was Elizabeth Patterson, an American. They were married in Baltimore in 1803 and her biographer has written that Jerome ordered Parisian *toilettes* for his bride from LeRoy. According to contemporary accounts her French fashions shocked society: C. Bourguignon-Frasseto, *Betsy Bonaparte* (Paris, 1988). In 1817 a Madame Petterson is listed in 'Grand Livre de Compte de LeRoy',

no. 4, f. 271 and a Miss Patersonn is listed in f. 413, also for 1817: Bibliothèque nationale, FR NA 5931.

5   For further information on the structure of the courts and their finances see P. Mansel, *The Court of France 1789–1830* (Cambridge, 1988); idem, *The Eagle in Splendour: Napoleon I and His Court* (London, 1987); idem, *Louis XVIII* (London, 1981).

6   For studies that examine the role of the eighteenth-century milliner, see J.M. Jones, 'The Taste for Fashion and Frivolity: Gender, Clothing and the Commercial Culture of the Old Regime', Princeton University, PhD dissertation, 1991; P.A. Parmal, 'Fashion and the Growing Importance of the Marchande de Modes in Mid-Eighteenth Century France', *Costume: The Journal of the Costume Society*, 31 (1991), pp. 68–77; N. Pellegrin, *Marchande de modes, les vêtements de la liberté, abécédaire des pratiques vestimentaires de 1780 à 1800* (Aix-en-Provence, 1989), and Roche, *La Culture des apparences*.

7   D. Roche provides an overview of the whole clothing system and its social meaning in France in the seventeenth and eighteenth centuries. He argues that there was a 'clothing revolution' in the late eighteenth century that involved 'fashion' and fast-moving consumption: *La Culture des apparences*. See also idem, *Histoire des Choses Banales: Naissance de la Consommation XVIIe–XIXe* (Paris, 1997). C. Fairchilds examines the importance of what she calls the 'consumer revolution' in France against the traditional view that London provided the model for Europe. She examines the production and consumption of 'populuxe' items (cheap copies of luxury goods), guild controls and the importance of the milliner and their innovations in retailing: C. Fairchilds, 'The Production and Marketing of Populuxe Goods in Eighteenth Century Paris', in J. Brewer and R. Porter, eds, *Consumption and the World of Goods* (London, 1993).

8   P. Perrot, *Les Dessus et les dessous de la bourgeoisie, une histoire du vêtement au XIXe siècle* (Paris, 1981; English translation, *A History of the Bourgeoisie: A History of Clothing in the Nineteenth Century* (Princeton, 1994)); R. Williams, *Dream Worlds, Mass Consumption in Late 19th Century France* (Berkeley, 1982); J. Coffin, *The Politics of Women's Work: The Paris Garment Trades, 1750–1915* (Princeton, 1996).

9   See A. Daumard, *Les Bourgeois et la bourgeoisie en France depuis 1815* (Paris, 1987); P. Pilbeam, ed., *Themes in Modern European History 1780–1830* (London, 1995); and idem, *The Middle Class in Europe, 1789–1914* (London, 1990).

10   See N. McKendrick, 'The Commercialisation of Fashion', in N. McKendrick, J. Brewer and J.H. Plumb, eds, *The Birth of a Consumer Society* (London, 1983).

11   For a consideration of arguments about 'luxury' see Roche, *La Culture des apparences*. See also engravings such as 'La Mère à la Mode – La Mère Telle Que Toutes Devraient Etre', *c.* 1800 and Anonyme, 'Luxe et Indigence', *c.* 1818.

12   For the continuation of this approach see the series of twentieth-century designer monographs, *Fashion Memoirs* (London and Paris, 1996).

13   D. de Marly, *The History of Haute Couture* (London, 1980); idem, *Worth, Father of Haute Couture* (London, 1980); F. Boucher, *Histoire du Costume en Occident, de l'Antiquité à Nos Jours* (Paris, 1967). For an acknowledgement of LeRoy's position in the hierarchy of historical 'designers', see H. Bouchot, *La Toilette à la Cour de Napoleon* (Paris, 1895); P. Seguy, *Histoire des modes sous*

l'Empire (Paris, 1988); and F. Ffoulkes, 'Louis Hippolyte LeRoy 1763–1829: Grandfather of Haute Couture', Winchester School of Art, unpublished MA dissertation, 1995.

14   McKendrick, 'The Commercialisation of Fashion'.

15   L. Weatherill, *Consumer Behaviour & Material Culture in Britain 1660–1760* (London, 1988); D. Hebdidge, *Object as Image: The Italian Scooter Cycle, Hiding in the Light: On Images and Things* (Paris, 1988); A. Vickery, 'Women and the World of Goods: A Lancashire Consumer and her Possessions, 1751–81', in Brewer and Porter, eds, *Consumption and the World of Goods*, pp. 274–301.

16   M. Douglas and B. Isherwood, *The World of Goods: Towards an Anthropology of Consumption* (Glasgow, 1979).

17   D. Roche, *Le Peuple de Paris* (Paris, 1981; English translation, *The People of Paris* (Oxford, 1987)).

18   Regarding the importance of fashion, see McKendrick, 'The Commercialisation of Fashion', and Roche, *La Culture des apparences*, and regarding fashion and its adoption by distinct social groups see Perrot, *Les Dessus et les dessous de la bourgeoisie*, p. 174. For contemporary Irish comments on the importance of fashion to French society, see *Lady Morgan in France*, ed. E. Suddaby and P.J. Yarrow (Exeter, 1971).

19   There were no fashion journals published in Paris between spring 1783 and March 1797, when the *Journal des Dames* was published. In September 1797 the *Journal des Dames et des Modes* commenced and continued to publish until 1839.

20   J.M. Jones, 'Repackaging Rousseau: Femininity and Fashion in Old Regime France', *French Historical Studies*, 18 (1994), pp. 939–67.

21   Grand Livre de Compte no. 4 (1812–21); Grand Livre de Compte no. 5 (1818–21).

22   Auger, 'Notice sur L.H. LeRoy', pp. 280–321; (1830), pp. 145–62 and 348–55.

23   Inventaire Après Décès de L.H. LeRoy, Archives Nationales (hereafter AN), Minutier Central, ET/CXVII/1138, 25 March 1829.

24   From 1793 until 1806 the street was known as Rue de la Loi: J. Hillairet, *Dictionnaire Historique des Rues de Paris* (Paris, 1963 and 1972).

25   *Recettes et Dépenses de l'Impératrice Josephine*, 1804–9, Musée de Malmaison.

26   LeRoy was to retain three years' surveillance of the business: Auger, 'Notice sur L.H. LeRoy', *La Mode* (1830), p. 352.

27   In 1824 LeRoy had a business association with Esther Gabrielle LeRoy (wife of Lazare Auger), Mademoiselle Genevieve Victoire Brunet and Madame Jeanne Agathe Morial (widow of Monsieur Jean Jacques Pillon). The three women were living at 36 rue de Rivoli: Archives de Paris, D32 U3 9 and D2 U3 1819. When LeRoy died in 1829 the documents showed that he had been in a business association for the sale of fashionable goods (*commerce de nouveauté*) with Madame Agathe Jeanne Morial (widow, Pillon), who lived at and worked from 36 rue de Rivoli, AN, Minutier Central, ET/CXVII/1138.

28   *Almanach du Commerce, 1841*.

29   Grand Livre no. 5, f. 67, 1818–21, salary 400 francs p.a. Esther married Lazare Auger, who was Hippolyte Auger's brother (the writer of LeRoy's obituary notice).

30   It is not possible to be sure of the exact number of people that LeRoy employed, as according to Roche many of those employed in the dressmaking trades were paid by the hour or day to carry out the work at home and may not

have been officially recorded: Roche, *The Culture of Clothing*, and Grand Livres nos 4 and 5.

31   Auger, 'Notice sur L.H. LeRoy' (1829), p. 312.

32   The one-piece chemise dress of the 1780s was a technical advance from the earlier eighteenth-century form of dress that consisted of a petticoat, gown and stomacher that had to be pinned or stitched together when worn, over the chemise and corset. It normally had gathering to achieve a fit over the bust. By the early 1800s this dress had developed into a simpler, smaller shape and a closer fit was achieved by different methods, including shaped pattern pieces and bust darts. The shape of the skirt was achieved by the cutting of side panels and controlled gathering. The opening was often at the centre back and was fastened by either hooks and eyes, buttons or laces. The use of linings, the development of finer sewing thread and increased skill in needlework helped to achieve a high quality of construction.

33   Normally LeRoy supplied the fabrics and other raw materials. The Empress Josephine supplied some fabrics and trimmings, but this may have been a reflection both of her particular interest and her unique status as patron of French manufacturers.

34   Auger, 'Notice sur L.H. LeRoy' (1829), p. 286.

35   'Although the barbarous practice of covering one's clothing with precious metals has been abolished, taste still reigns in France': *Journal de la Mode et du Gout*, April 1791, quoted in Jones, 'Repackaging Rousseau', p. 966; and 'luxury went out, but is now within reach of all citizens, since it resides in the comfort, propriety and elegance of form', in *Le Cabinet des Modes*, 21 September 1790, quoted in Roche, *The Culture of Clothing*, p. 148.

36   Duchesse d'Abrantès, *At the Court of Napoleon: Memoirs of the Duchesse D'Abrantès* (Gloucester, 1991), p. 251. For a study of the use of embroidery on LeRoy's garments see F. Ffoulkes, 'All That Glitters ... LeRoy and Embroidery', *Text: For the Study of Textile Art Design & History*, 24 (1996), pp. 17–21.

37   Auger, 'Notice sur L.H. LeRoy' (1830), p. 152.

38   Documents relating to the *corbeille de mariage* de Catherine de Wurtembourg, AN, 0/2/31.

39   Auger, 'Notice sur L.H. LeRoy' (1830), p. 320.

40   *Ibid.* (1830), p. 355.

41   LeRoy's opinions about his profession were recorded by Napoleon's civil service because LeRoy attempted to justify his refusal to have his products evaluated during the *estimation* that Napoleon insisted upon: documents relating to the *corbeille de mariage* de Catherine de Wurtembourg, AN, 0/2/31.

42   Two examples reveal LeRoy's concern for the financial side of his business. The first is a letter from LeRoy to Madame Lavalette, who controlled the Empress Josephine's wardrobe. In this letter LeRoy discussed several orders that were under way and asked for his expressions of admiration to be passed on to the Empress. However, this is then followed by a reminder that purchases have reached the maximum of 7,000 francs per month, imposed by Napoleon, and this must be dealt with as soon as possible (16 May 1809): Documents relating to the Empress Josephine, The Victoria and Albert Museum, 86.UU. 1, 2. The second example is a judgement of the 'Premiere Chambre de la Cour Royale de Paris' that was published in the *Gazette des Tribunaux* for 8 November 1826 which found against Madame Amelin and in favour of LeRoy. Madame Amelin

was ordered to pay 3,155 francs to LeRoy for goods supplied twenty-five years before in year IX (September 1800–1).

43 A play written by M. de Jouy had a character based on LeRoy played by the actor Hippolyte of the Vaudeville: Auger, 'Notice sur L.H. LeRoy' (1830), p. 316. LeRoy owned a house in the prestigious rue de la Chausée d'Antin, where he bought number 41 in 1821 for 135,000 francs: AN, Minutier Central, RE/CXVII/18. Before this in 1818 he had sold a house in the Bois de Boulogne, 7 rue Montmorency: AN, Minutier Central, ET/VII/621. He may have sold this house in order to purchase a country estate at Franconville, Val D'Oise, north of Paris. Perhaps the ultimate evidence of his status is that after his death he was buried in the new and expensive cemetery, later known as 'Père Lachaise'. His widow spent 1,000 francs on suitable mourning clothes for the domestic staff: AN, Inventaire Après Décès.

44 Important news about the court was sometimes thought to emanate from him. See the letter from the Empress Josephine to her daughter Hortense regarding the possibility of Prince Eugene's wedding: B. Chevallier and C. Pincemaille, *L'Impératrice Josephine* (Paris, 1988), p. 311.

45 E. Planta, *A New Picture of Paris* (London, 1814).

46 Auger, 'Notice sur L.H. LeRoy' (1829), pp. 315–16; Auger said that the sumptuous use of bronze and glass created a fairy-tale quality in the salons which was an important innovation soon copied by other lesser *boutiques*: *ibid.*, p. 315. For a further discussion of the experience of purchasing between merchant and client, see C. Sargentson, *Merchants and Luxury Markets* (London, 1996).

47 For more information about fashion journals, see M. Ginsburg, *An Introduction to Fashion Illustration* (London, 1980); Musée de la Mode et du Costume, *Modes & Revolutions 1780–1804* (Paris, 1989); R. Gaudriault, *Répertoire de la Gravure de Mode Française des Origines à 1815* (Paris, 1983); idem, *La Gravure de Mode Feminine en France* (Paris, 1983). For a discussion of the origins of the drawings and designs in fashion plates see Musée Galliera, *Le Dessin Sous Toutes ses Coutures* (Paris, 1995); Jones, 'Repackaging Rousseau'.

48 H. Auger, *Mémoires* (Paris, 1891).

49 Auger referred to the coronation of Napoleon as a ceremony that sanctioned a government of luxury: Auger, 'Notice sur L.H. LeRoy' (1829), p. 314.

50 The client number is approximate because sometimes it is not clear whether the same client is referred to or a relation of the client. Also many purchases within an account are commissions for other people. The number of clients is therefore likely to be an underestimation.

51 Other foreign titles were as follows: seven from Italy, one from Poland, one from Sweden, one from Monaco, one from Holland and two from Spain. These included French nationals, such as Hortense who became Queen of Holland.

52 I am referring to the American Elizabeth Patterson, once the wife of Jerome Bonaparte. See note 4.

53 The accounts of male clients require more examination; however one example of an outfit purchased for himself is as follows: Marshal MacDonald, Duc de Carante, purchased a Neapolitan masquerade costume in 1818: Grand Livre, 5, f. 15.

54 This loyalty was not restricted to French clients. The British aristocrat Lady Ailesbury made purchases between 1814 and 1819: Grand Livre, 4, ff. 381, 382 and 432.

55 Napoleon was supplied with several velvet and beaver hats by LeRoy, pur-
    chased by the Empress Josephine: Invoice January 1809, Documents – Empress
    Josephine. LeRoy also carried out repairs to Napoleon's imperial mantle, at the
    time of preparations for his second marriage, in March 1810: AN, 0/2/33.
    Napoleon's attention to appearances was also referred to by Mademoiselle
    Avrillon in her memoirs and quoted by P. Seguy, *Histoire des modes sous l'Empire*
    (Paris, 1988), p. 141. In 1807 Napoleon sent presents of a Sèvres dinner ser-
    vice to Tsar Alexander of Russia together with a carton of LeRoy's dresses for
    the Tsar's mistress, Elizabeth Antonovna. He is reported as saying, 'I chose them
    myself. You know I have a good understanding of fashion': C. Sutherland,
    Marie Walewska (London, 1986), p. 112.
56 According to Auger, LeRoy deliberately ousted Madame Germond from her
    position as Josephine's milliner: 'Notice sur L.H. LeRoy' (1829) p. 313.
57 The Empress Josephine retained a reputation for her stylish and fashionable
    appearance, as is shown by the following publication: Anon, *Court and Camp
    of Buonaparte* (London, 1831): 'All the fashions emanated from her, and every-
    thing she put on appeared elegant', p. 118.
58 Madame de Remusat, *Memoirs*, 2 vols (Paris, 1880). See also Ffoulkes, *LeRoy
    and Embroidery*; and *Soieries de Lyon. Commandes Impériales, Musée Historique
    des Tissus* (Avignon, 1982).
59 Documents relating to the Empress Josephine, Victoria and Albert Museum.
60 Napoleon attempted to impose a limit of 7,000 francs per month on Josephine's
    expenditure at Maison LeRoy; however, it was never really adhered to: *Recettes
    et Dépenses*.
61 *Ibid.*
62 *Ibid.*
63 Queen Hortense, Grand Livre de Compte, 4, ff. 11, 38, 60, 74, 102, 135, 148,
    192, 230, 323, 324, 1813–17; 5, f. 81, 1818–19.
64 There is, however, evidence of the close relationship that developed between
    LeRoy, his family and the Empress, and Auger related that after her death
    LeRoy's busts and paintings of her were for a long time draped in funeral
    crêpe and together treated like a shrine: Auger, 'Notice sur L.H. LeRoy' (1829),
    p. 153.
65 AN, 0/2/1217.
66 Between April and November 1810, she purchased goods from LeRoy to the
    value of 104,502 francs, 75 centimes: F. Masson, *Private Diaries of Empress
    Marie Louise* (London, 1922). Grand Livre, 4, ff. 1, 239, 441, 442, 467 and 476,
    1812–18; Grand Livre, 5, ff. 50, 51, 96, 124, 1818–21.
67 Some family members married into the aristocracy of other countries, such as
    Pauline Bonaparte, who married the Italian Prince Borghese, and Prince Eugene
    (Josephine's son who was adopted by Napoleon), who married the daughter of
    the king of Bavaria.
68 One example is Elisa Bonaparte, Princess of Piombino and Grand Duchess of
    Tuscany, who employed her lady-in-waiting Madame Laplace (who also had
    her own account) to send garments to her.
69 Grand Livre, 4, ff. 5, 43, 50, 115, 142, 201, 400, 412, 1812–16 and Grand
    Livre, 5, f. 66, 1818–19.
70 *Ibid.*
71 Duc de Rovigo, Grand Livre, 4, f. 44, 1812–13. Duchesse de Rovigo, including
    purchases for Mademoiselle Hortense, Leontine, Pauline and Marie, ff. 44, 90,

130, 163, 177, 205, 389, 423, 453 and 471, 1812–18. Mademoiselle Hortense Rovigo, f. 196, 1818–19.

72   'That, by Pa's strict command, I no longer employ
That, enchanting *couturière,* Madam LE ROI
But am forc'd, dear, to have VICTORINE, who – deuce take her!
It seems is, at present, the king's mantua-maker –
I mean *of his party* – and, though much the smartest,
LE ROI is condemn'd as a rank Bonapartist.

T. Brown, *The Fudge Family in Paris* (London, 1818), pp. 135–6.

73   Grand Livre, 4, f. 286.
74   *Ibid.*
75   Grand Livre, 4, f. 325; Grand Livre, 5, f. 1.
76   See Auger, 'Notice sur L.H. LeRoy' (1830), pp. 150–4.
77   *Ibid.*, pp. 155–8.
78   J. Raymond, *The Reminiscences and Recollections of Captain Gronow* (London, 1964), p. 100.
79   Grand Livre, 4, Madame Choisy, ff. 285 and 357 (1814–15) and Comtesse Choisi, ff. 444 and 445 (1815–16). Madame Clermont-Tonnere, ff. 288 and 314 (1814–16) and Duchesse de Clermon-Tonnerre, Grand Livre, 5, f. 13 (1818–21).
80   Respectively, Grand Livre, 4, f. 273 (1816–18), f. 434 (1815), f. 383 (1814–15) and f. 307 (1814).
81   The Duke of Wellington was the British Ambassador to France at this time.
82   Respectively, Grand Livre, 4, ff. 116, 193 and 276 (1813–15) and f. 467 (1817).
83   Grand Livre, 4, ff. 338, 339, 340 (1814), ff. 367, 439, 450 (1814–16).
84   *Ibid.*, ff. respectively, 372 and 435 (1814–17) and Grand Livre, 5, f. 57 (1819); Grand Livre, 4, f. 224 (1818); Grand Livre, 4, f. 478 (1818); Grand Livre, 4, f. 150 (1813).
85   Grand Livre, 4, ff. 3, 20, 144, 226, 326, 396 (1812–16).
86   Sutherland, *Marie Walewska*, pp. 112–13.
87   Grand Livre, 4, ff. 3–396.
88   *Ibid.*, respectively, f. 22 (1814); f. 281 (1814); f. 311 (1814); ff. 100, 171 (1813, 1816) and Grand Livre, 5, f. 82 (1819); see also Princess Schawsemberg's account: she made purchases for Princess Esterhazy.
89   Grand Livre, 4, f. 114 (1812–13).
90   *Ibid.*, ff. respectively, 76, 210, 240, 353, 466 (1813–19); f. 236 (1813–14); Grand Livre, 5, f. 88 (1820); Grand Livre, 4, f. 405 (1816) and f. 252 (1814–15).
91   *Ibid.*, ff. respectively, 380, (1815–16); 264 (1814); Grand Livre, 5, f. 26 (1818); Grand Livre, 4, ff. 159 and 395 (1813–16).
92   *Ibid.*, ff. 159 and 395.
93   According to Napoleon's civil service, LeRoy's profit margin was higher than other milliners due to his reputation.
94   I am continuing to examine these questions about the importance of the milliner to the Parisian clothing system during my research for a PhD thesis being undertaken at the University of Southampton. The title of my thesis is 'Dressing Royalty: The Luxury Clothing Industry for Women in Paris 1795–1848'.

PART FIVE

Identity and display

Romanticism and the urge to consume in the first half of the nineteenth century

Introduction

Writing on the relationship between the romantic movement and the emergence of modern consumerism, a recent commentator has observed that

> Individuals do not so much seek satisfaction from products, as from the self-illusory experiences which they construct from their associated meanings. The essential activity of consumption is thus not the actual selection, purchase or use of products, but the imaginative pleasure-seeking to which the product image lends itself, 'real' consumption being largely a resultant of this 'mentalistic' hedonism.[1]

Rather than a device for displaying wealth and status, motivated by economic considerations, fuelled by modern marketing and made possible by the possession of surplus income,[2] consumption can be viewed as an act of the individual imagination, conditioned by the individual's pursuit of pleasure. Early nineteenth-century observers, notably Coleridge, were aware of the existence of a new form of 'hedonistic self-consciousness', the product of romanticism, acting to define social behaviour,[3] and the imaginative underpinnings of consumer behaviour are repeatedly demonstrated in contemporary accounts of goods and their acquisition.

Young women were acutely conscious of the subtle messages contained in objects and even in the colours that objects assumed. Elizabeth Grant, the daughter of a lawyer and minor landowner who lived in Edinburgh in the first few decades of the nineteenth century, in a passing observation on the fashions of the day, expressed this to perfection.

> We were inundated this whole winter [1815–16] with a deluge of a dull ugly colour called Waterloo blue, copied from the dye used in Flanders for the calico of which the peasantry make their smock frocks or blouses. Every thing new was Waterloo, not unreasonably, it had been such a victory, such an event, after so many years of exhausting suffering. And as a surname to hats, coats, trowsers, instruments, furniture it was very well – a fair way of trying to perpetuate the return of tranquillity; but to deluge us with that vile indigo, so unbecoming even to the fairest! It was really a punishment.[4]

A 'Waterloo hat' in 1815 was a fashionable product with intense 'associated meaning'. It evoked a spirit of heroic nationalism, coupled with the emotions arising out of victory and the hope for peace. It conjured a poignant connection with a land at some distance from Britain, where a simple peasantry attired in traditional rural dress had had their lives and world ripped apart by modern warfare. Though Elizabeth Grant was repelled by the colour, she writes with the assumption that such association between events, places and artefacts was natural and commonplace; as, indeed, it had become by the early nineteenth century. She also assumes that it was natural that she and those who shared her social world would wish to acquire such products in order to express their sense of cultural belonging. The relationship between the 'Waterloo hat' with its complex associations and the desire among individuals to possess such an object is an illustration of romantic 'mentalistic hedonism'.

Popular romanticism

Spanning the years from c. 1775 to 1825,[5] with blander manifestations of some of the same ideas remaining powerful into the 1840s in the form of the Biedermeier movement, romanticism was a complex sociocultural phenomenon that emerged in Britain, Europe and North America partly as a reaction against the intellectualism and rationalism of the Enlightenment. As preached and practised by some of its foremost advocates, it was a movement that opposed modern consumerism and evoked a spirit of restraint. It was also elitist in many of its preoccupations. Wordsworth condemned the rise of urbanism and its attendant commercial evils and Blake criticised the new mass art-production techniques, the consequence of a brutal commercial age that had robbed art of its inspiration and reduced it to a mechanical 'industry' to meet the insatiable demand of a public without taste.[6] Yet to see romanticism as a rarefied movement of opposition is to minimise the degree to which it was rooted in and perpetuated earlier popular cultural developments.[7] Like the Enlightenment, it provided an affirmation of individualism. It took certain Enlightenment ideas, notably that of sensibility, and developed the concept into an intense preoccupation with the cultivation of individual emotions.[8] Though critical of the debasing power of the market, popular manifestations of romanticism were intimately tied to modern commercialism. Indeed, the movement flourished throughout the western world and was particularly popular among the middle classes, because its cultural products were manufactured and marketed by some of the most commercially minded producers of the age and because it was tied to the spirit of modern consumption.

Romanticism encouraged a focus on the self and the cultivation of unstated emotions, imagination and intuition. Its philosophy was transcendental and idealist. Its politics were revolutionary and passionately nationalistic. Its theorists and popularisers expressed an antipathy to some of the starker tendencies of contemporary life, seeking refuge in an idealised past of humane social relationships and solace in the natural world. Romanticism gave rise to a psychological state of 'longing and a permanently unfocused dissatisfaction',[9] which became one of the defining characteristics of the modern mindset. This was important for the encouragement of consumerism both in the early nineteenth century and since. There was an easy transition from longing for some hard-to-define emotional fulfilment to longing for those material objects that could act as proxy for the emotions and thus make them real.

In order to be experienced and expressed, romanticism was reified in the world of goods, and objects or even colours – such as Waterloo blue – became visible signs of an essentially amorphous state of mind. As a result of this relationship, the period witnessed major developments in the mass production, distribution and internationalisation of goods of personal consumption. Ready-made clothing and furniture, the large-scale publishing of books and magazines, and the technology of musical instruments all evolved at this time. Art became increasingly commercialised and the leisure and tourist industries came into existence. Houses became sites in which goods that were laden with emotional associations were located and, through dress and posture, the physical body was employed to evoke a romantic frame of mind.

The consumption of art and music

The cultivation of the emotions, which was a central expression of romanticism, was achieved for many through creativity in the arts. This encouraged a desire for the material objects and facilities that allowed access to the arts as both audience and practitioner: such things as books and magazines for poetry and fiction, musical instruments, sheet music and attendance at concerts, the purchase of art and attendance at art classes and galleries. Provincial art-making flourished as a consequence in the first thirty years of the nineteenth century. In Scotland, the portrait painter Henry Raeburn, knighted in 1822, was the first to establish a national reputation based on a local Edinburgh clientele. Women were primary consumers in this sphere. In the mid-eighteenth century most of the art to be found in middle-rank houses represented a male political and rational agenda. It was dominated by images of men in public life and was found in those rooms in the home that were given over to male socialising. There were relatively few images of women in domestic art collections, but sixty years later this was reversed. Early nineteenth-century art collections were female selected, containing many images of women and children, located in rooms that had evolved around a female domestic agenda and dominated by themes and iconographies that evoked the romantic spirit.[10] The mass consumption of art was encouraged by producers and through new institutions of middle-class patronage.

Provincial art unions were founded in all the major cities of Europe in the first two decades of the century, providing accessible galleries for the display of original art and facilities for the production of engravings. In Scotland as elsewhere, these tended to favour local subject matter, with Highland scenes dominating the output. By the mid-nineteenth century the consumption of art had permeated even the poorest sections of society.[11]

Women were also found among the growing ranks of art producers. The most notable were Angelica Kauffman and Maria Cosway, portrait artists specialising in female and child subjects, whose work was widely engraved for the popular market.[12] The former was also a successful decorative arts designer. Numerous miniature painters were women, and women also produced designs for fashionable china and textile manufacturers.[13] The early nineteenth century saw a flourishing trade in art classes and art schools for the lady amateur, some of them operated by distinguished artists or by their wives or daughters. Alexander Nasmyth created such a school in Edinburgh, which was run by his two daughters, who were both talented artists in their own right.[14] Art manuals aimed at the female consumer were also produced in large numbers.[15] With an emphasis on natural subjects and landscape, women were encouraged to develop their creative talents in the hope that art would give rise to emotional sensitivity and moral renewal.

Through modern advertising and the new technologies of print production the book industry was swiftly changing at this time.[16] Pictures in words were consumed in vast quantities in the form of romantic poetry and fiction, which reached an audience that was unsurpassed by any earlier genre of literature. The emphasis, again, was on an engagement with the emotions, particularly through the representation of landscape and nature, as well as depictions of the spirit of individual creativity, heroism or nationalism.[17] Certain romantic writers – Byron was the most dramatic case – exemplified in their private histories the romantic spirit that was depicted in their art. Life was art – and the art of biography, another popular commercial-romantic genre, evolved in this context.

Art and books were luxuries, areas of consumption that in previous ages had been the preserve of the rich. A third area of luxury consumption that became a mass phenomenon during the early nineteenth century was musical instruments and sheet music. Britain produced more musical instruments and published more music than any other European country and both areas of business were associated with remarkable technical and marketing innovation. The most popular instrument and the easiest to play was the piano, which developed to replace the harpsichord from the 1770s and was commonly regarded in Europe as quintessentially 'anglais'.[18] The company of John Broadwood – a Scot by background, but trading in London – produced 400 pianos each year in the twenty years to 1802 and by 1824, with steam-powered manufacture, was able to achieve an annual output of almost 1,700 instruments, at lower prices than before the turn of the century.[19] British makers coined the terms 'grand', 'cabinet' and 'cottage' to denote the different sizes of piano being made to suit the range of domestic accommodation and purchasing power that was found among the middle classes in Europe.[20] By 1810, most middle-class houses contained a piano. They were valuable pieces of furniture, prominently placed in the most public rooms in the house and clearly represented an important investment.[21] Other instruments such as harps were also commonplace. Elizabeth Grant favoured the harp over the piano.[22]

The new prominence given to musical instruments reflected the fact that music was widely considered to be the 'most romantic of all the arts'[23] and an appropriate vehicle for emotional expression among young women. It allowed gently raised girls, bound to the drawing room, to express their passion for nature, to empathise with the sufferings of others and indulge in a nostalgia-laden longing for the simple rural life. Music printing from type rather than more costly engraving was pioneered in Britain in the later eighteenth century, giving rise to the mass production of cheap sheet music on popular themes. The events of 1793 led the London-based composer-publisher Dussek to produce a hugely popular sonata entitled *The Sufferings of the Queen of France*.[24] Commercial engravings of the subject were also available to adorn the drawing room wall.[25] The same composer, responding to the vast demand for music to represent nationalist and military themes, produced such piano works as *The Naval Battle and Total Destruction of the Dutch Fleet by Admiral Duncan, Oct. 11, 1797,* depicting the various stages of the famed defence of Ireland at Camperdown. Again, it was mainly purchased and played by women.[26] Duncan, who lived in Edinburgh, was a hero to rival Nelson north of the border. A painting of his bold victory was commissioned from the London-based American artist John Singleton Copley to adorn a public building in his native Dundee. It was paid for by a voluntary local tax on property and became the subject of numerous engravings.[27]

Tourism and the leisure industry

A defining characteristic of the romantic movement was the preoccupation with 'expansion'. Expansion of emotional range, expansion of experience of places and time, and expansion of contact with physical space.[28] Domestic objects and architecture were often designed to evoke a sense of the exotic, or of places and times in the past that were laden with romantic associations.[29] The vogue for gothic design reflected this expansion, as did the craze in the 1820s for design motifs taken from ancient Egypt.[30] The preoccupation with travel was another aspect of expansion. As middle-class men became more urban, desk-bound and commerce driven, many developed a restless wanderlust of the kind that is illustrated in the poetry of Wordsworth, who found moral renewal in strenuous country walking.[31] Expansion and wanderlust, coupled with a romantic preoccupation with nature in its virgin state and with certain types of landscape, notably the sublime landscape of mountains, rivers and torrents, generated a desire to visit those areas of Europe where such awesome and 'unaltered' nature was to be found.

If the landscape was also rich in historical associations, it was doubly attractive to the romantic traveller.

Tourism had existed on a modest scale prior to the romantic age. The 'grand tour' of European centres of art and civilisation was long established as a central institution in the education of wealthy young men[32] and tours of sites of great antiquity had been popular among the intellectual elite since the mid-eighteenth century.[33] But romantic tourism was of a different character, available to women as well as men, undertaken by growing numbers of the ordinary middle classes as a regular event and increasingly defined by commercial considerations. By 1830 there were timetabled transport services to meet the demands of the tourist trade. Tourist hotels and inns were booming and personal guides were readily available. Typical of such tourists were John Bowman and John Dovaston, middle-aged friends from Lancashire, one a banker, the other a lawyer, who took a month-long trip to the Highlands in 1825.[34] Two years before they had made a similar tour through the Lake District.

Though practical men of business, while on holiday they conformed to the spirit of romanticism. To quote Bowman in Perthshire:

> sublimity sat enthroned on every cloud cap'd summit on which the eye could rest. Ben Arthur was now very near us, frowning in terrific grandeur. His top is dreadfully rended, as if by the explosion of some mighty subterranean power and is composed of huge pointed and shattered blocks, piled on end like a vast and complicated Druidical remain, which absolutely curl and overhang the frightful crater within. The sight of it made us absolutely shudder.[35]

Bowman's journal demonstrates the extent to which tourism had become regimented and consumption driven, despite the participants' ostensible motivation to achieve contact with nature in its undisturbed forms. It also reveals an international dimension so typical of the 'romantic experience', where ever it was found:

> At the inn we met with several Italian gentlemen who had just returned from Staffa and had been highly gratified. One of them spoke excellent English and was a man of superior manners and attainments. They were very warm in their admiration of Scotch scenery, and allowed that . . . it was not equalled on the Continent. The gentleman named above had walked through Switzerland with Mr Hutchinson a few months before he effected the liberation of Lavalette; had ascended Etna etc etc . . .[36]

For individuals unable to visit the Highlands in person, a vicarious experience was possible through music – the wild island of Staffa was immortalised in music just a few years later in Mendelssohn's instantly popular 'Hebrides Overture' ('Fingals Cave')[37] – and also through reading. In the 1760s there were only seven published descriptions of personal tours and travels in Scotland. Fifty-three were published in the 1820s, some of them bestsellers.[38] Novels and poetry provided powerful images of romantic landscapes. By the 1820s it was easy to buy engraved images of Highland or Lake District scenery. Souvenir trinkets designed to evoke an emotional association were also produced from this time. The coming of photography and the railway made romantic tourism accessible to a wider group and intensified its commercial and consumption-driven characteristics.

The craze for visiting the Highlands in order to indulge in the 'romantic experience' had a critical impact on the economy of the region and on the ordinary people that lived there. It brought prosperity to those landowners who invested in the inns and transport services and gave employment to some of the peasantry, though of a type that was divorced from their usual occupations. But more than that, it generated a cultural blindness to some of the discomforting realities of life in that part of Britain. Dorothy Wordsworth's recollections of her Highland tour of 1803 in the company of her brother William and their friend Coleridge, provide a telling account of the beauties of the landscape alongside frequent expressions of lack of sympathy for the people that lived there. The manifest poverty of the latter is attributed to slovenliness and their language and preoccupations dismissed as barbaric.[39] Romantic tourists preferred a landscape devoid of people – or with figures alone and safely placed at a distance, as in Wordsworth's poem *The Solitary Reaper*, 'Behold her, single in the field, Yon solitary Highland Lass!'. The ambiguity of an impoverished peasantry living in the richest country in the world was hard to accommodate among lowland Scots, never mind among English or European visitors. The ruthlessness of clearance policies was also incompatible with a cultural agenda based on pleasure seeking. It was easier to ignore the phenomenon when it came into sight, a facility provided in later decades by the buffer of a commercialised tourist industry. Dorothy Wordsworth mentioned the local people in tones of exasperation because she and her party relied on them to get by on their travels; later tourists did not need them and wrote as though there were no indigenous population living in the Highlands. The aestheticisation of the region inevitably meant that when disaster finally struck in the form of the famines and evictions of the 1840s, middle-class tourists hardly noticed until it became a subject for newspaper enquiry and entered the sphere of everyday politics.

Tourism evolved hand in hand with a developing vogue for country house visiting, particularly of houses in romantic landscapes. Encouraged by the owners, who sought to impress with their taste and wealth and who also hoped to enhance their incomes through investment in the tourist infrastructure on their estates, the middle classes flocked to observe at first hand how the vastly wealthy furnished their houses and conducted their lives.[40] Jane Austen in *Pride and Prejudice* (1813) provides a typical illustration in her account of Elizabeth Bennet's tour of the Peak District, in the company of her aunt and uncle from London. In addition to observing the Derbyshire countryside, they also visit a number of 'great houses', so many, indeed, that Elizabeth remarks 'she must own that she was tired of great houses: after going over so many, she really had no pleasure in fine carpets or satin curtains'. Highland landowners made their houses available to respectable visitors for a small fee, donated to a favoured charity, or more often the perquisite of the butler or housekeeper. Walter Scott allowed visitors to Abbotsford, but was soon overwhelmed with the demand. Tourists became a plague in his life, appearing at all times of the day to demand access to this shrine to romanticism. 'Talking of Abbotsford', he wrote in 1825, 'it begins to be haunted by too much company of every kind, but especially foreigners. I do not like them . . .'.[41]

Just as romantic tourism was encouraged by reading, the interest in country house visiting was stimulated by published descriptions of upper-class lifestyles in illustrated magazines and also in fiction, the latter termed 'silver fork' novels. Enormously popular in the 1820s and 1830s, such novels were notable for their emphasis on elite clothing and deportment and particularly for their accounts of dining and other social rituals – which included copious descriptions of table services, the decoration of rooms, the role of servants and such minutiae as the number of silver forks that were required to eat fish in fashionable circles. Often written by impecunious aristocrats and always with an emphasis on fashionable London life, 'silver fork' novels included details of the names of real shops, or restaurants, or suppliers of luxury services – a form of 'advertising *orné*' which doubtless brought financial benefits to the authors.[42] This enhanced knowledge of wealth and its attendant luxuries, gleaned by the middle classes through popular tourism and enhanced by the reading of carefully targeted commercial literature, both reflected and fuelled an urge to consume.

Nationalism and possessions

Romanticism stimulated the rise of modern nationalism. Coinciding with long years of war in Europe and with the early stages of modern state building, the romantic spirit – though a truely international phenomenon – encouraged an emotional identification with the historical processes that defined national differences. Signalling an attachment to national identity was commonly achieved through possessions. A striking example is furnished by Scotland, where textiles and clothing of a particular type – supposedly of great antiquity, but in practice not – were adopted in the early nineteenth century as non-threatening symbols of a distinct cultural identity that could be held simultaneously with political attachment to Great Britain.[43] Since Scotland was widely regarded in both its history and landscape as epitomising the essence of romanticism, non-Scots eager to signal their romantic credentials also adopted the dress and paraphernalia of Scottishness. English and foreign tourists in Scotland decked themselves in tartan and kilts. And during his visit to Paris in 1828, Sir Walter Scott was surprised to discover that Russian ladies at court were all dressed in tartan.[44] The demand was such that it spawned new areas of textile production. Manufacturers were supported by 'ancient' documents that purported to show the different tartans of the various clans. The fact that these were newly invented did not diminish the romantic wish to identify with the potent symbolism of tartan.[45]

Nationalism generated a need for heroes, men who embodied the nobility of the nation, who defended the people from threat from outside or were leaders in struggles to achieve political freedom. Seafaring heroism was especially popular in Britain. There was a passionate interest in all matters relating to Nelson, a romantic figure with a poignant love life, who made the ultimate sacrifice of his own life for his country. This preoccupation was translated into many different types of consumer objects, as shown in Edinburgh during the building of the New Town. Largely intended for middle-class occupancy, New Town houses, built by speculative builders with an eye to current fashions, contained elaborate interior plaster work and chimney pieces that evoked in their design the essence of romanticism. One of the largest producers of chimney surrounds was the firm of Rammage and Fergusson of Leith, who manufactured in Scots pine and painted gesso, in cheap imitation of carved white marble. One of their most popular designs, usually found in drawing rooms,[46] depicts a pensive young woman in swirling muslin dress, leaning against an anchor and looking out to sea where she espies a ship in the distance, tossed about on the ocean. The figure is Emma Hamilton, archetype of the grieving woman awaiting the return of her love, or possibly Britannia, mourning the loss of her sailors at sea. These chimney pieces were embellished with a range of seaside imagery such as shells and starfish, seaweed and coral. They also contain references to the union between Scotland and England in the form of thistles intertwined with roses and have images of plenty in the form of cornucopias of fruit and grain.[47]

Biedermeier and the taming of romanticism

In its pure form, romanticism had many disturbing implications for the ordinary middle classes. Its nihilistic tendencies, brooding introspection, emotional excess and rejection of many aspects of rational modernity were often seen as socially dangerous. The response to the publication of Goethe's *Sorrows of Young Werther* in 1774, the clarion-call for romanticism, is indicative of this. Enormously popular with young people throughout Europe, there was an immediate vogue for emulating the style of Werther in clothing and demeanour. Yellow breeches and blue top coats were widely adopted by young men as a sort of uniform, to be worn while engaged in pensive wanderings in solitary places. But Werther was a character who pursued a married woman, who descended into melancholy and depression when that lady rejected him and who finally killed himself for love.[48] Such behaviour was not considered by an older generation to be a morally acceptable model for the young and nor was the behaviour depicted in many popular works of fiction, particularly those that fell within the romantic gothic genre.

The response in literature, as in everyday life, was a taming of romantic ideas into forms that could be more easily accommodated within prevailing notions of moral relationships and social stability. That taming was manifested in a frame of mind and way of living, roughly spanning the years from 1815 to the 1840s and prefiguring many aspects of Victorianism, that within the European context is generally known as the 'Biedermeier'.[49] The name is derived from Gottlieb Biedermeier, a smug, wealthy, old-fashioned provincial philistine, who first appeared as a comic character in a popular German magazine of 1855. Initially used as a term of derision for a social type and style of life that had become passé, by 1900 'Biedermeier' had been adopted to describe the arts, decorative arts and other aspects of material life that were distinct to the wealthy middle classes in the first half of the nineteenth century.

In literature, the essence of Biedermeier 'taming' was to be found in the domestication of the romantic spirit and the association that was drawn between extremes of romantic feeling and youthful immaturity. This was particularly marked in popular fiction in Britain,[50] as in the work of Walter Scott, whose *Waverley*, published in 1814, like *Werther*, was an instant Europe-wide romantic bestseller, but with subtle differences in tone and plot. Waverley is a fanciful and ill-disciplined young man, whose emotional excesses and wanderlust are cured by his experience of life. The story ends with the hero's transition to maturity, social conformity and the achievement of domestic harmony through a suitable marriage. In this, as in other novels of the type, there is a considerable preoccupation with the character and trappings of the home. Romanticism was tamed by bringing it within the orbit of family and domestic emotions and buttressing those emotions with a particular style of material life. Domesticated music making was one feature of this. Increasingly elaborate notions of good relationships between parents and children, which translated into a massive paraphernalia of goods to define infancy and childhood, was another. As, indeed, was the growing desire for a domestic existence away from city pressures, with an inward-looking privacy and capacity to indulge in the balming influence of nature through a private garden, however small.

The vogue for engagement with nature in a form that was morally and socially compatible with family values was secured through the reading of another type of popular literature. The 1820s saw the first proliferation of provincial novels describing countrified and suburban styles of living. The most important author in this genre was Mary Russell Mitford, whose short stories, collectively published under the title *Our Village*, enjoyed unsurpassed popularity among the middle classes. Describing simple village life in the recent past, setting the ordinary lives and loves of familiar rustic figures in a background of picturesque landscapes and cottage gardens, the stories first appeared in print in 1819 in the *Ladies Magazine*, whose principal fare hitherto had comprised accounts of fashionable dress for women. Within a few months, the tales of *Our Village* were said to have quadrupled the sales of that journal. The conjoining of cosmopolitan high consumerism with evocations of rural simplicity and provincial cottage culture seems a paradox, but was, in reality, easily accommodated within the tamed romantic psyche of the British middle classes. Five volumes of stories of *Our Village* were published between 1824 and 1832, Miss Mitford made a fortune from these objects of consumption and the middle classes reinvented their ways of material existence.[51] The Scottish parallel, though with more darkly Calvinist undertones, was the stunningly popular *Annals of the Parish* (1821) by John Galt, whose romantic credentials were reinforced by his friendship with and later biography of Byron.

Luxury and loss

Underpinning the relationship between romanticism and the urge to consume was a preoccupation with loss. Lost love, lost causes, the loss of life and the loss of riches were central concerns in this sometimes melancholy age. Tragic events that in the past may well have been addressed through solace in religion were now, at a time of increasing secularisation, articulated and resolved through material possessions and through objects and clothing as symbols of a state of mind. One of the striking outcomes of the preoccupation with luxury and loss was the aestheticisation and commodification of death and mourning. This began in the 1820s with the new garden cemeteries that were built on the outskirts of large cities to house the grand funery monuments of the urban middle classes. The new cemetery in Glasgow – the Necropolis – was typical (Plate 25). Founded out of necessity, given the dangerously unhealthy state of antique churchyards in a burgeoning industrial city,

25 View of the Necropolis, Glasgow. From Peter Buchan, *Glasgow Cathedral and Necropolis* (Glasgow, 1843)

it swiftly came to be described in local guide books in terms that evoked the picturesque and romantic landscape, gave prominence to the architecture of the monuments and dwelt at length on the melancholy beauty of the place. The cemetery here, as elsewhere, became an object for the tourist's gaze.[52] The commodification and attendant commercialisation of death gathered force in the 1830s and 1840s through the elaboration of mourning dress and mourning rituals to become one of the defining characteristics of Victorian material culture. By the mid-nineteenth century, an industry employing vast numbers had been founded to service the doleful business of death and to salve, in appropriate fashion, the attendant sense of personal loss.

Financial loss was also a major preoccupation in a world where so many of the newly enriched middle classes had a recent background in poverty and hardship. The first thirty years of the nineteenth century saw much economic instability which inevitably resulted in loss of wealth and frequent bankruptcies. Genteel poverty became a new and socially accepted phenomenon and a stock characteristic of many figures in literature.[53] The 1820s saw much legislation on the subject of bankruptcy and popular pressure to decriminalise such personal tragedy through the abolition of imprisonment for debt.[54] Romantic interpretations of financial loss stressed the human dimension, elevated the emotional impact, accorded a certain heroic status to those who struggled to overcome their crises and sought sympathetic understanding for those individuals who were unable to succeed in a ruthlessly competitive commercial world.

Art at this time reflected the middle-class preoccupation with luxury and loss. One of the most popular pictures to be exhibited at the Royal Academy in London in 1815, and also widely engraved for the mass market, was David Wilkie's 'Distraining for the Rent'. A classic romantic genre scene, it shows a Scottish rural family in a state of great distress, in the main room of their farmhouse and having their domestic property inventoried by court officials prior to sale for non-payment of rent. Friends and neighbours plead for their cause, but to no avail. Though a modest interior, there are numerous objects that are up-to-date and fashionable, such as chairs, the bed and a washstand with china basin and jug. Yet there is no implied criticism of such consumption; indeed, the emotions evoked by the image are those of sympathy and understanding for the loss. The picture was a social commentary on the wave of bankruptcies and evictions that beset the farming classes in the period of economic downturn following the end of the French wars. The objects that are about to be lost are the cement of family life and emotional attachments. Though popular with the middle-class public, who empathised with the situation, it caused a storm among the aristocratic elite, who saw it as an attack on landlords. One noble critic was outraged that the artist had not made it clear that the tenants were shiftless and idle and the 'distraint' was wholly justified.[55]

Financial loss was not only felt by the working population. Land-owners who indulged in excessive expenditure during the heady days of wartime prosperity found themselves in desperate situations by the 1820s. This was particularly true and poignant among Highland lairds, many of whom lost their estates and clan lands at this time. Colonel Alastair Ranaldson Macdonell, fifteenth Chief of Glengarry, was a romantic consumer in spectacular and eccentric style. Though educated in Eng-land and on the 'grand tour', throughout adulthood from the 1790s to 1820s he indulged in a 'fantasy' Highland life. Dressed in tartan with a retinue of clan followers similarly attired at his own expense – includ-ing pipers and bardic poets – he hunted, gave balls, hosted Highland games, founded Gaelic societies and promoted his own brand of mytho-logised clan 'traditions'. He owned a fine estate and several houses. Invergarry House was let along with the shooting rights from 1810. His main residence was Garry Cottage, a modest but picturesque villa on the Tay about a mile from Perth. He also had a summer house at Inverie on Loch Nevis, a bizarre place built to his own instruction and unusual for the fact that half of the house – comprising the dining room, drawing room and several bedrooms – was constructed in the ancient wattle system, with Scots fir beams rising from a clay floor and a ceiling of beams and woven hazel.[56]

Macdonell of Glengarry was a cultivated romantic – in the words of Walter Scott, 'this gentleman is a kind of Quixote in our age, having retained, in their fullest extent, the whole feelings of clanship and chieftainship, elsewhere so long abandoned. He seems to have lived a century too late . . .'.[57] Scott's fictional Jacobite Fergus McIvor in *Waverley* was modelled on Glengarry and the flamboyance of the man is equally captured in the great swagger portrait by Raeburn, painted in 1812. But by the mid-1820s decades of extravagance had brought him to the brink of ruin. He died in 1828 as the result of a steamship accident – a decidedly unromantic fate – and left his estate in such a parlous situation that his family were forced to sell the whole of the property. His wife and children moved to Edinburgh and his heir, who was a minor at the time of his father's death, later emigrated to Australia. Clan tradition swiftly characterised Glengarry as a romantically heroic failure.

26 The Antiquary's 'Sanctum sanctorum', from Sir Walter Scott, *The Antiquary* (London, n.d.)

Walter Scott, a friend and soulmate of Glengarry, provides a further illustration of that form of romantic heroism that could be constructed out of the relationship between luxury and loss. A lawyer by profession, from an ordinary bourgeois background, Scott's great financial folly was Abbotsford, a house that he built in the borders of Scotland in the 1820s in emulation of a gothic castle and that he filled with artefacts in great profusion to lend material substance to his ideas about the past (Plate 26). He was successful in his professional practice and deeply involved in the commercial world as a partner in a publishing firm. His income was vast and entirely absorbed by his conspicuous, almost manic consumption of objects to embellish Abbotsford. When he was bankrupted in 1826, the result of mismanagement in the book trade and in a climate of speculative upheaval, Scott was forced to sell his family home in Edinburgh, to retreat to Abbotsford in broken health and spirits, to witness the early death of his wife and spend his remaining few years attempting to pay off his creditors through the relentless production of new fiction for a romance-hungry public. His struggle to achieve an honourable acquittal of his debts was well publicised and widely applauded. He invented himself as a tragic hero, an image that was promoted following his death in 1832 in numerous biographies. Throughout this time, he continued to consume and to add to the fabulous and fabulised contents of Abbotsford.[58]

Conclusion

Romantic consumerism was not just the preserve of the literary elite or of fanciful and foolish lairds in Scotland. In his business and family life, Scott was typical of the middle classes and the middle classes certainly identified with him and with his ultimate tragedy. His refuge in the material world was equally common. Scott was a classic exemplar of the self-conscious, mentalistic hedonism that underpinned consumerism during the romantic age and which was certainly to be found among the more prosaic elements of the middle-class population elsewhere. It was a phenomenon that was to remain powerful throughout the nineteenth century in many areas of middle-class life. The Victorian sentimentalisation of objects had its foundations in romanticism, as did their adoption of gothic architecture and the vogue for themes of chivalry in popular poetry and art. Indeed, romantic consumerism retains a popular vigour even today, most notably in the tourist industry and in many areas of mass leisure. A holiday in the Highlands is normally undertaken in the late twentieth century in order to engage in a similar aesthetic experience to that which was sought almost two centuries ago. Though 'sun, sand and sex' do exist in north-west Scotland, these are not commodities that we tend to look for in a holiday in that part of the world. What we seek, of course, is an escape into a transcendental nature; an indulgence in a past world of greater excitement, colour and humanity than we think we have today; a brief encounter with Eden. All of which is made more enjoyable with up-to-date maps and tourist guide books and when viewed from the comforts of reliable trains or fast cars, with decent B&Bs or country house hotels to lodge in and friendly tea rooms and craft shops to visit along the way.

Notes

1   C. Campbell, *The Romantic Ethic and the Spirit of Modern Consumerism* (Oxford, 1987), p. 89.
2   The broad argument behind much of the consumerism literature: see N. McKendrick, J. Brewer and J.H. Plumb, *The Birth of A Consumer Society: The Commercialization of Eighteenth-Century England* (1982).
3   Campbell, *Romantic Ethic*, p. 73.
4   E. Grant, *Memoirs of a Highland Lady* (Edinburgh, 1997), vol. 2, p. 35.
5   The symbolic starting point is often regarded as the publication in 1774 of Goethe's novel *The Sorrows of Young Werther*.
6   M. Eaves, *The Counter-Arts Conspiracy: Art and Industry in the Age of Blake* (Ithaca, 1992), ch. 4.
7   M. Brown, 'Romanticism and Enlightenment', in Stuart Curran, ed., *The Cambridge Companion to British Romanticism* (Cambridge, 1993), pp. 25–47.
8   See F.W. Hilles *From Sensibility to Romanticism: Essays Presented to Frederick Pottle* (Oxford, 1965); G.J. Barker-Benfield, *The Culture of Sensibility: Sex and Society in Eighteenth-Century Britain* (Chicago, 1992).
9   Campbell, *Romantic Ethic*, p. 87.
10   For details, see S. Nenadic, 'Print Collecting and Popular Culture in Eighteenth-Century Scotland', *History*, 82 (1997), 203–22.
11   P. Anderson, *The Printed Image and the Transformation of Popular Culture, 1790–1860* (Oxford, 1994), provides examples.
12   W. Roworth, ed., *Angelica Kauffman: A Continental Artist in Georgian England* (London, 1992); S. Lloyd, *Richard and Maria Cosway: Regency Artists of Taste and Fashion* (Edinburgh, 1995).
13   One of the most notable was Lady Dianna Beauclerk, an impoverished aristocrat who produced designs for Wedgwood.
14   See F. Irwin, 'Lady Amateurs and Their Masters in Scott's Edinburgh', *The Connoisseur*, 187, December 1974.
15   F. Irwin, 'Amusement or Instruction? Watercolour Manuals and the Woman Amateur', in C. Campbell Orr, ed., *Women in the Victorian Art World* (Manchester, 1995), pp. 149–66.
16   D. Vincent, *Literacy and Popular Culture: England, 1750–1914* (Cambridge, 1991).
17   See L.J. Swingle, 'Wordsworth's "Picture of the Mind"', in K. Kroeber and W. Walling, eds, *Images of Romanticism: Verbal and Visual Affinities* (New Haven, 1978), pp. 81–90.
18   C. Ehrlich, *The Piano: A History* (Oxford, 1990), p. 17.
19   A. Loesser, *Men, Women and Pianos: A Social History* (New York, 1954), pp. 234–5.
20   *Ibid.*, p. 250.
21   S. Nenadic, 'Middle Rank Consumers and Domestic Culture in Edinburgh and Glasgow, 1720–1840', *Past and Present*, 145 (1994), pp. 122–56.
22   The Musgrove girls in Jane Austen's *Persuasion* are also harp players.
23   H.G. Schenk, *The Mind of the European Romantics: An Essay in Cultural History* (London, 1966), p. 201.

24   Loesser, *Men, Women and Pianos*, p. 252.
25   This was one of the main items in the inventory of stock of Edward Jee, a bankrupt Birmingham print publisher in 1799: Nenadic, 'Print Collecting', p. 209.
26   Loesser, *Men, Women and Pianos*, p. 253.
27   An exhibition of contemporary paintings and other images celebrating this event was held in the National Gallery of Scotland to mark the 200th anniversary of Admiral Duncan's victory.
28   V. Nemoianu, *The Taming of Romanticism: European Literature and the Age of Biedermeier* (Cambridge, MA, 1984), p. 25.
29   *Ibid.*, p. 71.
30   For instance, the Carron Iron Company manufactured a 'Pyramid' stove to reflect this vogue: Scottish Record Office, GD58/16/3, Design Book.
31   Schenk, *The Mind of the European Romantics*, p. 164.
32   C. Hibbert, *The Grand Tour* (London, 1987).
33   T.C. Smout, 'Tours in the Scottish Highlands from the Eighteenth to the Twentieth Centuries', *Northern Scotland*, 5 (1983), pp. 99–121.
34   J.E. Bowman, *The Highlands and Islands: A Nineteenth-Century Tour* (Gloucester, 1986), p. ix.
35   *Ibid.*, p. 41.
36   *Ibid.*, p. 104.
37   For an account of romanticism in music, including the work of Mendelssohn, see C. Rosen, *The Romantic Generation* (Cambridge, MA, 1996).
38   S. Nenadic, 'Land, the Landed and Relationships with England: Literature and Perception, 1760–1830', in S.J. Connolly *et al.*, eds., *Conflict, Identity and Economic Development: Ireland and Scotland, 1600–1939* (Preston, 1995), p. 151.
39   D. Wordsworth, *Recollections of a Tour Made in Scotland*, introduced by C.K. Walker (New Haven, 1997).
40   A. Tinniswood, *A History of Country House Visiting: Five Centuries of Tourism and Taste* (Oxford, 1989).
41   *The Journal of Sir Walter Scott, 1825–32 from the Original Manuscript at Abbotsford* (Edinburgh, 1891), p. 13.
42   See A. Adburgham, *Silver Fork Society: Fashionable Life and Literature from 1814 to 1840* (London, 1983), pp. 213–15.
43   P. Womack, *Improvement and Romance: Constructing the Myth of the Highlands* (Basingstoke, 1988).
44   Scott, *Journal*, p. 299.
45   H. Trevor-Roper, 'The Invention of Tradition: The Highland Tradition of Scotland', in E. Hobsbawm, ed., *The Invention of Tradition* (Cambridge, 1983).
46   Dining room fireplaces were much plainer, normally of unembellished dark marble suitable for an essentially 'male' space.
47   D. Black, *Mr Adam's Chimneypiece: A Drawing Room Mystery* (Smailholm, 1995).
48   S. Pratt Atkins, *The Testament of Werther in Poetry and Drama* (New Haven, 1938).
49   See Nemoianu, *The Taming of Romanticism*, p. 4; H. Bisanz, ed., *Vienna in the Biedermeier Era, 1815–1848* (New York, 1986).
50   Jane Austen's *Northanger Abbey*, first published in 1818, is a satire on the gothic romance, as is also Thomas Love Peacock's *Nightmare Abbey*.
51   M. Russell Mitford, *Selected Stories from Our Village* (London, *c.* 1890). Details on publication are taken from the Introduction.

52 See, G. Blair, *Biographical Sketches of the Glasgow Necropolis* (Glasgow, 1857).

53 Commonly seen in Mitford's *Our Village*; also in the novels of Jane Austen and in Elizabeth Gaskell's *Cranford*, another set of stories of village life, first published in 1851.

54 L.V. Markham, *Victorian Insolvency: Bankruptcy, Imprisonment for Debt and Company Winding-Up in Nineteenth-Century England* (Oxford, 1995).

55 A.S. Marks, 'Paintings of David Wilkie to 1825', unpublished University of London PhD thesis (1968).

56 N.H. MacDonald, *The Clan Ranald of Knoydart and Glengarry: A History of the MacDonalds or Macdonells of Glengarry* (Edinburgh, 1995).

57 Scott, *Journal*, p. 120.

58 See C. Wainwright, *The Romantic Interior: The British Collector at Home, 1750–1850* (New Haven, 1989), chs 6 and 7 on Abbotsford.

11 ✆ CHARLOTTE KLONK

The National Gallery in London and its public

In 1868 Mary Ann Hoggins wrote to her friend Amelia Hodge about a visit to the National Gallery. After looking around for a while, she had turned to an elderly gentleman who was studying the works carefully and asked what he thought a particular portrait would cost, there being no prices on the pictures. 'What do you think that old party said,' she reported, amazed:

> but that them picters had cost thousands to the nation, which the government had bought them cheap at that. I looked at him scornful as haven't been away from the country to be took in like that, an says, 'You ought to know better, at your time o' life, to give yourself to such a falsity. 'An,' I says, 'I may be countrybred, but I've seen a-many better down the City-road as might be had frame and all,' I says, 'for eleven or twelve shillin's ...'.[1]

To mistake a public picture gallery for a market store would not have been so outrageous in the eighteenth century as it had become by the middle of the nineteenth century. In the eighteenth century, all public art exhibitions functioned, more or less openly, as market-places for artists' wares.[2] When the National Gallery was founded, however, a different notion prevailed. Its value was widely seen to lie precisely in the fact that it provided a realm for a different kind of consumption, a non-material, spiritual one. In an essay of 1848 on the National Gallery, Charles Kingsley, addressing himself to working people, laid out this vision for the museum:

> Therefore I said picture-galleries should be the townsman's paradise of refreshment ... There, in the space of a single room, the townsman

27 T.H. Shepherd, *Trafalgar Square*, c. 1843

> may take his country walk – a walk beneath mountain peaks, blushing
> sunsets, with broad woodlands spreading out below it; . . . and his hard-
> worn heart wanders out free, beyond the grim city-world of stone and
> iron, smoky chimneys, and roaring wheels, into the world of beautiful
> things . . .[3]

Never mind that landscape art was the genre least represented in the
National Gallery's collection of old master paintings, Kingsley's image
of the museum as an idyllic retreat had become a commonplace by
the mid-nineteenth century. The conception of museums as places
of aesthetic contemplation, set apart from the commercial world, lay
behind the foundation of the many national museums which sprang up
all over Europe in the first half of the nineteenth century.[4]

The National Gallery (Plate 27) was, in fact, one of the last
of the European state-founded museums to open. Although national
galleries were presented as refuges from social life, the way in which
their role was tied up with contemporary redefinitions of the nation
gave them considerable social importance.[5] Who understood what by
the term 'national' with regard to the museum; who was believed to be
representative of the nation; and what role the public consumption of
art was assumed to play in British society of the early nineteenth
century will be the subject of the following discussion.[6]

A gallery for the nation

In what sense might an art gallery be 'national'? One obvious way would be if the function of the gallery were to display exclusively the artistic products of a particular nation. Yet this was never the case with the National Gallery – or, indeed, with any of the other national galleries that were founded at around this time across Europe.[7] The idea, then, was less specific: that a national art gallery would contribute, in some way, to the national sense of identity. For Kingsley, the National Gallery was a proud emblem of national (English!) inclusiveness: 'In . . . the National Gallery alone the Englishman may say, "Whatever my coat or my purse, I am an Englishman, and therefore I have a right here. I can glory in these noble halls . . .".'[8] However, which nation was to be served by the Gallery became more contentious than ever in the years before and after the Reform Bill in 1832. The unprecedented popular agitation for the extension of the franchise was a clear sign to the government that the middle classes were no longer content to accept the sectional interests of the great landholders as representative of the nation as a whole.

The term 'nation' was, as has often been pointed out, a relatively recent invention in the terminology of political discourse, promoted by the revolution in communications.[9] Following the American and the French Revolutions it came to mean 'the body of citizens whose collective sovereignty constituted them a state which was their political expression'.[10] Thus its usage was initially political, referring first to a territory rather than to the supposed cultural and ethnic unit that the term was later to denote.[11] It was in this political sense that radicals, starting with John Wilkes in 1777, had urged the government to purchase an art collection for the nation.[12] In 1793, the Louvre opened to the public, demonstrating to the world the new French conception of citizenship and nationhood. Behind it lay the conviction that 'the joint ownership of nationalized art would forge communal bonds of belonging and loyalty to the state sufficient to dissolve preexisting differences of origin, class, race, and language'.[13] Similarly, British radicals wished to make the art treasures of the country a shared possession of the people, rather than the private property of the rich and powerful alone.[14]

Since the days of Hogarth, British aristocratic art collectors had been repeatedly attacked for their unpatriotic preference for old (and thus foreign) masters at the expense of native art.[15] As the dominant force in political life, their reluctance to establish public collections also came under fire in the years after the opening of the Louvre. In an attempt to ward off such criticism, some patrician art patrons, following the example of the Marquis of Stafford in 1806, started to open their collections to the public on a regular basis. A year earlier a group of them, including the Marquis and Sir John Leicester, had founded the British Institution, to which they lent generously from their own collections.[16] These were not freely accessible public enterprises – a shilling entrance fee was charged at the British Institution and, although the private collections were mainly free of charge, tickets had to be applied for and the applicant to be known to the family – but they showed that the arts were of concern to the ruling class.

That art reflected the rise and fall of societies, and the more civilised a society was the more its art flourished, had become a commonplace by the eighteenth century.[17] David Hume had argued the position,[18] and it appeared particularly in the work of other Scottish writers in the second half of the century.[19] The idea was taken up again by the aristocratic founders of the British Institution when, in 1805, they outlined the purpose of the institution in a pamphlet. Here, however, the emphasis was on the generous patronage system which was required if the arts were to develop: 'the pre-eminence, which the imitative arts attained in certain distinguished periods of ancient Greece and modern Italy, was produced, not by fortuitous circumstances, but by great and splendid patronage . . .'.[20]

It was one thing to demonstrate the flourishing of the arts under the elite's auspices, another to make it a state concern. With the example of France in mind, the British ruling class feared that a state-sponsored national institution, such as the National Gallery, would undermine their dominance.[21] But, in fact, the government, when it eventually bought the Angerstein collection for the nation, and installed it initially in its former owner's house at Pall Mall (Plate 28), continued the tradition of leaving the nation's artistic heritage in the hands of an elite of rich connoisseurs.

In their first formal meeting, held on 7 February 1828, the Trustees referred to the museum as the 'Royal National Gallery'.[22] What is striking about this is that (in contrast to other national galleries such as the Royal Museum of Berlin) no royal collection formed the nucleus of the National Gallery, nor was royal money provided to fund its building.[23] In Berlin, even the position of the museum (opposite the monarch's residence) symbolically asserted the leading role played by royal patronage in national life. In England prior to 1870, by contrast, there was, as David Cannadine has argued, a strong current of hostility towards any moves to enhance royal standing and power.[24]

28 F. Mackenzie, *Principal Original Room of the National Gallery, c.* 1830 to 1834

London saw no ostentatious building projects such as those on which other European cities were then embarking. By European standards, the National Gallery appeared mean and meagre, both before and after its move to Trafalgar Square (Plate 29). When the National Gallery opened in the new building, the *Times*, for example, judged that it was 'disgraceful to the national respectability to tolerate the existence, much more the original erection, of such a honeycomb of cells for the exhibition of those great works of art'.[25] In Europe similar public buildings were being designed to testify to the power of the state or of the monarch. Britain lacked this drive. Instead 'the squares and suburbs, railway stations and hotels, were monuments to the power and wealth of the *private* individual'.[26]

So, when the trustees privately started to call the National Gallery 'Royal' its significance was quite different from what it would have been in a Continental European context. The use of the term 'Royal' can best be understood as a defensive gesture on the part of the old elite, asserting its own claim to lead the nation in matters of taste.[27] The British aristocracy at that stage had no wish (or need) to promote the role of royalty as the head of the nation.

29 Charles Joseph Hullmandel, *The Louvre and 100 Pall Mall, c.* 1830

The function of the museum: the improvement of morals or of manufacture?

Tied in with this dispute was the question of the role art played in society and, consequently, what function the National Gallery should fulfil. Since the eighteenth century, artists had campaigned for public

support by using the argument that art was of public importance because its cultivation had the capacity to 'descend to the subordinate
Branches of Design' and so make home industry more competitive
internationally.[28] This argument was invoked more and more after the
turn of the century in support of calls for the establishment of a gallery
for the nation. It was an argument which was particularly congenial to
a large section of radicals. When in 1835 the House of Commons
appointed a Select Committee for the first time to enquire into the
state of the arts, it was this argument which chiefly appealed to the
utilitarian-inspired radicals who dominated its membership. The Committee was chaired by William Ewart, who was associated with James
and John Stuart Mill and the Benthamites. Of its fifteen members, only
three, apart from the chair, attended all its meetings; many members
did not even attend a single one. The three constant attendees were
the radicals, Joseph Brotherton and Henry Thomas Hope, and the
Benthamite, John Bowring.

Benthamism played a very prominent role in the world of British
political radicalism in the years immediately before and after the 1832
Reform Bill. In common with the other radicals, the Benthamites
agitated for the democratic reform of the British constitution and set
themselves against the entrenched system of inherited privilege: the
patronage system, the Church Establishment and the power of the local
magistracy.[29] But while other radicals concentrated on a single issue
(for instance, tariff reform, factory reform or the extension of the franchise) what made the Benthamite 'Philosophic Radicals' distinctive
was their integration of their attitude towards particular issues within
a philosophically stringent overall programme, and they went on to
become the strongest voice in opposition to the government after many
of their group were elected to Parliament in 1832.[30]

Notoriously, Benthamite utilitarianism gave the arts no distinctive value. It was Bentham, after all, who put the worth of poetry on a
level with that of push-pin.[31] The 'arts and sciences of amusement' –
under which category fell the fine arts – were valued by Bentham solely
for the pleasure directly produced by them, a pleasure which in any
case was only available to a small section of the population.[32] What
Bentham termed 'the arts and sciences of utility', on the other hand,
included knowledge applicable to manufacturing and were thus indirectly productive of utility. As John Stuart Mill noted, however,
Bentham's disciples did not go as far as Bentham himself in their regard
for the cultivation of the arts.[33] Bentham saw no need for the cultivation of the fine arts at public expense in rich and prosperous nations;

this he felt would be done by individuals.[34] The radicals who became members of the Select Committee, by contrast, argued for public patronage of the fine arts by claiming that they too acted as a stimulus to manufacturing and commerce. Witness after witness in the Committee's meetings answered variations of the following question: 'Do you consider the English manufactures superior as far as regards the manufacture of the goods, but inferior in that portion of them which is connected with the arts?'[35] Unanimously, they answered 'yes'. Great Britain was quantitatively ahead of other countries in terms of industrial output, but French luxury goods, such as fashionable clothing, china and furniture, were squeezing British manufactures both in foreign markets and at home. Consequently, in their report the Committee drew the conclusion that

> to us, a peculiarly manufacturing nation, the connexion between art and manufactures is most important; – and for this merely economical reason (were there no higher motive), it equally imports us to encourage art in its loftier attributes; since it is admitted that the cultivation of the more exalted branches of design tends to advance the humblest pursuits of industry, while the connexion of art with manufacture has often developed the genius of the greatest masters in design.[36]

The Philosophic Radicals lost their strong voice in Parliament towards the end of the 1830s and their vision of a people united against aristocratic privilege started to fall apart. The rise of the Chartist movement on the one hand, and the Anti-Corn Law groups on the other, testified to the emergence of a distinct class-consciousness among the working and middle classes and led to increasing conflict between the two groups. Beginning with the Birmingham Riots in 1839, the 1840s – years of hunger and acute distress among agricultural and industrial workers – saw a series of violent clashes between Chartist supporters and the police. One of the most riotous assemblies, brutally dispersed by the police, happened directly in front of the National Gallery in March 1848.[37] Although the Chartist insurrections were suppressed by the end of the 1840s, the movement engendered a strong sense of working-class identity which was to continue in the politics of the labour movement in the second half of the century.[38]

This increasing separation between the classes reinforced rather than challenged the conservatives' hierarchical view of art and its consumers.[39] Artists who had made it to the top of the art establishment wished to establish themselves as above commerce and so they played down the connection between the cultivation of the high arts and improvement in manufactures. When the first President of the Royal Academy, Joshua Reynolds, gave his first 'Discourse' to fellow academicians in 1769, he remarked that an institution like the Academy 'has often been recommended upon considerations merely mercantile'.[40] He went on to say, though, that the arts ought to concentrate on higher aims and pay no attention to 'inferior ends'.[41] Another President of the Academy, Martin Archer Shee (1830–50), was even more adamant regarding the need to disconnect the fine arts from commercial interests. Before his appointment, Shee wrote some poems on the nature of art, the first of which appeared in 1805. In the preface to his *Rhymes on Art*, he noted:

> It has of late become so much the fashion, to view every thing through the commercial medium, and calculate the claims of utility by the scale of 'The Wealth of Nations,' that it is to be feared, the Muses and Graces will shortly be put down as unproductive labourers, and the price current of the day considered as the only criterion of merit.[42]

A little earlier he argued that:

> The arts treated commercially, . . . never did, and never can flourish in any country. The principle of trade, and the principle of the arts, are not only dissimilar, but incompatible. Profit is the impelling power of the one – praise, of the other. . . . Noble and national objects are not to be effected by common and contracted means . . .[43]

It was this idea, that art was valuable precisely because it was not connected with the concerns of everyday life (also expressed in Kingsley's vision of the National Gallery as a refuge quoted earlier) which increasingly came to dominate over the old art and manufacture argument. Instead of looking to the National Gallery to improve the working man's taste for the benefit of manufacturing, a separate institution was erected for that purpose in South Kensington in 1852. The South Kensington Museum (now the Victoria and Albert Museum) was restricted to applied art and mainly devoted to the education of the working classes in industrial design.[44] In 1853, shortly before he was appointed as the first Director of the National Gallery, Charles Eastlake recommended a division of the nation's collections between fine and applied art.[45] This system had been adopted in Berlin and was advocated in England by the much respected Director of the Royal Museum there, Dr Gustav Waagen, in his evidence to the Parliamentary Select Committee in 1836. However, it was John Ruskin who was most explicit about the need for a separation between institutions of a

primarily utilitarian kind and the National Gallery, whose purpose was
to be a temple for precious works of art to be appreciated for their
own sake.[46]

Not that the working class was not thought of as a desirable
part of the National Gallery's public, but the focus of the 1836 Select
Committee Report on the benefit of the connection between the arts
and manufactures gave way in later parliamentary enquiries to a different
interest in the labouring classes' presence in the Gallery: their moral
improvement.[47] While the Select Committee in 1836 looked for an
'improvement in taste',[48] the 1850 Select Committee sought to promote 'the improvement in the character of visitors'.[49] This latter report
also noted that the central location of the National Gallery brought
disadvantages unnoticed by any of the former enquiries:

> It appears . . . that the Gallery is frequently crowded by large masses
> of people, consisting not merely of those who come for the purpose
> of seeing the pictures, but also of persons having obviously for their
> object the use of the rooms for wholly different purposes; either for
> shelter in case of bad weather, or as a place in which children of all
> ages may recreate and play, and not infrequently as one where food
> and refreshments may conveniently be taken.[50]

The Report linked this issue with the rapid deterioration of the condition of the pictures, whose cleaning had caused a sharp controversy in
the 1840s. It is clear that this was, in fact, caused by the Gallery's
position in the polluted centre of London, with industry nearby. But
the dust and what was called the 'impure atmosphere'[51] were also, it
was argued, due to the large crowds which flocked to the National
Gallery. Over 575,000 people attended the Gallery in 1850 and almost
twice as many in 1851, during the Great Exhibition, a number which
levelled off at around 700,000 a decade later.[52] This anxiety about the
supposed impurity of crowds related to a wider current issue. Around
1840 public concern had begun to shift from the working conditions of
the poor to their living conditions and the insufficient sanitary arrangements of towns.[53] The fear was that filthy living conditions such as
those in the centre of London would lead to a rapid spread of disease
which could not be limited to the poor but would reach the 'best-
housed and best-fed'.[54] Thus it is no surprise that there was concern
about the 'state of health' of the pictures, particularly since it was
reported that on 'days on which the guard, after being changed, returns
to St. George's Barracks, . . . numerous crowds of persons, without
apparent calling or occupation, . . . come in large bodies . . . and fill the

rooms'.[55] On 17 June 1850 the then Keeper, Thomas Uwins, was asked by the chairman of the Select Committee, Lord Seymour, if he had observed many people frequenting the National Gallery 'without any regard for the pictures'. Uwins gave the following answer:

> I must imagine that to be the case, from many things that I have myself observed take place in the Gallery. I have seen that many persons use it as a place to eat luncheons in, and for refreshment, and for appoint-ments. . . . I have observed a great many things which show that many persons who come, do not come really to see the pictures. . . . On [one occasion], I saw some people, who seemed to be country people, who had a basket of provisions, and who drew their chairs round and sat down, and seemed to make themselves very comfortable; they had meat and drink; and when I suggested to them the impropriety of such a proceeding in such a place, they were very good-humoured, and a lady offered me a glass of gin, and wished me to partake of what they had provided; I represented to them that those things could not be tolerated.[56]

While the Select Committee of 1841, chaired by the Benthamite John Hume,[57] still received plenty of reassurances as to the good conduct of the visitors, including 'mechanics that come . . . to see the pictures, and not to see the company',[58] fear of improper behaviour in the Gallery made itself felt in the Report of 1850. The interest in art as a means of instruction to the working man and woman had been displaced by a notion of art as a vehicle of moral refinement.

In the years of increasing popular unrest from 1837 onwards it was not just conservatives but also middle-class radicals who came to attribute value to the fine arts in terms of its capacity to produce moral improvement. Most famously, John Stuart Mill took issue with Bentham in 1838 for his opinions on art. Although he claimed that Bentham was actually much keener on music, painting and sculpture than was generally believed, Mill argued that Bentham's rationalistic and utilitarian understanding of human nature made him ignorant 'of the deeper springs of human character' (i.e. emotional needs not governed by selfish interests) and that this 'prevented him (as it prevents most Englishmen) from suspecting how profoundly such things enter into the moral nature of man, and into the education both of the individual and of the race'.[59] Like Ruskin, to whom he refers his readers when discussing the nature of beauty in art, Mill valued art because it pro-vided 'noble grounds for the noble emotions'.[60] Art was capable of cultivating aspects of human nature which lay barren in a culture driven by self-interest, capable of 'feeding and encouraging those high feelings, on which we mainly rely for lifting men above low and sordid objects, and giving them a higher conception of what constitutes success in life'.[61] 'The more prosaic our ordinary duties', Mill continues – indirectly justifying institutions like the National Gallery and the freedom of access to them:

> the more necessary it is to keep up the tone of our minds by frequent visits to that higher region of thought and feeling, in which every work seems dignified in proportion to the ends for which, and the spirit in which, it is done; . . . there is, besides, a natural affinity between goodness and the cultivation of the Beautiful, when it is real cultivation, and not mere unguided instinct.[62]

Similarly, George Foggo, who had worked closely with John Hume during the latter's enquiries as chair of the Select Committee on National Monuments and Works of Art in 1841, when questioned by another Committee in 1853, stated that, in his view, 'a National Gallery should be for the instruction and improvement of the intellect and the moral condition of the people'.[63] Although Foggo continued to criticise the management of the Gallery in a radical vein for its undemocratic character, his understanding of art's value to society represented a shift from its utilitarian consequences to its role in the cultivation of the nation's mind.

There had, of course, always been non-Benthamite reformers. Thomas Wyse, for example, made his name as an advocate of educational reform and became a member of Melbourne's administration in 1839 and served again under Russell in 1846. Among the committees Wyse was appointed to was the Fine Art Commission, which enquired into the decoration of the newly rebuilt Palace of Westminster, and the first Select Committee on the state of the arts in the country (which, however, he never attended).[64] Wyse, a Catholic MP from Ireland, published a book on education in 1836 in which he specifically addressed the role of aesthetic instruction. He insisted on the need for state-controlled, nation-wide, comprehensive primary education, teaching which would concentrate on education in the spiritual and 'certainly not in the mechanical and material sense'.[65] Aesthetic appreciation was to play a central part in this. In Wyse's estimation, it cultivated those feelings which were conducive to the growth of the intellectual and moral faculties, and introducing it into the curriculum would eventually produce a less coarse and vulgar and more refined nation:

> Bull baits, and boxing matches, and cock-fights, might perhaps still
> continue; but this [the widespread instruction in the arts] would be one
> more means of weaning the people from those gladiatorial amusements
> natural only to an uncivilised or degenerate populace. Though we should
> not form a nation of amateurs, which is not to be looked for, we should
> form a nation capable of knowing and loving the arts; we should multi-
> ply the moral tendencies, we should augment the moral pleasures . . .[66]

Wyse clearly hoped to polish the rough proletarian manners of the lower
classes (cock-fights and the like were, of course, lower-class pastimes)
into a more restrained, moderate – in the end, bourgeois – mode;[67] in
making art accessible to the working class, the National Gallery would
be a refuge for recreation in the Kingsleyan sense, but also a tool of
social refinement. It was in this spirit that the Select Committee of
1850 both evoked the fear of unruly behaviour by the lower classes and
enquired into the possibility of their moral improvement.

The argument that art could be a force for moral improvement
was not new, of course. It had been advanced by artists a century earlier
when they promoted their plan for an academy of art. In a pamphlet
published in 1755 they gave two arguments. The first was the one
discussed above, namely that art promotes the quality of design. The
second, however, went as follows: 'The Love of Pleasure is implanted in
every Heart as the necessary Sweetener of Life; and, consequently, can
never be reprehensible, but when irregular or inordinate'.[68] Art, the
argument continues, is 'the most innocent, the most refined, and the
most laudable Kind' of entertainment and a force for moral improvement.[69] Art is of value negatively, in that it diverts the appetites that
would otherwise find expression in coarser and more destructive forms,
and positively, in that, by engaging in pleasures of the more elevated
kind, the senses of those who participate in them would become polished and refined. Different as they are in other respects, it is this sense
of the social importance of art that both Reynolds's academic art theory
and the more reception-oriented aesthetic treatises of other eighteenth-
century writers have in common. For Reynolds, the cultivation of art
was a means of overcoming the tyranny of the coarser pleasures by
training perception of more essential and abstract truths. In his tenth
Discourse he had warned his audience that

> to him who has no rule of action but the gratification of the senses,
> plenty is always dangerous: it is therefore necessary to the happiness of
> individuals, and still more necessary to the security of society, that the
> mind should be elevated to the idea of general beauty, and the contem-
> plation of general truth.[70]

Other writers on aesthetics, even if they assumed the existence of different faculties for moral and aesthetic judgements, nevertheless saw a close connection between the two.[71] The cultivation of the arts is 'chiefly the duty of the opulent, who have the leisure to improve their minds and their feelings', Henry Home, Lord Kames, argued in his aesthetic treatise,

> The fine arts are contrived to give pleasure to the eye and the ear, disregarding the inferior senses. . . . In this respect, a taste in the fine arts goes hand in hand with the moral sense, to which indeed it is nearly allied. Both of them discover what is right and what is wrong.[72]

For eighteenth-century thinkers the level of civilisation of a society corresponded to the degree of sensory refinement apparent in its artistic productions.[73]

The distinctively new aspect of the nineteenth-century discussion, however, was the connection that was established between the value of aesthetic contemplation and the fact that it was independent of social reality – what Kingsley invoked when he referred to picture galleries as 'the townsman's paradise of refreshment' or John Stuart Mill identified as the 'higher purpose in life' which raises a man above the self-regarding everyday concerns of enriching himself and raising 'in the world himself and his family'.[74] This conception came to England from Germany via the powerful proselytising of Carlyle and Coleridge[75] and was based on Kant's doctrine of the disinterested nature of aesthetic pleasure.[76] However, it should be emphasised that for Schiller, and, following him, for a tradition of post-romantic thought, the autonomy of art was no barrier to its fulfilling an important social function. On the contrary, according to Schiller, it is art's autonomy that ensures the freedom of the aesthetic experience and it is this freedom that allows art to play its cultivating (*bildende*) role in relation to the individual:

> All improvement in the political sphere is to proceed from the ennobling of character – but how under the influence of a barbarous constitution is character ever to become ennobled? To this end we should, presumably, have to seek out some instrument not provided by the State, and to open up living springs which, whatever the political corruption, would remain clear and pure. . . . This instrument is Fine Art; such living springs are opened up in its immortal exemplars. . . . Art . . . is absolved from all positive constraint and from all conventions introduced by man; both rejoice in absolute *immunity* from human arbitrariness.[77]

Nor did Schiller's insistence on the autonomy of art imply that the content of art was unaffected by the society in which it is produced. On the contrary:

> The artist is indeed the child of his age, but woe to him if he is at the same time its ward or, worse still, its minion! . . . His theme he will, indeed, take from the present; but his form he will borrow from a nobler time, nay, from beyond time altogether, from the absolute, unchanging, unity of his being.[78]

By the 1840s this new German philosophical understanding of art had taken hold quite broadly in England,[79] and Charles Eastlake was one of its most prominent and influential spokesmen. Eastlake had lived on the Continent, principally in Rome, from 1816 to 1830, and there he became closely acquainted with many German artists and writers.[80] It was this knowledge which helped him secure his appointment in 1841 as secretary to the Fine Art Commission (whose President was another sympathiser with German art history, Prince Albert).[81] While still in Rome, Eastlake started writing an essay 'On the Philosophy of the Fine Arts', which was published in 1848 together with other articles, some of which he had written for the much publicised reports of the Commission. It was through these writings that a wider public came to learn about a conception of art which identified its value with the way that the unity of works of art communicates internal harmony and completeness. For Eastlake, influenced by Friedrich Schelling's philosophy of Nature, the fundamental principle of natural beauty was that each object should realise its own individuality:

> the visible qualities in an object which are truly *its own*, constitute the relative beauty of that object. The qualities may, or may not, be intrinsically beautiful, but, such as they are, they represent the outward recommendations of that particular example.[82]

Art, Eastlake believes, must give expression not just to individuality – character, as he, following Schelling, calls it – but to life ('the highest character') and mind ('the highest life').[83] It is, Eastlake argues, the unique merit of painting that it is able to act as a vehicle for this latter form of character, and so to convey moral qualities in a beautiful form:

> The less restricted means, and therefore less exclusively abstract treatment of form, which painting, as compared with sculpture, employs, its variety and individuality of character, its command of colour and light as vehicles of expression, and its 'power of dealing with the eye,' constitute a language which leaves it free to assert the claims of the moral human being consistently with the full use of the best attributes of art.[84]

In Germany, the emphasis on the distinctiveness and individuality of character of genuine works of art led to a displacement of the eighteenth-century hierarchy of art. 'Don't let the fundamental conditions be missing and the revived art will, like the art of former times, show already in her first works the end of her destination', Schelling declared in his lecture on art and nature which Eastlake refers to in his essay 'On the Philosophy of the Fine Arts'. 'In the formation of the particular characteristic already', Schelling continued, 'is, . . . , the grace present . . .'.[85] On this view, first articulated by Johann Gottfried Herder and later more systematically adopted for art history by August Wilhelm Schlegel, Carl Friedrich Rumohr and Johann David Passavant, nations and ages came to be seen as embodying distinct identities, which determined the characters of both their members and of their cultural products.[86]

In order to make the distinctiveness of each school of art apparent to the spectator, Eastlake wanted to show them in their early as well as late phases in the National Gallery. Eastlake was not an undiscriminating enthusiast for early Italian art like the Pre-Raphaelites; yet, shortly after he arrived at the Gallery, he proposed to acquire several works which were not within the established canon of art. In response to one particular proposal he received a letter from the trustee Sir Robert Peel, then Prime Minister, informing him that the policy of the Gallery should be to acquire

> works of sterling merit that may serve as examples to the Artists of this country rather than purchase curiosities in painting valuable certainly as illustrating the progress of art, or the distinctions in the style of different Masters, but surely *less valuable* than works approaching to perfection.[87]

Peel clearly perceived the works deposited in the National Gallery in the same way that he regarded the reserves of bullion in the Bank of England.[88] They were imperishable guarantees of aesthetic value. Consequently, more works by Annibale Carraci and several Guino Renis were acquired instead of those which Eastlake wanted to buy in order to illustrate the developing history of art.

When Eastlake became Director in 1855, he used the increased powers this gave him to acquire many of the now celebrated early Renaissance works in the collection. Meanwhile, opposition to the collection and arrangement of art according to historical principles had weakened. Two years before his appointment as Director, the Select Committee of 1853 officially acknowledged the merit of a comprehensive historical acquisition policy:

> The intelligent public of this country are daily becoming more alive to the truth, which has long been recognised by other enlightened nations, that the arts of design cannot be properly studied or rightly appreciated by means of insulated specimens alone; that in order to understand or profit by the great works, either of the ancient or modern schools of art, it is necessary to contemplate the genius which produced them, not merely in its final results, but in the mode of its operation, in its rise and progress, as well as in its perfection. . . . In order, therefore, to render the British National Gallery worthy of the name it bears, Your Committee think that the funds appropriated to the enlargement of the collection should be expended with a view, not merely of exhibiting to the public beautiful works of art, but of instructing the people in the history of that art, and of the age in which, and the men by whom, those works were produced.[89]

Where once art was supposed to educate by refining taste via the senses, education in art was now seen to involve the intellect as well: the mind must play an active role in the imaginative reconstruction of the contexts that gave artistic works their identity. The education of the public lay now in their contemplation of the achievements of different artists and different nations. In doing so, the hope was that they would acquire on the one hand a sense of their own harmoniousness suitable for their role as the moral subjects of the nation and, on the other, an awareness of their nation's distinctiveness.[90] In the words of Waagen: 'an historical arrangement . . . by following the spirit of the times and the genius of the artists, would produce an harmonious influence upon the mind of the spectator'.[91] Not only was a visual training in comparison between different paintings necessary for this, but also an increasingly refined knowledge of the historical circumstances which had contributed to the production of the works under consideration. What this involved was explained by Eastlake in an essay that he had produced 'to assist the intelligent observation of works of art':

> Thus without limiting the degrees of knowledge which may add to the interest capable of being derived from works of art, it is quite clear that *some* mental preparation is necessary in addition to the exercise of the eye. The interest of the ordinary spectator is in short especially dependent on associations, and it is desirable that these should be analogous to the nature and character of the object. For such an observer, therefore, a knowledge of the history of the art, and of its criticism, the connexion of its epochs and styles with general history, and of course a sufficient familiarity with the subjects of representation may be pronounced to be indispensable.[92]

While the specialist (as Eastlake saw himself) had the eye to distinguish fakes from originals, to recognise harmonious unity, to attribute works to artists accurately, and, generally, to appreciate quality, the 'ordinary' visitor aimed at by the Gallery was the learned bourgeois citizen of the nineteenth century. Given Eastlake's list of the mental equipment needed for the appreciation of art, it is clear that the newly systematised and historicised museum, ordered according to art historical principles, came closer to Ruskin's concept of a temple of treasures for the educated, separate from those art institutions dedicated to the instruction of the working classes, than to the early nineteenth-century radical vision of the museum as a space which would forge communal bonds across the different classes and groups of the nation. Despite rhetoric which advocated the use of the museum for the instruction of the working class, the consumption of art in the nineteenth-century public picture gallery became intellectually as exclusionary as the private collections of the eighteenth century had been physically.

Notes

1   This satire comes from *Fun*, 4 April 1868, p. 38.
2   On the increasing criticism of the commercial aspect of art exhibitions in the nineteenth century, see Andrew Hemingway, 'Art Exhibitons as Leisure-Class Rituals in Early Nineteenth-Century London', in Brian Allan, ed., *Towards a Modern Art World*, Studies in British Art 1 (New Haven and London, 1995), pp. 95–108.
3   Charles Kingsley, *His Letters and Memories of His Life* (1877), ed. Fanny Kingsley, (London, 1894), vol. I, p. 129.
4   See Gwendolyn Wright, ed., *The Formation of National Collections of Art and Archaeology*, Studies in the History of Art 47 (Washington, 1996).
5   Similarly, the interior of the museum was not a world apart, but inevitably reflected changes in the social connotations of consumption and perception in the first half of the nineteenth century (I am currently preparing a publication on this subject). A very helpful descriptive account of the changes in the interior decoration of British galleries is Giles Waterfield, 'Picture Hanging and Gallery Decoration', in Giles Waterfield, ed., *Palaces of Art: Art Galleries in Britain 1790–1990* (London, 1991), pp. 49–65.
6   Over the last decade or so there has been a growing interest in the history and development of museums and art galleries. This new critical attention departs from narratives of the development of individual institutions by looking at the way in which museums accord particular significance to objects and construct a public in their display strategies. A pioneering work in the field was an article by Carol Duncan and Alan Wallach, 'The Universal Survey Museum', *Art History*, 3 (1980), pp. 448–69. Carol Duncan has recently published a book, bringing together her research over many years: *Civilizing Rituals: Inside Public Art Museums* (London and New York, 1995). The literature on museums is

immense and growing constantly. I can here give only a selection related to my subject and period: Andrew McClellan, *Inventing the Louvre: Art, Politics, and the Origin of the Modern Museum in Eighteenth-Century Paris* (Cambridge, 1994); Debora J. Meijers, *Kunst als Natur: Die Habsburger Gemäldegalerie in Wien um 1780*, trans. Rosi Wiegmann, Schriften des Kunsthistorischen Museums Wien 2 (Vienna, 1995); Tony Bennett, *The Birth of the Museum* (London, 1995). Older literature on the National Gallery includes the following: Charles Holmes and C.H. Collins Baker, *The Making of the National Gallery* (London, 1924); Philip Hendy, *The National Gallery London* (London, 1960). A comprehensive account of the foundation of the National Gallery can be found in Gregory Martin, 'The Founding of the National Gallery in London', *The Connoisseur*, 185 (1974), pp. 280–7; 186 (1974), pp. 26–31, 124–8, 200–7; 187 (1974), pp. 49–53, 108–13, 202–5, 278–83. See also Felicity Owen, 'Sir George Beaumont and the National Gallery', in *'Noble and Patriotic': The Beaumont Gift* (London, 1988), pp. 7–16. These publications tell the story of the National Gallery as largely driven by individuals, their decisions and practical concerns. Although Ivan Gaskell is undoubtedly right in asserting that recent writing on museums 'ignores the fact that museums are constituted of people, as well as of buildings and collections' (*Art Bulletin*, 77 (1995), p. 673), the decisions on which these people base their activities shape and are shaped by larger social debates. Two recent accounts which do discuss the National Gallery in the context of nineteenth-century social and political concerns are Duncan, *Civilizing Rituals*, pp. 34–47; and Colin Trodd, 'Culture, Class, City: The National Gallery, London and the Spaces of Education, 1822–57', in Marcia Pointon, ed., *Art Apart* (Manchester, 1994), pp. 33–49. Trodd's discussion of the role of art education in the National Gallery presents the issue as structured by a simple binary opposition between bourgeois interests and the working class. Duncan, on the other hand, pays attention to the differences of vision between radicals and conservatives in government. In my view, however, none of them quite realises the changes in the debate surrounding the National Gallery and the different and contentious conceptions of art and its assumed role within the nation that were at issue.

7   British art in the National Gallery was, however, greatly increased in 1847 when Robert Vernon, an army contractor in horses, bequeathed his 157-strong collection of work by British artists to the nation (although it found no space in the building at Trafalgar Square and was never displayed there).

8   Kingsley, *His Letters*, vol. I, p. 137.

9   In Benedict Anderson's estimation, 'nothing perhaps more precipitated this search [for the imagined community of nations], nor made it more fruitful, than print-capitalism, which made it possible for rapidly growing numbers of people to think about themselves, and to relate themselves to others, in profoundly new ways': *Imagined Communities: Reflections on the Origin and Spread of Nationalism*, 2nd edn (London, 1991), p. 36.

10   Eric J. Hobsbawm, *Nations and Nationalism since 1780: Programme, Myth, Reality*, 2nd edn (Cambridge, 1992), pp. 18–19.

11   According to Roger J. Smith, cultural nationalism rose with the popularisation of Scott's writing in the nineteenth century and was theoretically elaborated in Coleridge's treatise of 1830, 'On the Constitution of the Church and State': *The Gothic Bequest: Medieval Institutions in British Thought, 1688–1863* (Cambridge, 1987), pp. 133–70.

12 William T. Whitley, *Artists and Their Friends in England 1700–1799*, vol. 1 (London and Boston, 1928), pp. 325–8.

13 Andrew McClellan, 'Nationalism and the Origins of the Museum in France', in Wright, ed., *The Formation of National Collections*, p. 37.

14 In 1818, for example, the radical weekly *Examiner* took the opportunity of the opening up of Sir John Fleming Leicester's private collection to ridicule the feebleness of official efforts to make art accessible to the people: see Janet Minihan, *The Nationalization of Culture: The Development of State Subsidies to the Arts in Great Britain* (London, 1977), p. 20. A comparison of the Louvre and the National Gallery in London is the subject of Carol Duncan's second chapter in *Civilizing Rituals*, pp. 21–47.

15 Ian Pears, *The Discovery of Painting: The Growth of Interest in the Arts in England 1680–1768* (New Haven and London, 1988), pp. 181–206.

16 Peter Fullerton, 'Patronage and Pedagogy: The British Institution in the Early Nineteenth Century', *Art History*, 5 (1982), pp. 59–72.

17 Francis Haskell, *History and its Images: Art and the Interpretation of the Past* (New Haven and London, 1993), pp. 201–16.

18 See, for example, David Hume, 'Of the Rise and Progress of the Arts and Sciences', in idem *Essays and Treatises on Several Subjects* (London, 1753), vol. I, pp. 156–92.

19 Andrew Hemingway, 'The "Sociology" of Taste in the Scottish Enlightenment', *Oxford Art Journal*, 12 (1989), pp. 3–35.

20 *An Account of the British Institution for Promoting the Fine Arts in the United Kingdom* (London, 1805), p. 23.

21 Linda Colley, 'Whose Nation? Class and National Consciousness in Britain 1750–1830', *Past and Present*, 113 (1986), p. 113.

22 *Minute Book, Royal National Gallery: Minutes of the Board Meetings 7/2/1828– 2/12/1847*, vol. 1, National Gallery Archive. The last entry which explicitly refers to the 'Directors of the Royal National Gallery' occurs, to my knowledge, in the minutes of a meeting on 7 April 1843 (p. 271).

23 Renate Petras, *Die Bauten der Berliner Museumsinsel* (Berlin, 1987), p. 34.

24 'The abiding political influence which the monarch wielded made it dangerous; the real power of the nation made it unnecessary; and the localized nature of society, reinforced by the provincial press, combined with the lack of a sufficiently splendid metropolitan setting, made it impossible': David Cannadine, 'The Context, Performance and Meaning of Ritual: The British Monarchy and the "Invention of Tradition", c. 1820–1977', in Eric Hobsbawn and Terence Ranger, eds, *The Invention of Tradition* (Cambridge, 1983), p. 116.

25 *The Times*, 10 April 1838, p. 5.

26 Cannadine, 'The Context, Performance and Meaning of Ritual', p. 113.

27 In 1825 Sir Robert Peel gave a speech in which he praised the king for having bought the collection in the National Gallery for the nation, although he must have known that there was no ground for such gratitude: William Whitley, *Art in England 1821–1837* (New York, 1930), p. 91.

28 This quote comes from an anonymously published pamphlet, *The Plan of an Academy for the better Cultivation, Improvement and Encouragement of Painting, Sculpture, Architecture, and the Arts of Design in General* (London, 1755).

29 Joseph Hamburger, *Intellectuals in Politics: John Stuart Mill and the Philosophical Radicals* (New Haven and London, 1965), pp. 30–1.

30 The Philosophic Radicals who were elected into Parliament in 1832 were a group around James and John Stuart Mill. They were, however, not very close to John Bowring, who had become Bentham's closest ally in his last years. When Bowring became editor of the *Westminster Review* in 1824, the Mills and their friends contributed to it only reluctantly: *ibid.*, p. 17.

31 'Prejudice apart, the game of push-pin is of equal value with the arts and sciences of music and poetry. If a game of push-pin furnish more pleasure, it is more valuable than either': Jeremy Bentham, *The Works of Jeremy Bentham*, ed. John Bowring (Edinburgh, 1843), vol. II, p. 253.

32 *Ibid.*, p. 253.

33 John Stuart Mill, 'The Works of Jeremy Bentham', *The London and Westminster Review*, 31 (1838), p. 487.

34 Bentham, *The Works*, p. 255.

35 *Report from the Select Committee on Arts and their Connexion with Manufactures*, House of Commons, 1836, p. 19.

36 *Ibid.*, p. iii.

37 Rodney Mace, *Trafalgar Square: Emblem of Empire* (London, 1976), p. 135.

38 Eric J. Evans, *The Forging of the Modern State: Early Industrial Britain, 1783–1870*, 2nd edn (Harlow, 1996), p. 276.

39 It was John Stuart Mill who divided his contemporaries into two groups, the 'Movement' class (following Bentham's radicalism) and the 'Conservative' class (influenced by Coleridge's thinking): Mill, 'The Works of Jeremy Bentham', p. 468.

40 Joshua Reynolds, *Discourses on Art*, ed. Robert R. Wark, 2nd edn (New Haven and London, 1981), p. 13.

41 *Ibid.*

42 Martin Archer Shee, *Rhymes of Art*, 2nd edn (London, 1805), p. lvii.

43 *Ibid.*, pp. xxi–xxii.

44 Minihan, *The Nationalization of Culture*, ch. 4.

45 *Report from the Select Committee on the National Gallery*, House of Commons, 1853, p. 460, and *Report from the Select Committee*, 1836, p. 11.

46 Elizabeth Helsinger, 'Ruskin and the Politics of Viewing: Constructing National Subjects', *Nineteenth-Century Contexts*, 18 (1994), p. 130.

47 Colin Trodd detects an ambiguity in quotations from people connected with the National Gallery: 'While on the one hand they assert the desirability of working class people in the museum, they, on the other hand, express anxiety about their behaviour and suitability', 'Culture, Class, City', pp. 33–49. Trodd, however, does not link this ambiguity to a shift in attitudes in response to the events of the 1840s, nor does he see the changes in the understanding of art inflected in this.

48 *Report from the Select Committee*, 1836, p. 141.

49 *Report from the Select Committee on the National Gallery*, House of Commons, 1850, p. 6.

50 *Ibid.*, p. iv.

51 *Ibid.*

52 *Report from the Select Committee*, 1853, p. 829; and 'Reports of the Director of the National Gallery', 1856–64, *Minute Book, National Gallery: Minutes of Board Meetings 12/11/1855–11/2/1871*, vol. 4, National Gallery Archive.

53 Christopher Hamlin, 'Providence and Putrefaction: Victorian Sanitarians and the Natural Theology of Health and Disease', *Victorian Studies*, 28 (1985), pp. 381–411.

54 Robert Ferguson in the June 1840 issue of the *Quarterly Review*, quoted in R.P. Wallins, 'Victorian Periodicals and the Emerging Social Conscience', *Victorian Periodicals Newsletter*, 8 (1975), p. 55.

55 *Report from the Select Committee*, 1850, p. iv.

56 *Ibid.*, p. 6.

57 In order to allow the working class easy access to the National Gallery, Hume had, in the early 1840s, pressed the Trustees to print cheap catalogues and, when this was not forthcoming, arranged for the printing himself: *Letter from Joseph Hume*, 7 July 1842, History File, National Gallery Archive, NG5/51/1842. At this stage, however, the catalogue was no more than a list of the names of artists and titles of the pictures in the collection.

58 This quote comes from a statement by John Peter Wildsmith, attendant in the Gallery, *Report from the Select Committee*, 1841, p. 137. For other statements of this kind, see also pp. 130–4.

59 Mill, 'The Works of Jeremy Bentham', p. 504.

60 The quote is from Ruskin's definition of poetry in *Modern Painters*: Edward Tyas Cook and Alexander Wedderburn, eds, *The Works of John Ruskin* (London, 1904), vol. V, p. 28. For Mill's recommendation of Ruskin, see James Mill, *Analysis of the Phenomena of the Human Mind*, ed. John Stuart Mill, 2 vols in 1 (London, 1869), vol. II, pp. 252–5.

61 John Stuart Mill, 'Inaugural Address at St. Andrews' (1867), in Francis A. Cavenagh, ed., *James and John Stuart Mill on Education* (Cambridge, 1931), p. 192.

62 *Ibid.*, pp. 194–5.

63 *Report from the Select Committee*, 1853, p. 511.

64 *Report from the Select Committee*, 1836, p. ii.

65 Thomas Wyse, *Education Reform; Or, The Necessity of a National System of Education* (London, 1836), p. 94. Wyse stressed the importance of religious teaching, albeit teaching which was imparted separately by the pastors of the various denominations.

66 *Ibid.*, p. 198.

67 Peter Stallybrass and Allon White, *The Politics and Poetics of Transgression* (London, 1986).

68 *The Plan of an Academy*, p. iv.

69 *Ibid.*

70 Reynolds, *Discourses on Art*, p. 170. See also John Barrell, *The Political Theory of Painting from Reynolds to Hazlitt* (New Haven and London, 1986), pp. 69–162.

71 Hemingway, 'The "Sociology" of Taste', pp. 3–35.

72 Henry Home (Lord Kames), *Elements of Criticism* (Edinburgh, 1762), vol. I, pp. 6–7.

73 For an understanding of the function of art as sensual refinement, see also David Hume, 'Of the Delicacy of Tastes and Passions', in idem, *Essays and Treatises on Several Subjects*, vol. I, p. 4.

74 Mill, 'Inaugural Address', pp. 191–2.

75 Rosemary Ashton, *The German Idea* (Cambridge, 1980), chs 1 and 2.

76 Immanuel Kant, *Kritik der Urteilskraft* (1790), ed. Wilhelm Weischedel, *Werkausgabe* (Wiesbaden, 1957), vol. 10. See Michael Podro, *The Manifold in Perception* (Oxford, 1972).

77 Friedrich Schiller, 'Ninth Letter', in idem *On the Aesthetic Education of Man*, (1793–94), trans. Elizabeth M. Wilkinson and L.A. Willoughby (Oxford, 1967), p. 55.

78   *Ibid.*, pp. 55–7. Carlyle, who was deeply influenced by Schiller's understanding of the moral function of art, quoted a similar passage from Schiller's 'Ninth Letter' in his *Life of Friedrich Schiller*, (1825), (London, 1898), p. 202.

79   William Vaughan, *German Romanticism and English Art* (New Haven and London, 1979), p. 80.

80   David Robertson, *Sir Charles Eastlake and the Victorian Art World* (Princeton, 1978), p. 11.

81   Thomas Sherrer Ross, 'The Decoration of the New Palace of Westminster, 1841–1863', *Journal of the Warburg and Courtauld Institutes*, 17 (1954), pp. 322–3.

82   Charles Eastlake, 'On the Philosophy of the Fine Arts', in idem, *Contributions to the Literature of the Fine Arts*, 2nd edn (London, 1870; 1st pub. 1848), p. 362. For a discussion of this text with a slightly different emphasis, see Vaughan, *German Romanticism*, pp. 85–90.

83   *Ibid.*, p. 363.

84   *Ibid.*, p. 392.

85   Friedrich W.J. Schelling, *Über das Verhältniß der bildenden Künste zu der Natur* (Munich, 1807), p. 63.

86   Vaughan, *German Romanticism*, pp. 73–80; Michael Podro, *The Critical Historians of Art* (New Haven and London, 1982).

87   *Minute Book, Royal National Gallery*, Meeting of the Trustees, 13 May 1844, p. 254.

88   Boyd Hilton, 'Peel: A Reappraisal', *The Historical Journal*, 22 (1979), pp. 589–96.

89   *Report from the Select Committee*, 1853, p. xvi. The radical Select Committee Report of 1836 had already criticised the preponderance in the National Gallery's collection of sixteenth-century Renaissance works, particularly by the Carracci, a balance that reflected the aristocratic predilections of the eighteenth century. Rather they recommended 'those of the era of Raphael, or of the times just antecedent to it': *Report from the Select Committee*, 1836, p. x. However, the crucial difference between the two reports in 1836 and 1853 is that the earlier committee still recommended the acquisition of work on the grounds that it should form a collection of models of quality rather than illustrate the history of art.

90   The foundation of the National Portrait Gallery in 1856 also testifies to the increasing role historical awareness played in the construction of the national identity in Britain in the nineteenth century. Here, however, artistic harmony was not a consideration in the selection of the works for display: Marcia Pointon, *Hanging the Head* (New Haven and London, 1993), pp. 227–44; Charles Saumarez Smith, *The National Portrait Gallery* (London, 1997), pp. 9–26.

91   *Report from the Select Committee*, 1836, p. 11.

92   Charles Eastlake, 'How to Observe', in idem, *Contributions*, p. 221.

INDEX ෨෧

Note: Page references in *italics* indicate illustrations. 'n' after a page reference indicates a note number.